Forest Policy, Laws, Legislation and Constitution of India

Forest Policy, Laws, Legislation and Constitution of India

Dr. Girish B. Shahapurmath
M.Sc. (Forestry) Ph.D.
Assistant Professor of Forest Management
Department of Natural Resource Management
College of Forestry, Sirsi (UK), Karnataka

Dr. Hanumantha, M.
M.Sc. (Forestry) Ph.D.
Assistant Professor of Forest Utilization
Department of Forest Products and Utilization
College of Forestry, Sirsi (UK), Karnataka

SSPH

SATISH SERIAL PUBLISHING HOUSE
403, Express Tower, Commercial Complex
Azadpur, Delhi-110033 (India)
Phone : 011-27672852, Fax : 91-11-27672046
e-mail : info@satishserial.com, hkjain1975@yahoo.com
Website : www.satishserial.com

Published by :

SATISH SERIAL PUBLISHING HOUSE
403, Express Tower, Commercial Complex, Azadpur, Delhi-110033 (INDIA)
Phone : 011-27672852 Fax : 91-11-27672046
E-mail : info@satishserial.com, hkjain1975@yahoo.com

ISBN 978-93-88020-65-7

Composed, Designed & Printed in India

About the Authors

Dr. GIRISH B. SHAHAPURMATH, M.Sc. (Forestry) Ph.D.
Assistant Professor of Forest Management
Department of Natural Resource Management
College of Forestry, Sirsi-581 401, Karnataka
University of Agricultural Sciences, Dharwad, India
E-mail: girishbshahapur@gmail.com /
shahapurmathgb@uasd.in

- Specialization in Silviculture and Agroforestry, Forest Management, Remote Sensing and GIS.
- Post Graduate Diploma in Agricultural Extension and Management (PGDAEM) by MANAGAE, Hyderabad during 2014-15.
- Post Graduate Diploma Computer Applications (PGDCA) by Infotech Computer Education and Manipal Institute of Computer Education (MICE) during 2008-09.
- Total 16 years of experience in the field of forestry (Teaching, Research and Extension).
- Presently working as Assistant Professor of Forest Management in Department of Natural Resource Management at College of Forestry, SIRSI (University of Agricultural Sciences, Dharwad, Karnataka (India).
- Recipient of "Outstanding Scientist Award" in Forestry by The Society of Tropical Agriculture, New Delhi, India in 7th International Conference on Agriculture, Horticulture and Plant Sciences held at Shimla (H. P.) during June 28-29, 2018.
- Recipient of "Best Teacher Award-2016" for outstanding contribution in the field of Forestry on the occasion of International Conference on "Rural Livelihood Improvement by Enhancing Farmers' Income through Sustainable Innovative Agri and Allied Enterprises (RLSIAAe)" organized by the Society for Upliftment of Rural Economy, Varanasi (India) during 30th October to 1st November, 2018 held at Birla Institute of Technology, Patna.
- Recognized as a Life Member for the "Society for Upliftment of Rural Economy, Varanasi (Membership No. LM/245/2018).
- First prize for Best Poster Presentation on Multistoreyed Cropping of Teak-perennial vegetables-legume based Agroforestry system

Presented in National Symposium (Silver Jubilee) on "Agroforestry Knowledge for Sustainability, Climate Moderation and Challenges Ahead" held at National Research Centre for Agroforestry, Jhansi (UP) from 15-17 December, 2008.

- First Prize for Best Poster presentation on "Forest Law and Models" presented in "National Kaanoonu Utsava" Ehibition held at Sirsi from 07.06.2014 to 06.07.2014 organized by Karnataka High Court, Bengaluru and District Law Service, Karwar and Bar Association, Sirsi.
- Worked as Principal Investigator and CO-Principal Investigator for 10 Research Projects.
- Field of interest - Silviculture and Agroforestry, Forest Management and Policy, Sustainable Forest Management, Remote Sensing and Geographical Information System in Forestry.
- Developed the course materials as reference books and for competitive exams, such as ASRB, IFS, ACF, RFO, KPSC, etc., in the field of forestry for students' purpose.
- Attended more than 15 Trainings/Summer/Winter schools, short courses, Seminars, Workshops, Conferences and undergone Agricultural Massive Open Online Courses (Ag MOOC).
- Published more than 100 publications including Research papers in NAAS rated journal/Research notes/Papers presented and published in symposium/seminar/conference/workshop/Training/ international conference/Popular articles published in journals/ newspapers/Books/chapters in books.

Dr. Hanumantha, M., M.Sc. (Forestry), Ph.D.
Assistant Professor of Forest Utilization
Department of Forest Products and Utilization
College of Forestry, SIRSI- 581 401, Karnataka
University of Agricultural Sciences, Dharwad, India

- Total 18 years of experience in the field of Forestry (Teaching, Research and Extension)
- Specialization in Wood Anatomy, Wood Science, Wood Products, Non-Timber Forest Products and Forest Mensuration
- Completed 18 months course of *"Instruction and Practical Training in Forestry and Allied subjects"* (RFO, Training) at State Forest Service College (SFSC), Coimbatore, Tamil Nadu from 01-04-2005 to 30-09-2006
- Post Graduate Diploma in Agricultural Extension and Management (PGDAEM) by MANAGE, Hyderabad during 2014-15
- Developed Course Materials as reference books and for competitive examinations (IFS, ACF, RFO) in the field of Forestry (Silviculture, Silviculture of Species, Forest Management, Forest Mensuration, Forest Policy and Legislation and ACF Solved Question papers in Forestry)
- Developed Lecture Notes on Wood Anatomy, Wood Science, Wood Products and Non-Timber Forest Products
- Participated in Two summer and winter school training
- Completed Eight Agriculture Massive Open Online Courses (AGMOOC)
- Recipient of "Young Scientist Award" for contribution in the field of Forestry by Society for Scientific Development in Agriculture and Technology (SSDAT). Received in International Conference on Global Research Initiatives for Sustainable Agriculture and Allied Sciences (GRISAAS-2018) during 28-30th October, 2018 held at Rajasthan Agricultural Research Institute, Durgapura, Jaipur, Rajasthan, India.
- Awarded National Young Leader Programme Award by Ministry of Youth Affairs and Sports, New Delhi and UAS, Dharwad for the year 2015-16 (awarded on 10-04-2017) for contribution towards NSS activities.
- Awarded First Prize for Best Poster/Chart presentation on "Forest Law and Models" in "National Kaanoonu Utsava" Ehibition held at

Sirsi from 07.06.2014 to 06.07.2014 organized by Karnataka High Court, Bengaluru and District Law Service, Karwar and Bar Association, Sirsi.

- Worked as Principal Investigator and Co-Principal Investigator for 13 Research Projects.
- Published more than 100 publications including Research papers in NAAS rated journal/Research notes/Papers presented and published in symposium/seminar/conference/workshop/Training/international conference/Popular articles published in journals/news papers/Books/chapters in books.

Hon'ble
Vice Chancellor

UNIVERSITY OF AGRICULTURAL SCIENCES, DHARWAD
KRISHI NAGAR, DHARWAD-581 005
KARNATAKA STATE, INDIA

Foreword

The term "policy" is not tightly defined but is used in different ways on different occasions. Often, it can mean "a course of action adopted and pursued". A policy can be explicitly stated or not. It can also be planned or it can emerge through evident behaviour. It is, thus, often viewed either as a rational system based on deliberate aims and plans or as a consequence of political activity arising from a series of decisions. In any case, a policy needs to provide guidance and a sense of direction over a certain period of time in order to be useful. People complain that central government, a ministry or other stakeholders "do not have a policy" when decisions are made on an ad hoc basis or are incoherent or contradictory. A policy is intended to guide and determine present and future decisions and actions. It usually comprises two elements: a set of aspirations, goals or objectives an outline of a course of action to achieve them.

A national forest policy is considered to be a negotiated agreement between government and stakeholders (i.e. all those who depend on or benefit from forests or who decide on, control or regulate access to these resources) on the orientations and principles of actions they adopt, in harmony with national socio-economic and environmental policies, to guide and determine decisions on the sustainable use and conservation of forest and tree resources for the benefit of society.

A national forest policy is not to be unilaterally imposed by government. Ideally, it is an agreement among bodies that represent different forest interests and is formally adopted by government. Who should be involved in its development is, thus, a key question, as the selection of the participants influences which interests are taken into account. It is difficult to imagine a national forest policy that can be relevant and useful without being firmly placed within the broader aims of society. Forest policies, thus, not only have to cover issues under the competence of the forestry administration and its agencies, but they also need to contribute to overarching policies, including those responsible for national development or economic and poverty strategies. They also need to be consistent with policies issued by other government authorities, e.g. on environmental protection, climate change, agriculture, industry and trade.

Thus, a forest policy is a policy for people, not for the forestry administration. Being an agreement among government and stakeholders, a national forest policy is endorsed by government and implemented through legal, economic and informational instruments, and by other stakeholders with their respective means. Ultimately, through government endorsement, a formal national forest policy is the official position of the government, as a clear statement of a country's goals and objectives, made public so that all parties know the directions being pursued and the outcomes to be achieved. If different actors, each pursue their particular interests and change course frequently, larger goals or longer-term objectives are unlikely to be reached. Thus, there are a number of good reasons for jointly developing and using an agreed forest policy. The process of bringing stakeholders with diverse interests together to negotiate an agreement is extremely valuable in itself. A mutually accepted forest policy builds a sense of joint ownership, which is essential for its implementation. The involvement of stakeholders beyond the forest sector gives the policy legitimacy across society. Wide buy-in is particularly advantageous, when negotiating with powerful ministries, such as agriculture, energy, planning or finance. A national forest policy provides excellent guidance for developing more coherent institutional frameworks and policy instruments, including forest legislation.

A national forest policy can guide the planning and operations of forestry stakeholders including administrations and agencies at various levels. A national forest policy facilitates communication, coordination and collaboration across government, non-governmental organizations and the public. A national forest policy can provide a solid basis for international policy discussions and for strengthening technical assistance co-operation. The national forest policy can serve as a reference to guide decisions on emerging issues, particularly those where quick, difficult or controversial decisions must be made.

Integrating forest issues in broader policies addressing national sustainable development as well as the challenges associated with changes taking place at the global level may involve some risk (e.g. loss of control) but can open up considerable opportunities. For example, India, the Republic of Korea and the United States of America have linked forests and forest management to wider development agendas by making them part of "Green Deal" programmes, and Costa Rica and the Republic of Korea have made natural resources a central part of their national development strategies. Efforts are under way in many countries to improve integration of forest and climate change policies as well as forest and energy policies.

Textbooks on Forest Policies, Forest Laws and Legislations suitable for undergraduate and post graduate students are very few particularly in Forestry Colleges in India. This textbook on "Forest Policies, Laws and Constitution of India" by Dr.Girish B. Shahapurmath and Dr.Hanumantha, M., is a timely and welcome contribution in the forestry field. The authors have a considerable experience in teaching, research and extension in forestry / agroforestry and have presented the subject matter critically and systematically. This book will serve as a valuable source of information for the academicians in forestry institutes and also for the students for the preparation of competitive examinations in forestry discipline. I congratulate the authors for the hard work they put in, the systematic selection of topics and well documented and meticulous presentation.

I am hopeful that this text book will adequately meet the needs of students of forestry colleges and would be widely welcomed. I extend my best wishes to Dr.Girish B. Shahapurmath and Dr.Hanumantha, M., for the success of their book.

May, 2019
Dharwad, Karnataka

Dr. M.B. CHETTI
(Vice Chancellor)
University of Agricultural Sciences, Dharwad
and Former Assistant Director General (HRD)
ICAR, New Delhi

Preface

Forestry, as a subject, is being taught to students of the Forest Colleges in different Agricultural Universities in India. This subject had been introduced as a subject for degree courses in most of the Indian Agricultural Universities. Indian Council of Agricultural Research (ICAR) provided an opportunity to start state-run forestry colleges in various State Agricultural Universities (SAUs) in the country. Earlier as per the recommendation of the National Commission on Agriculture, ICAR had started a course in 'Farm Forestry' during 1976 in all SAUs. There was a growing concern among the academicians and politicians alike that the students of forestry should have a greater exposure and access to natural forests. There has been increased public awareness of natural resource policy, including forest management. A national forest policy is not to be unilaterally imposed by government. Ideally, it is an agreement among bodies that represent different forest interests and is formally adopted by government. Who should be involved in its development is, thus, a key question, as the selection of the participants influences which interests are taken into account. It is difficult to imagine a national forest policy that can be relevant and useful without being firmly placed within the broader aims of society. Forest policies, thus, not only have to cover issues under the competence of the forestry administration and its agencies, but they also need to contribute to overarching policies, including those responsible for national development or economic and poverty strategies. They also need to be consistent with policies issued by other government authorities, e.g. on environmental protection, climate change, agriculture, industry and trade. Therefore, this book has been written to meet the requirements of the students of the Forest Colleges as well as those of the students preparing for competitive examinations.

The book covers mostly the present syllabi of the Forest Colleges as well as those of the competitive examinations (Indian Forest Service and State Forest Services). I claim no originality in writing this book except for the arrangement and presentation of the subject matter. A large number of books, journals and proceedings of symposia and workshops have been consulted. A list of these references is given at the end of book as references/bibliography.

I, therefore, gratefully acknowledge the help taken from "Forest Policy and Law" by S.S.Negi., "Indian Forestry" by K. Manikandan and S. Prabhu., "Indian Polity for Civil Services Examinations" by M. Laxmikanth and other publications mentioned in the references.

I am greatly indebted to Dean (Forestry) for constant guidance and help during the time of writing the book and improving it substantially. I am equally grateful to all the faculty members of College of Forestry, Sirsi (UAS, Dharwad, Karnataka) and officers of Karnataka Forest Department for their valuable suggestions and help in writing the book as well as for reading through the chapters and making very valuable improvements.

Place: Sirsi, Karnataka
Date: 1st January, 2019

Dr. Girish B. Shahapurmath
Assistant Professor of Forest Management
Department of Natural Resource Managment
College of Forestry, Sirsi (UAS, Dharwad)
Karnataka, India

Contents

Chapter 1

Forestry Administration and Oragnization

History of Forests in India

- There is enough evidence to show that dense forests once covered India. The changing forest composition and cover can be closely linked to the growth and change of civilizations. Over the years, as man progressed the forest began gradually depleting. The growing population and man's dependence on the forest have been mainly responsible for this.
- All ancient texts have some mention of the forest and the activities that were performed in these areas. Forests were revered by the people and a large number of religious ceremonies centred on trees and plants. The ***Agni Purana*, written about 4000 years ago**, stated that man should protect trees to have material gains and religious blessings. Around 2500 years ago, Gautama Buddha preached that man should plant a tree every five years. Sacred groves were marked around the temples, where certain rules and regulations applied.
- When **Chandra Gupta Maurya came to power around 300 BC**, he realized the importance of the forests and appointed a high officer to look after the forests. **Ashoka stated that wild animals and forests should be preserved and protected**. He launched **programmes to plant trees** on a large scale. These rules continued even during the Gupta period.
- During the Muslim invasions a large number of people had to flee from the attacks and take refuge in the forests. This was the beginning of a phase of migration to the forest. They cleared vast areas of forests to make way for settlements.
- The Muslim invaders were all keen hunters and therefore, had to have patches of forests where they could go hunting. This ensured that the trees in these areas were not felled, and the forest ecology was not tampered with. The Mughals showed more

interest in gardens and their development. Akbar ordered the planting of trees in various parts of his kingdom. Jahangir was well known for laying out beautiful gardens and planting trees.

- During the early part of the British rule, trees were felled without any thought. Large numbers of trees, such as the sal, teak, and sandalwood were cut for export. The history of modern Indian forestry was a process by which the British gradually appropriated forest resources for revenue generation. Trees could not be felled without prior permission and knowledge of the authority. This step was taken to ensure that they were the sole users of the forest trees.
- But after some time, the British began to regulate and conserve. In 1800, a commissioner was appointed to look into the availability of teak in the Malabar forests. In 1806, the Madras government appointed Capt. Watson as the commissioner of forests for organizing the production of teak and other timber suitable for the building of ships.
- **In 1855, Lord Dalhousie framed regulations for conservation of forest in the entire country. Teak plantations were raised in the Malabar hills and acacia and eucalyptus in the Niligiri Hills.**
- In Bombay, the conservator of forest, Gibson, tried to introduce rules prohibiting shifting cultivation and plantation of teak forests. **From 1865 to 1894, forest reserves were established** to secure material for imperial needs. From the **18th century, scientific forest management systems** were employed to regenerate and harvest the forest to make it sustainable. **Between 1926 and 1947, afforestation was carried out on a large scale in the Punjab and Uttar Pradesh.** In the early 1930s, people began showing interest in the conservation of wild life.
- During World War I forest resources were severely depleted as large quantities of timber were removed to build ships and railway sleepers and to pay for Britain's war efforts. Between the two wars, great advancements in scientific management of the forests were made, with many areas undergoing regeneration and sustained harvest plans being drawn up. Sadly, emphasis was still not on protection and regeneration but on gaining maximum revenue from the forests. **World War II made even greater demand on the forest** than World War I had done.

- With the independence of India in 1947, a great upheaval in forestry organization occurred. The princely states were managed variably, giving more concessions to the local populations. The transfer of these states to the government led to deforestation in these areas. But some forest officials claim that the maharajas cut down a lot of their forests and sold them. This may have been the case in some instances, but a lot of forest had existed and has been lost since the government took over these states.
- **The new Forest Policy of 1952 recognized the protective functions of the forest and aimed at maintaining one-third of India's land area under forest**. Certain activities were banned and grazing restricted. Much of the original British policy was kept in place, such as the classification of forest land into two types.
- The next 50 years saw development and change in people's thinking regarding the forest. A constructive attitude was brought about through a number of five-year plans. Until 1976, the forest resource was seen as a source of earning money for the state and therefore, little was spent in protecting it or looking after it.
- In 1976, the governance of the forest came under the concurrent list. 'Development without destruction' and 'forests for survival' were the themes of the next two five-year plans, aiming at increasing wildlife reserves and at linking forest development with the tribal economy. But a large gap between aim and achievement exists still.

Highlights of History

- The ancient scriptures (epics like Ramayana and Mahabharata) give attractive descriptions of forests like ***Dandakaranya, Nandavan, Khandavavan***.
- During **300 BC, Chandragupta Maurya** recognized the importance of forests and appointed a high official to look after the forests of his kingdom assisted by a number of subordinates.

  The year 1864 is regarded as the beginning of forest administration in India.
- **Brandis was appointed as the first Inspector General of Forests** with a mandate to advise the government on all questions

connected with forest administration and generally to introduce a system of management and conservation throughout all forests in the territories under the Government of India.

History of Forest Management

History of Forest Management is divided into five distinct periods:

I) Pre-British period (1526-1700)

II) Early-British period (1750-1900)

III) Late-British period (1900-1947)

IV) Post-Independence period (1947-1975)

V) Post-Independence period (1985-till date)

I. Pre-British period (including epic period - 1526-1700)

- Dhandakaranya and Nandana vanas (Epic period)
- Dravidians (Rishimunis)
- Buddhism and Jainism (Both appreciated nature)
- Kautilya formed Arthashastra that envisages functions and importance of forests (400 BC)
- Ashoka emphasized on symbiotic relationship between man, trees and animals (300 BC)
- Moghul invasion (1526-1700)-Avenue planting and canal plantations.

II. Early-British period (1750-1900)

- Concepts of sustainable yield, Rotation, Normal forests and control of forests (1800).
- British introduced agriculture into forestry and establishment of Nilambur teak plantation (1842)
- Commercial interference i.e. committee constituted on harvestable material mainly evergreen forests (1850)
- Beginning of forest administration in India (1864)
- Brandis–First Inspector General of Forests (IGF) introduced scientific forest management and forest administration (1855)

- Scientific forest management started with introducing sustainable yield and normal forests (1864)
- First ever Indian Forest Act was passed (1865)

III. Late British Period (1947-1975)

- Importance was given for Industrial plantations
- Second World was (1939-1945) – Loss of large area forests
- Howard retired as IGF under British rule
- Indian Forest Act, 1927 was enacted

IV. Post-Independence period (1947-1975)

- National Forest Policy revised (1952)
- Emphasis on agriculture
- Functional classification of forests, such as :
  - Protection forests
  - National forests
  - Village forests and
  - Tree lands

V. Post-Independence period (1985-till date)

- Wildlife (Protection) Act, 1972
- Forest Conservation Act, 1980
- National Forest Policy, 1988
- Biodiversity Act, 2002 – Biological Diversity Act was signed by India (UN convention on biodiversity)
- Recognition of Forest Rights - 2006

Central Forestry Administration and Organization

- In India, the Forestry administration and organization has developed both at the State and Central Government levels over a period spanning more than 135 years.

- The Ministry of Environment and Forests (MoEF) is the controlling Ministry for forests and environment at the Central Governmental levelheaded by a Minister.
- **Inspector General of Forests** (IGF) is the **technical head of the forest service in India** and is an **Officer of the Indian Forest Service.**

There are two additional IGFs designated as:

a) Additional IGF (General)

b) Additional IGF (Wildlife)

Duties IGF

i) Wildlife

ii) Forest Conservation and Protection

iii) Forest survey and utilization

iv) Forest policy

Duties of Deputy Inspector General of Forests (DIGF)

i) Research and Training

ii) Forest Conservation

iii) Wildlife

iv) Forest fires and protection

v) Forest survey and utilization

vi) Wastelands

Duties of Assistant Inspector General of Forests (AIGF)

i) Research and Training

ii) Wildlife

iii) Forest statistics

iv) Industries

v) Wastelands

vi) Forest Conservation

Central Board of Forestry (CBF)

In 1948, a conference of the forest ministers of various states decided that central forestry organization should look after various forestry activities at the national level. It consists of Ministers (States and Union), Members (Loksabha and Rajyasabha), Secretary (MoA) and Secretary (CBF).

NAEB (1992) - National Afforestation and Eco-Development Board was constituted with the mandate to act as a catalyst in afforestation and eco-development of stress sites. It is headed by Minister of Environment and Forests (MoEF) who functions as its chairman. **National Afforestation and Eco-Development Board (NAEB) was set up in August 1992 for promoting the Afforestation, tree planting, ecological restoration and eco-development activities in the country**. It gives special attention to the regeneration of degraded forest areas and lands adjoining forest areas, national parks, sanctuaries and other protected areas as well as the ecologically fragile areas like the Western Himalayas, Aravallis, Western Ghats, etc. Major function of the NAEB is to evolve mechanisms for ecological restoration of degraded forest areas and adjoining lands through systematic planning and implementation, in a cost effective manner. Another major function is to restore through natural regeneration or appropriate intervention the forest cover in the country for ecological security and to meet the fuel wood, fodder and other needs of the rural communities.

ICFRE (1986, Dehradun) – Indian Council of Forest Research and Education is an autonomous organization under MoEF. The Director General of ICFRE is the Chief Executive of the ICFRE. The ICFRE functions through its headquarter at "**Dehradun**".

IIFM ((1982, Bhopal) – Indian Institute of Forest Management was established in 1982 as an autonomous institute under the Ministry of Environment and Forests.

FSI (1981) – Forest Survey of India is a government organization in India under the union Ministry of Environment and Forests for conducting forest surveys and studies. **The organization came into being in June, 1981. It is headquartered at Dehradun, Uttarakhand, India**. The objective of the organization is monitoring periodically the changing situation of land and forest resources and present the data for national planning; conservation & management of environmental preservation and implementation of social forestry projects.

IGNFA (1938, Dehradun) - Indira Gandhi National Forest Academy is an organisation/subordinate office under the Ministry of Environment and Forests (India), which was originally as Indian Forest College, established in 1938 for training senior forest officers. It **is situated in the New Forest campus of Forest Research Institute (FRI), Dehradun.** IGNFA is currently functioning as a Staff College for the officers of the **Indian Forest Service** (IFS). The primary mandate of the Academy is to impart knowledge and skills to the professional foresters and help them to develop competence for managing the country's forest and wildlife resources on a sustainable basis. In the Academy, training is provided at different levels of seniority in the Indian Forest Service besides training the new entrants to the service.

Indian Forest Service (IFS) was created in 1966 under the All India Services Act, 1951. Previously, the Imperial Forestry Service existed during the British Raj from 1865 to 1935. Officers are recruited via a rigorous competitive examination and then trained for about two years by the Central Government. Their services are placed under various State cadres and joint cadres, even though they have the mandate to serve both under the State and Central Governments. The main mandate of the service is the implementation of the National Forest Policy which aims to ensure environmental stability and maintenance of ecological balance which are vital for sustenance of all life forms, human, animal and plant. IFS officers while in field postings in respective state cadres work for conservation, protection and development of forests and wildlife along with an aim to enhance livelihood opportunities of forest dependent communities of rural and tribal areas.

State Forestry Administration and Organization

There is a separate forest ministry in each state or union territory under the charge of minister. The structure, levels and functions of the State Forest Department are as follows:

1. **Principal Chief Conservator of Forests (PCCF)** (Head of Forest Force): Head of the Forest Department in each state. The senior-most IFS Officer.
2. **Principal Chief Conservator of Forests (PCCF)** - Wildlife
3. **Additional Principal Chief Conservator of Forests** (APCCF)

4. **Chief Conservator of Forests** (CCF)-Head of various wings of the forest department or functioning as regional controlling officers for different regions of the state.
5. **Conservator of Forests** (CF)-Officer in-charge of territorial or functional circles under PCCF or CCF.
6. **Deputy Conservator of Forests** (DCF)-Head of Division - DCF is in-charge of a territorial or functional division (DFO-Divisional Forest Officer).
7. **Assistant Conservator of Forests** (ACF) - Head of Sub-division -ACF assists DCF in performance of various duties. He may also be in-charge of a forest sub-division.
8. **Range Forest Officer (RFO)** - Head of Range - RFO is in-charge of a territorial or functional range. RFO has been referred as the backbone of the forest department.
9. **Forester** - Head of Section
10. **Forest Guard** - Head of Beat
11. **Watcher** -Watch and ward

Forest Development Corporations

After the recommendation in the Interim Report of the National Commission on Agriculture **(NCA, 1972)** on **'Production of Man-made Forests'**, many State Governments in India established **Forest Development Corporations (FDCs)** to work on commercial lines by raising industrial plantations of teak, eucalyptus, bamboo, etc., to enhance the production of forest produce, to restore the productivity of degraded forest areas, to harvest and undertake trade to timber and Non-Timber Forest Products (NTEPs), to own and run forest based industries, to provide support to farmers for marketing their forest product, and to provide consultancy in raising bio-aesthetic plantations, etc. Most of the FDC were created during 1970s.

FDCs exists in 22 states (except in Assam, Manipur, Mizoram, Nagaland, Rajasthan and Sikkim) and in the UT of Andaman & Nicobar Island. Most of the states have only one FDC but two states have more than one forest related corporation, namely Karnataka (Karnantaka FDC, Forest Industries Corporation, & Cashew Development Corporation).

1. **Andhra Pradesh**: **Andhra Pradesh Forest Development Corporation (APFDC)** established in 1975 has an annual turnover of about Rs. 60 crores at present.
2. **Andaman and Nicobar Island:Forest Plantation and Development Corporation**, a Government of India undertaking, was established in 1977 mainly to harvest timber, to manage the inaccessible forest and to undertake cultivation of red oil palm, rubber, spices, etc.
3. **Arunachal Pradesh**: **Arunachal Pradesh Forest Corporation** was established in 1977 mainly to harvest and market timber in the leased forest area by the Forest Department in Tirap and Changlang districts of the state as well as to establish a few wood based industries.
4. **Bihar**: **Bihar Forest Development Corporation (FDC)** was established in 1975 mainly for harvesting and marketing of NTEPs of which tendu leaf was a major product.
5. **Chhattisgarh**: Though **FDC was created in 1976, after bifurcation of the state from Madhya Pradesh in 2000,** it was re-established in 2001, and the annual turnover is of about Rs. 45 crores at present.
6. **Gujarat**: **The FDC was created in 1976** has an annual turnover of about Rs. 30 crores.
7. **Haryana**: **Haryana Forest Development Corporation (HFDC)** was established in December 1989 under the Companies Act, 1956. The annual turnover is of the order of Rs. 37 crores at present.
8. **Himachal Pradesh**: **Himahcal Pradesh State Forest Development Corporation** was established in 1974. The turnover at present is about Rs. 150 crores with approximate profit of Rs. 15 crores.
9. **Jammu and Kashmir**: **The Jammu & Kashmir State Forest Corporation**, a statutory body, was established under the Jammu and Kashmir State Forest Corporation Act, 1978.
10. **Jharkhand**: **Jharkhand Forest Development Corporation** was re-established in 2002 after bifurcation of the state from Bihar to carry on the earlier activities of the Bihar Forest Corporation mainly to harvest NTEPs.

11. **Karnataka**: (i) **The Karnataka Forest Development Corporation (KFDC)** was established in 1971 with the main objective to raise plantations to commercially viable species (rubber, pulpwood, teak and bamboo).

    ii) **The Karnataka State Forest Industries Corporation** was incorporated in the year 1973, under the Companies Act, 1956 with the main objective to harvest forest produce for supply to pulpwood and rayon industries, processing of wood, and manufacture of furniture and wood based construction material.

    iii) **Karnataka Cashew Development Corporation** was incorporated in 1978 under the Companies' Act, 1956, with the main objective of taking over the existing cashew plantation for intensive development and to raise new cashew plantation in the state to attain increased productivity.

12. **Kerala : Kerala Forest Development Corporation** was established in 1975, in Kottayam with specific purpose to raise industrial plantations, spices, cashew, tea, coffee, etc. and to process and trade.

13. **Madhya Pradesh**: **Madhya Pradesh Rajya Van Vikash Nigam** was established in 1975 with the main objective to replace low value and inferior forests with high value multi-utility species.

14. **Maharashtra**: The FDC created in 1974 has an annual turnover of about Rs. 130 crores at present.

15. **Meghalaya**: Meghalaya FDC was established in 1975 under Companies Act, 1956 with authorized share capital of Rs. 2 crores mainly to harvest timber from government forests and to enter into timber trade.

16. **Odisha**: Odisha FDC came into being in 1990 by merging all forest corporations of the state which is including Odisha Forest Corporation (1962).

17. **Punjab**: **The Punjab State Forest Development Corporation** was established in 1983 under the Companies Act, 1956 and the annual turnover is nearly Rs. 34 crores, at present.

18. **Tamil Nadu**: (i) **Tamil Nadu Forest Plantation Corporation Limited (TAFCORN**) was incorporated under the provisions of

the Companies Act, 1956 and 1974 with the main objective to raise, maintain and harvest pulpwood and cashew to meet the needs of industries and to supply firewood to meet the fuelwood needs of the public.

ii) **Arasu Rubber Corporation** is a Government of Tamil Nadu Company functioning under the Tamil Nadu Company functioning under the Tamil Nadu Department of Environment and Forest since 20th August, 1984.

iii) **Tamil Nadu Tea Plantation Corporation Limited (TANTEA)**, an undertaking of the State Government of Tamil Nadu, India was established in 1968, to rehabilitate Sri Lankan repatriates trained in the fine art of tea culture.

19. **Tripura**: **Tripura Forest Development and Plantation Corporation Limited (TFDPC)** was established in the year 1976 under the Companies Act, 1956 and the present turnover is Rs. 45 crores with net profit of Rs. 16 crores.

20. **Uttar Pradesh**: **Uttar Pradesh Forest Corporati**on was established in 1974 under State's Local Bodies Act and not under Company's Act like other States FDCs. The annual turnover is of the order of Rs. 300 crores at present.

21. **Uttarakhand**: Till the creation as a separate state in November 2000 the activities of Uttar Pradesh Forest Corporation were extended in Uttarakhand. After the creation of a separate state, **Uttarakhand Forest Corporation** was established in 2001, and the activities identical to UP Forest Corporation have been continuing.

22. **West Bengal**: **The West Bengal Forest Development Corporation (WBFDC)** came into existence in 1974 and has an annual turnover of Rs. 90 crores and net profit of about Rs. 5 crores.

Ranks in Union Ministry and State Government

Grade	Union Ministry Designation
Apex Scale	Director General of Forests (वन महानिदेशक)
HAG + Scale	Additional Director General of Forests (अपर वन महानिदेशक)
Higher Administrative Grade	Inspector General of Forests (वन महानिरीक्षक)
PB-4	Additional Inspector General of Forests (अपर वन महानिरीक्षक)
PB-4	Deputy Inspector General of Forests (उप वन महानिरीक्षक)
PB-4	Director (निदेशक)
PB-3	Assistant Inspector Gerneral of Forests (सहायक वन महानिरीक्षक)

Grade	State Government Designation
Apex Scale	Principal Chief Conservation of Forests (प्रधान मुख्य वन संरक्षक)
Higher Administrative Grade	Additional Principal Chief Conservation of Forests (अपर प्रधान मुख्य वन संरक्षक)
PB-4	Chief Conservation of Forests (मुख्य वन संरक्षक) Regional Chief Conservation of Forests (क्षेत्रीय मुख्य वन संरक्षक)
PB-4	Conservation of Forests (वन संरक्षक)
PB-3	Deputy Conservation of Forests (उप वन संरक्षक) Divisional Forest Officer (वन प्रमंडल पदाधिकारी)
PB-3	Probationary Officer (प्रशिक्षु पदाधिकारी)

Indian Council of Forestry Research and Education (ICFRE)

The Indian Council of Forestry Research and Education (ICFRE) is an autonomous organisation or governmental agency under the Ministry of Environment and Forests, Government of India. Headquartered in Dehradun, its functions are to conduct forestry research; transfer the technologies developed to the states of India and other user agencies; and to impart forestry education. The council has 9 research institutes and 4 advanced centres to cater to the research needs of different bio-geographical regions. These are located at Dehradun, Shimla, Ranchi, Jorhat, Jabalpur, Jodhpur, Bengaluru, Coimbatore, Allahabad, Chhindwara, Aizawl, Hyderabad and Agartala.

Type	Autonomous Organisation
Established	1986
Parent institution	Ministry of Environment and Forests (India)
President	Maanas
Director	Maanas
Location	P.O. New Forest, Dehradun, Uttarakhand, India 248006
	30.345192°N 78.002193°E Coordinates:
	30.345192°N 78.002193°E
Campus	Urban
Acronym	ICFRE
Website	www.icfre.org//

History

ICFRE is the largest organization responsible for forestry research in India. ICFRE was created in 1986, under the Ministry of Environment and Forests (India), to direct and manage research and education in forestry sector in India. ICFRE is headed by a Director General with headquarters at Dehradun. ICFRE became an autonomous council under the Ministry in 1991.

Mandate

The mandate of the ICFRE is to organise, direct and manage research and education in the forestry sector, including in co-operation with FORTIP (UNDP/FAO Regional Forest Tree Improvement Project), UNDP and World Bank on economically important species. ICFRE established a National Bureau of Forest Genetic Resources (NBFGR).

Research perspective

- Conservation, protection, regeneration, rehabilitation and sustainable development of natural forest ecosystems.
- Revegetation of barren, waste, marginal and mined lands.
- Research on tree improvement.
- Enhancing productivity of wood and non-wood forest produce per unit of area per unit time by application of scientific and technological methods.
- Research on improved utilisation, recovery and processing of forest produce for value addition and employment generation.
- Ecological rehabilitation of all fragile ecosystems, such as mountains, mangroves, deserts, etc.
- Socio-economic and policy research for developing strategies towards attracting people's participation in forest management.

Research Institutes

Institute and their locations, sorted alphabetically					
Name	**Acronym**	**Established**	**City**	**Jurisdiction**	**Website**
Arid Forest Research Institute (AFRI)	AFRI	1988	Jodhpur	Rajasthan, Gujarat, Dadra and Nagar Haveli	afri.res.in
Forest Research Institute (FRI)	FRI	1906	Dehradun	Punjab, Haryana, Chandigarh, Delhi, U.P., Uttarakhand	fri.icfre.gov.in
Himalayan Forest Research Institute (HFRI)	HFRI	1977	Shimla	Himachal Pradesh, Jammu and Kashmir	hfri.icfre.gov.in
Institute of Forest Biodiversity (IFB)	IFB	2012	Hyderabad	Telangana, Maharashtra	frc.icfre.gov.in
Institute of Forest Genetics and Tree Breeding (IFGTB)	IFGTB	1988	Coimbatore	T.N., Kerala, A & Nicobar, Lakshadweep, Pondicherry	ifgtb.icfre.gov.in
Institute of Forest Productivity (IFP)	IFP	1993	Ranchi	Bihar, Jharkhand, Sikkim, West Bengal	ifpranchi.co.in
Institute of Wood Science and Technology (IWST)	IWST	1938	Bengaluru	Karnataka, Telangana, Andhra Pradesh, Goa	iwst.icfre.gov.in#/

Rain Forest Research Institute (RFRI)	RFRI	1988	Jorhat	North-east India	rfri.icfre.gov.in
Tropical Forest Research Institute (TFRI)	TFRI	1988	Jabalpur	M.P., Chhattisgarh, Maharashtra, Odisha	tfri.icfre.gov.in

Advanced Research Centres

Institute and their locations, sorted alphabetically					
Name	**Acronym**	**Established**	**City**	**Jurisdiction**	**Website**
Advanced Research Centre for Bamboo and Rattan (a unit of RFRI)	ARCBR	2004	Aizawl	North-east India	www.icfre.org
Centre for Forestry Research and Human Resource Development (satellite centre of TFRI)	CFRHRD	1995	Chhindwara	M.P., Chhattisgarh, Maharashtra, Odisha	www.icfre.org
Centre for Social Forestry and Eco-Rehabilitation (a centre of ICFRE)	CSFER	1992	Allahabad	Eastern U.P., North Bihar, Vindhya Range	www.icfre.org
Centre for Forest Based Livelihood and Extension[2][14]	CFLE	2013	Agartala	Tripura	tripurainfo
Centre for Urban Forestry Research (a centre of AFRI)	CUFR	(Planned)	Gandhinagar	Gujarat	

Institutes under the Indian Council of Forestry Research and Education

- Advanced Research Centre for Bamboo and Rattan, Aizawl
- Arid Forest Research Institute, Jodhpur
- Centre for Forest-based Livelihoods and Extension (CFLE), Agartala
- Centre for Forestry Research and Human Resource Development, Chhindwara
- Centre for Social Forestry and Eco-Rehabilitation, Allahabad
- Forest Research Institute (India), Dehradun
- Himalayan Forest Research Institute, Shimla
- Institute of Forest Biodiversity, Hyderabad
- Institute of Forest Genetics and Tree Breeding, Coimbatore
- Institute of Forest Productivity, Ranchi
- Institute of Wood Science and Technology, Bengaluru

- Rain Forest Research Institute, Jorhat
- Tropical Forest Research Institute, Jabalpur
- Van Vigyan Kendra (Forest Science Centres)

Other National Institues

Other research institutes under the Ministry of Environment and Forestry

Subordinate offices

- Forest Survey of India, Dehradun
- Botanical Survey of India, Kolkata
- Directorate of Forest Education, Dehradun
- Indira Gandhi National Forest Academy, Dehradun
- National Institute of Animal Welfare, Faridabad
- National Zoological Park, New Delhi
- National Museum of Natural History, New Delhi
- Zoological Survey of India, Kolkata
- Wildlife Crime Control Bureau (WCCB)

Authorities

- Central Zoo Authority of India, New Delhi
- National Biodiversity Authority, Chennai
- National Ganga River Basin Authority, New Delhi
- National Tiger Conservation Authority, New Delhi

Centres of Excellence

- Centre for Environment Education, Ahmedabad
- C.P.R. Environmental Education Centre, Chennai
- Centre for Animals and Environment, Bengaluru
- Centre of Excellence in Environmental Economics, Chennai
- Foundation for Re-vitalisation of Local Health Traditions, Bengaluru
- Centre for Ecological Sciences, Bengaluru
- Centre for Environmental Management of Degraded Ecosystem, Delhi

- Centre for Mining Environment, Dhanbad
- Salim Ali Centre for Omithology and Natural History (SACON), Coimbatore
- Tropical Botanic Garden and Research Institute, Thiruvananthapuram

Under State Governments

- Kerala Forest Research Institute
- Kerala Forest Research Institute, Pecchi, Thrissur
- Forest College and Research Institute, Tamil Nadu Agricultural University, Mettupalayam
- Forest Research Institute, Kanpur, Uttar Pradesh Forest Department
- Gujarat Forest Research Centre, Rajpipla, Gujarat
- State Forest Department, Jammu
- State Forest Research & Training Institute, Raipur, Chhattisgarh
- State Forest Research Institute, Jabalpur, Madhya Pradesh
- State Forest Research Institute, Chennai, Tamil Nadu
- State Forest Research Institute, Itanagar, Arunachal Pradesh

Forest Research Institute, Dehradun

The **Forest Research Institute** is an institute of the Indian Council of Forestry Research and Education and is a premier institution in the field of forestry research in India. It is located at Dehradun in Uttarakhand, and is one of the oldest institutions of its kind. In 1991, it was declared a deemed university by the University Grants Commission.

Established as Imperial Forest Research Institute in 1906, Forest Research Institute (FRI), Dehradun, is a premier institution under the Indian Council of Forestry Research and Education (ICFRE). Styled in Greeko Roman Architecture by C.G. Blomfield, the main building is a National Heritage which was inaugurated in 1929.

The Indian Council of Forestry Research and Education (ICFRE) is the apex body in the national forestry research system to develop a holistic forestry research through planning, promoting, educating and coordinating research education and extension of all aspects of forestry.

The following forestry research institutes and centres under the Council are responsible for undertaking research in their respective eco-climatic zones:

- Forest Research Institute, Dehradun
- Arid Forest Research Institute, Jodhpur
- Rain Forest Research Institute, Jorhat
- Institute of Wood Science and Technology, Bengaluru
- Tropical Forestry Research Institute, Jabalpur
- Institute of Forest Genetics and Tree Breeding, Coimbatore
- Himalayan Forest Research Institute, Shimla
- Institute for Forest Productivity, Ranchi
- Centre of Social Forestry and Eco-rehabilitation, Allahabad
- Institute of Forestry Research and Human Resources Development, Chhindwara

In addition, **the Indian Plywood Industries Research and Training Institute, Bengaluru**, an autonomous body of the Ministry, is a premier institution engaged in research and training activities on mechanical wood industries technology. **The Indian Institute of Forest Management, Bhopal**, an autonomous organization of the Ministry also undertakes training, research and consultancy in forest management.

(*Source:* National Portal Content Management Team)

List of Universities and Colleges of India

Working in the Field of Forestry

- Forest Research Institute, Dehradun
- PDKV University, Akola
- Arid Forest Research Institute, Jodhpur
- Aspee College of Forestry and Horticulture, Navsari Agricultural University, Navsari, Gujarat
- College of Forestry and Hill Agriculture, Ranichauri, G.B. Pant University of Agriculture and Technology, Pantnagar
- College of Forestry, Dr. Balasaheb Sawant Konkan Krishi Vidyapeeth University (BSKKV), Dapoli, Maharashtra

- College of Forestry, Kerala Agricultural University
- College of Forestry, Ponnampet, UAHS, Shimoga
- College of Forestry, Sirsi, University of Agricultural Sciences, Dharwad
- College of Horticulture and Forestry, Maharana Pratap University, Jhalawar, Rajasthan
- Department of Forest Sciences, Desh Bhagat University (DBU), Mandi, Gobindgarh, Punjab
- Department of Applied Science, North-Eastern Regional Institute of Science and Technology (NERIST), Nirjuli, Arunachal Pradesh
- Department of Ecology and Environmental Science, Assam University, Silchar, Assam
- Department of Forestry, Dr. Panjabrao Deshmukh Krishi Vidyapeeth University (PDKV), Akola, Maharashtra
- Department of Forestry, Hemwati Nandan Bahuguna Garhwal University
- Department of Forestry, Jawaharlal Nehru Agricultural University, Jabalpur, Madhya Pradesh
- Department of Forestry, Wildlife and Environment Science, Guru Ghasidas University, Bilaspur
- Dr. Yashwant Singh Parmar University of Horticulture and Forestry, Nauni, Solan, Himachal Pradesh
- Forest College and Research Institute, Tamil Nadu Agricultural University, Mettupalayam, Tamil Nadu
- Forest Department, Forest Rangers College, Angul, Odisha
- Forest Research Institute University, Dehradun
- Indian Institute of Forest Management, Bhopal
- Gujarat Forest Research Institute, Gujarat Forest Rangers College, Rajpipla, Gujarat
- Faculty of Forestry, Sher-e-Kashmir University of Agricultural Sciences and Technology of Kashmir, Ganderbal, Jammu and Kashmir.

Chapter 2

Forest Policy
(Definition, Scope and Legal Approaches to Forest Management)

The necessity of a vigorous forest policy was strongly indicated from the earliest days of British occupation in India.

First step towards conservation policy: The first step towards development of conservation was an order issued by the "**Bengal Bombay Joint Commission**" appointed to enquire into the internal circumstances of the Malabar (Kerala) and make regulations prohibiting the felling of teak trees of girth less than 21 inches (53.34 cm)

Royalty on teak trees: The declaration of royalty on teak trees claimed by the former governments was vested in the East India Company and any further unauthorised felling of such trees was banned. Further, British government appointed a special officer for the preservation and improved production of teak and other timbers suited for ship building.

First Conservator: Captain Watson of the Police was appointed as the first conservator of forests in India, in **1806** (in Madras). Watson succeeded in establishing a timber monopoly throughout Malabar, Travancore (Kerala) and practically extinguished private rights in the forests.

Beginning of scientific forestry in India: Dr.Mcclelland was appointed as the superintendent of forests declaring all forests as a government property. The province of Pegu (city in Myanmar, Burma) was annexed in 1852. For nearly hundred years, teak had been one of the most important exports from Rangoon (Yangon, former capital of Burma) and the forests have been claimed as Royal property by the Alompra dynasty (Burma).

Outline of permanent forest policy: In 1855, the government of India laid down for the first time the outline of a permanent policy for forestry in the country in response to the report submitted by Dr.Mcclelland. This was a great step for laying the foundations of Indian forestry. Later **Brandis was appointed as the IGF to the Government of India**, who introduced measures for the protection and improvement of forests.

Charter of Indian Forestry, 1855: Dr.Mcclelland, Superintendent of forests of Pegu suggested (Report submitted to GOI) that certain restrictions need to be placed on the unchecked exploitations of forests by private parties. This formed the basis of the memorandum of the government issued on 3rd August, 1855 by Lord Dalhousie (then Governor General of India).

This has come to be known as the **"Charter of Indian Forestry".** This has laid down for the time the outline of policy for forest conservancy. It was an act of far sighted statesmanship and marked the first concrete step towards the scientific conservation and management of forests in India.

National Forest Policies

The following Forest Policies have been formulated after the **Charter of Indian Forestry** of 1855 are:

1. **Forest Policy, 1894 (19th October, 1894)**
2. **National Forest Policy, 1952 (12th May, 1952)**
3. **National Forest Policy, 1988 (7th December, 1988)**
4. **National Forest Policy, 2018 (Draft)**

What is a national forest policy and why should a country have one?

The term "**policy**" is not tightly defined but is used in different ways on different occasions. Often, it can **mean "a course of action adopted and pursued". A national forest policy is a policy for society, not for forestry administration**. A policy can be explicitly stated or not. It can also be planned or it can emerge through evident behaviour. It is, thus, often viewed either as a rational system based on deliberate aims and plans or as a consequence of political activity arising from a series of decisions. In any case, a policy needs to provide guidance and a sense of direction over a certain period of time in order to be useful. People complain that central government, a ministry or other stakeholders "do not have a policy", when decisions are made on an ad hoc basis or are incoherent or contradictory.

A policy is intended to guide and determine present and future decisions and actions. It usually comprises two elements:

- A set of aspirations, goals or objectives
- An outline of a course of action to achieve them.

In this book, a national forest policy is considered to be a negotiated agreement between government and stakeholders (i.e. all those who depend on or benefit from forests or who decide on, control or regulate access to these resources) on the orientations and principles of actions they adopt, in harmony with national socio-economic and environmental policies, to guide and determine decisions on the sustainable use and conservation of forest and tree resources for the benefit of society.

A national forest policy is not to be unilaterally imposed by government. Ideally, it is an agreement among bodies that represent different forest interests and is formally adopted by government. Who should be involved in its development is, thus, a key question, as the selection of the participants influences which interests are taken into account. As Byron (2006) observes, it is difficult to imagine a national forest policy that can be relevant and useful without being firmly placed within the broader aims of society. Forest policies, thus, not only have to cover issues under the competence of the forestry administration and its agencies, but also they need to contribute to overarching policies, including those responsible for national development or economic and poverty strategies. They also need to be consistent with policies issued by other government authorities, e.g. on environmental protection, climate change, agriculture, industry and trade. Further, they need to be in line with a country's forest-related international commitments. ***Thus, a forest policy is a policy for people, not for the forestry administration.***

Being an agreement among government and stakeholders, a national forest policy is endorsed by government and implemented through legal, economic and informational instruments, and by other stakeholders with their respective means. Ultimately, through government endorsement, a formal national forest policy is the official position of the government, as a clear statement of a country's goals and objectives, made public so that all parties know the directions being pursued and the outcomes to be achieved. If different actors, each pursue their particular interests and change course frequently, larger goals or longer-term objectives are unlikely to be reached. Thus, there are a number of good reasons for jointly developing and using an agreed forest policy:

- The process of bringing stakeholders with diverse interests together to negotiate an agreement is extremely valuable in itself.
- A mutually accepted forest policy builds a sense of joint ownership, which is essential for its implementation.
- The involvement of stakeholders beyond the forest sector gives the policy legitimacy across society. Wide buy-in is particularly advantageous when negotiating with powerful ministries, such as agriculture, energy, planning or finance.
- A national forest policy provides excellent guidance for developing more coherent institutional frameworks and policy instruments, including forest legislation.
- A national forest policy can guide the planning and operations of forestry stakeholders including administrations and agencies at various levels.
- A national forest policy facilitates communication, coordination and collaboration across government, non-governmental organizations and the public.
- A national forest policy can provide a solid basis for international policy discussions and for strengthening technical assistance co-operation.
- The national forest policy can serve as a reference to guide decisions on emerging issues, particularly those where quick, difficult or controversial decisions must be made.

How does a forest policy relate to forest laws, national forest programmes, strategies and action plans?

A forest policy sets out a broad vision or goal and a long-term direction about forests and their use but does not usually specify in detail the instruments or practices to implement it. One key instrument for implementing the forest policy is the forest legislation. Some countries do not have a forest policy statement and consider the legislation to contain or express the policy, providing the main framework that guides government action. However, the primary purpose of legislation is the distribution and enforcement of rights and responsibilities related to forests, not to lay down an agreed vision, goal or strategy.

"Forest policy and forest law are complementary tools: the policy provides direction and law establishes rights and responsibilities".

Does a policy have to be within the legislation or must the legislation be within the policy?

Obviously, any government policy needs to be consistent with the constitution and other laws of a country. However, all laws, including those pertaining to forests, are made with certain policies in mind. Thus, a policy, i.e. an agreement on strategic direction, needs to be developed before any aspect of it can be made legally binding. After all, translating the rights and duties contained in policy into law is a technical procedure, not a political one. Thus, experts in formulating legislation will say "give me the policy and I will draft the law". In practice, wherever no such policy statement is available, revising forest legislation is a more or less explicit process of policy development and formulation. In cases where a forest policy statement has been agreed, forest legislation can be amended accordingly to implement the policy.

Legislation is usually considered a key instrument for implementing a forest policy, setting out rights and obligations and institutionalizing the rules through primary legislation (parliamentary-level) and secondary legislation (regulations, decrees, ordinances and bye-laws, for example). Legislation prohibits certain conduct, provides for sanctions and offers a solid foundation for action in the face of political changes in government. However, using forest laws as the basis for policy guidance has some undesired consequences. Not all policy aspects can be covered in sufficient detail in the legislation, and specifications in legal acts are subject to legal procedures. Thus, resorting to the judiciary is a way of delaying, if not stopping, a specific action. Moreover, legal instruments are usually inadequate in terms of providing guidance or the flexibility to address emerging issues. Neither are they easily accessible or understandable to all. Nonetheless, in the face of conflict and in the absence of other mechanisms to settle disputes, law takes precedence over policy. Only the former can be challenged through the courts for a judgment based on legislation, not policy. For these reasons, legal advisers often recommend putting no more than core rights and responsibilities into forest legislation.

Table 1 summarizes the main differences between forest policy and legislation.

Sometimes legislation needs to be repealed or revised because it is out of step with the new policies, vision and goals. However, amendments may not be required to implement a revised forest policy if non-governmental entities, such as forest industries undertake the major functions and if their practices are already regulated by broader laws, such as those that govern planning or protect the environment.

The term "**forest policy**" is also sometimes confused with "**national forest programme**" (NFP). A term agreed by countries in the international dialogue on forests, NFP denotes a comprehensive forest policy framework built on a number of specific principles, which can be loosely clustered in three groups:

- National sovereignty and country
- Leadership;
- Consistency within and integration beyond the forest sector, and participation and partnership (FAO, 2001).

This framework builds on the iterative process of developing/ revising and implementing national forest policies and of translating international commitments into action on the ground.

Forest legislation can be drafted after policy decisions are made, not vice versa.

Table 1: Main differences between forest policy and forest law

S.No	Forest Policy	Forest Law
1.	Can be adopted and amended through different procedures and by different bodies, according to each specific situation	Adopted and amended by Parliament or the Head of State through procedures determined by the Constitution or legislation
2.	Non-legally binding	Legally binding
3.	Provides guidance by specifying visions, goals and how to reach them	Specifies rights and duties based on a policy vision or goals
4.	Can be general, so it can be adapted to meet different and changing circumstances	Must be specific to enable judicial dispute settlement and applied universally across jurisdictions
5.	Soft mechanisms to deal with non-compliance	Judicial powers to punish non-compliance
6.	Amended by those bodies that adopt the policy, through their respective procedures	Constitutionally or legally determined procedure needed for amendments

"NFPs are a comprehensive framework for a country's forest policy. NFP processes and platforms are used to develop or revise forest policy, strategies and programmes and facilitate their implementation".

How does a National Forest Policy link to other policies?

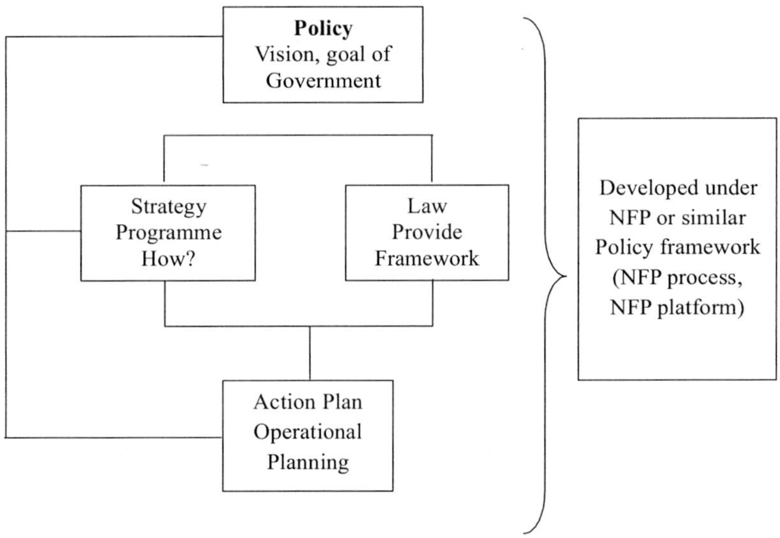

Fig. The relationship between Policy, Strategy, Law and Action Plans

Forest policy-makers have become increasingly aware, especially over the past decade, that forests cannot be managed sustainably, if other land and natural resource users do not recognize the importance of these resources. One reason for poor policy implementation and a lack of impact of many beautifully written policies and plans in the past was that they often were out of touch with the realities around forests and the wider societal developments.

For instance, in many countries, the rate of deforestation remained high despite explicit forest policies to reduce deforestation. In other cases, food production, shelter, infrastructure or broader economic development took precedence over ambitious afforestation programmes. Such examples underline the critical need to link forest policies with and to incorporate forest aspects into wider national policies – so as to make forest policies relevant and to enhance society's recognition of the value and benefits of forests and sustainable forest management. However, all too often, communication and collaboration with and among those responsible for developing and implementing these wider policies are absent. ***Forest policy goals need to be clearly linked to national development strategies.*** The below diagram illustrates the relationship between Policy, Strategy, Law and Action Plans.

Factors affecting Forest Policy

The following factors or considerations have a bearing on the forest policy of nation or state:

A. The National priorities, such as:

i) Conservation of forests

ii) Biodiversity Conservation

iii) Wildlife Conservation and protection

iv) Ecological security

v) Research and training needs

vi) Survey of forest resources

B. Regional priorities, such as:

i) Generating revenue

ii) Maintaining the water cycle

iii) Wildlife conservation and protection

C. Lacal priorities, such as:

i) Meeting local timber and non timber needs

ii) Rights and concessions

iii) Tribals

iv) Generation of employment.

❑❑❑

Chapter 3

National Forest Policies (NFP 1894, NFP 1952 and NFP 1988)

I. Highlights of Forest Policy, 1894 (19th October, 1894)

On the basis of Dr.Voelker report, entitled "**Improvement of Indian Agriculture**", the Govt. of India formulated the forest policy, 1894. This is the first national forest policy in India enacted under pre independence era.

Salient features

The salient features of the forest policy of 1894 are given below:

1. The main object of forest management is to promote the general well being of the country.
2. The maintenance of adequate forest cover is emphasized for the preservation of climatic and physical conditions and to meet the basic requirement of the people.
3. The government owned forests have been classified as follows:
   a) **Preservation of Forest:** Forest whose preservation is required on climatic and physical grounds.
   b) **Commercial Forest:** Forest for supplying valuable timber and other commercial products.
   c) Minor Forest
   d) Pasture Lands
4. This policy emphasis on permanent cultivation rather than shifting cultivation.
5. The policy gives importance to the fulfillment of the basic needs of the local people.
6. Obtaining maximum revenue is the main goal instead of conserving forest reserves.

Drawbacks / Limitations of NFP, 1894

1. It was formulated to satisfy the needs of the British Government.
2. It gives priority mainly to agriculture than forestry.
3. This facilitates easy diversion of forest lands for non-forestry purposes.
4. No guidelines for research and training in forestry.
5. Less stress is emphasized on the problems like shifting cultivation, forest fire, etc
6. No guidelines on conservation and preservation of biodiversity.
7. No specific provisions for management of wildlife.
8. Less emphasis is given on the management of catchments and forest on it.

Summary of First Forest Policy, 1894

After the establishment of a structured forestry set up in 1864, with the appointment of Dr. Dietrich Brandis as the first Inspector General of Forest, the first National Forest Policy was formulated in 1894. This document, which was circular No. 22-F dated **19th October, 1894, was based on 8th and 9th Chapters of Dr. Voelcker's Report on "Improvement of Indian Agriculture" and Review of Forest Administration in British India for 1892-93.** These documents differed in their approach considerably. While Dr. 27Voelcker attempted to recommend the role of forestry as subservient to agriculture, the Inspector General of Forest adopted a conservative approach and discussed in detail the principles, which should underlie the management of a state forest in India.

However, efforts were made to accommodate both viewpoints and to produce a document, which lays down the general policy regarding management of forests in British India. As per the policy, forests, being state property were broadly classified under four headings, namely Forest for Preservation, Forest for Commercial purposes, Minor Forests and Pasture Lands. Though, the aim of this policy was to manage state forests for public benefit, certain regulation of rights and restriction of privileges for the use of forest by the neighbouring populations was provided in this policy. Further, para 6 of the policy clearly mentioned: whenever an effective demand for cultural land exists and can only be supplied from forest, the land should ordinarily be relinquished without hesitation. This Forest Policy of 1894 did not accord proper recognition to forestry which was called for and in respect of land use, it was placed next to the agriculture.

The first Indian Forestry Act was passed in 1865 to control indiscriminate felling and initiate the preparation of working plans that would regulate yield. The first statement of National Forest Policy in 1894 emphasized the need to demarcate, reserve, and conserve forests. While this was excellent from the point of view of genetic resource conservation and wildlife, soil, and water protection, it did neither rationalize or maximize yields of forest products nor did it endear forestry officials to local populations, because forest officers carried out a policing function. Even today, it is not uncommon to hear foresters talk of forests "burdened with rights" implying that, in their opinion, non-foresters should be excluded from the forests. Yet, even under the 1894 policy, which later served as a model for other countries of the British Commonwealth, if a demand for agricultural land arises that can be met only from a forest, it should be conceded without hesitation (subject to certain reasonable conditions); further, forests that yield only inferior timber, fuelwood, or fodder, or that are used for grazing, should be managed mainly in the interest of the local population.

The Forest Policy of 1894 was the first official move towards regulating the rights and concessions enjoyed by the forest-dependent communities.

Important features

1. Rights and Concessions

'The Forest Policy of 1894 was the first official move towards regulating the rights and concessions enjoyed by the forest-dependent communities. The cardinal principle to be observed is that the rights and privileges of individuals must be limited, otherwise than for their own benefit, only in such degree as is absolutely necessary to secure that advantage (NFP 1894, para 2).

However, the Policy also clarified that every attempt should be made for the full and easy satisfaction of the needs of the forest-dependent people. Considerations of income should be made secondary to the full satisfaction of local needs...no restrictions should be placed upon reasonable local demands merely in order to increase the state revenue. (NFP 1894, para 8).

2. Grazing

The Forest Policy of 1894 was the most elaborated of all the policies in explaining the modalities of grazing in the various classifications of the forests.

The question whether any particular area can be made to support a greater number of cattle by preserving the grass and cutting it for fodder, or by permitting grazing upon it, is one that must be decided by the local circumstances of each case. (NFP 1894, para 11).

3. Fuelwood

Similar to grazing, supply of fuelwood was not an issue at the time of the Forest Policy of 1894 because the Government was of the view that the demand of fuelwood could be easily met from the margins of forest tracts without causing much harm to the valuable timber species. For the class three forests , the Policy specially mentioned that: These must be managed mainly in the interests of the population of the tracts which obtained its forest requirements from this source. (NFP 1894, para 9).

4. Shifting Cultivation

Though the Forest Policy of 1894 made it amply cleat that the claims of cultivation are stronger than the claims of forest preservation, it was against the honeycombing of a valuable forest by patches of cultivation and maintained that cultivation must be permanent. On the question of shifting cultivation, it stated that: A system of shifting cultivation which denudes a large area of forest growth in order to place a small area under crops, costs more to the community than it is worth, and can only be permitted under due regulation, where forest tribes depend on it for their sustenance. (NFP 1894, para 7).

II. Highlights of National Forest Policy, 1952 (12th May, 1952)

NFP, 1952 was the first forest policy of Independent India, which overcomes the short comings in the 1894 policy. This policy is formulated on the basis of paramount needs of our country that are as follows :

1. Need for evolving a system of balanced and complementary land use.

2. Need for checking the denudation in mountain region, soil erosion in river banks and invasion of sea sands on coastal tracks and shifting sand dunes in deserts.
3. Need for the establishment of tree lands, wherever possible.
4. To manage the progressively increasing demands (grazing, wood and firewood).
5. Need for the sustained supply of timber and other forest produce.
6. Need for the realization of the maximum annual revenue in perpetuity.

Main features of NFP, 1952

1. The forest is to be for the maintenance of physical conditions of the country.
2. This policy classifies the forest as follows:
    a) **Protection Forests:** These are the forests which are essential for the preservation of physical and climatic conditions of the county.
    b) **National Forests:** These forests are maintained and managed to meet the national needs (defence, communication industry and other purpose).
    c) **Village Forests:** These forests are maintained for providing firewood, small timber and other forest produces to local people and grazing for cattle.
    d) **Tree Lands:** These are the areas through which the scope of the ordinary peoples outside the forest is satisfied. These are essential for the amelioration of physical condition of the country.
3. This policy advocated a functional classification of India's forests, apart from legal classification (Reserved forest, Protected forest, Village forest and Un-classed forest) to focus attention on the specific object of management in each case into Protection forests, National forests, Village forests and Tree Lands.
4. The policy also suggested to keep a minimum of $^{1}/_{3}{}^{rd}$ of country's total land area under forests with **60% in the Himalayas and other hilly tracts** liable to erosion and **20% in the plains**.

Recommendations of National Commission on Agriculture (NCA), 1976

The NCA constituted in 1970, suggested the need for a revised forest policy in their report of 1976. The NCA concluded that National Forest Policy should rest on two important points, viz.:

1. Meeting the requirements of goods, i.e. industrial wood for forest based industries, defence, communications and other public purposes and small timber, fuelwood and fodder for rural community.
2. Satisfaction of the present and future demands for protective and recreational functions of the forests.

To meet these requirements, NCA suggested a revised forest policy. Revised National Forest Policy (draft) recognises the following vital needs of forest management :

i) For providing maximum goods and services for the public well-being and economic progress of the country.

ii) Need for checking denudation and erosion in the mountainous region, tree less river banks and wastelands.

iii) Need for realizing maximum productivity of the forests to meet increasing requirement of individual raw material, timber and other forest produce.

iv) Providing small timber, firewood and grazing for rural population. However, indiscriminate and harmful grazing to be strictly controlled.

To fulfill the above needs, the policy suggests that on an average, 33% of the land area should be dedicated to forest, comprising of **60% in the hills** and **20% in the plains.**

The policy clearly spells out the multiple purposes, for which the forests will be managed. For example:

a) **Environmental conservation:** To manage and provide for rehabilitation and improvement of forests for their protective influences, specially soil and water conservation.

b) **Production:** To meet the demands of existing and developing industries and the national requirements of timber for defence, communication and domestic needs.

c) **Social:** To meet the social needs of the community, such as recreation, agricultural timber, fuelwood and regulated grazing for rural people.

Summary of the National Forest Policy of 1952

The need for the formulation of the national forest policy became imperative after the attainment of Indian independence. Again, for removing the shortcomings of the Forest Policy of 1894, it was strongly advocated to formulate a new policy. Many fundamental changes had taken place in Indian economy since 1894. The pressure on all forms of land, including forests, had increased due to the rapid increase of population. The value of forests was recognised not only in the physical field, such as conservation of moisture, prevention of erosion and increase in rainfall but also in the economic field, such as development of agriculture, industry and communications. Hence, the conservation and development of forest resources had assumed an unprecedented importance in the economic life of the nation.

Revolutionary changes had occurred in the political field. India had become a sovereign democratic republic and the constitutional changes had conferred a large measure of autonomy on the States in the administration of forests. In view of all these facts and considerations, a forest policy was re-enunciated to suit the changed circumstances.

The Government of India enunciated the National Forest Policy on 12 May, 1952.

The new policy replaced the policy of 1894. This policy was built upon the earlier one which "still holds good" and also covered the omissions in it. Particularly, the protective and productive functions of forests as well as realisation of maximum revenue were covered in it. The policy prescribed that it was desirable to have one-third of the total land area for maintaining as forests. This policy called for a detailed survey for the proper land use. Soil conservation aspects were emphasized in this policy. It urged the forest tribes to be weaned away from the practice of shifting cultivation. Further, the need for wide publicity on the value of forests was pointed out in this policy. Villagers residing in the neighbourhood of forest must be permitted to enjoy greater use of its products for the satisfaction of their domestic and agricultural needs. Such use should in no event be permitted at the cost of national interest. In the Forest Policy of 1894, there was a provision for relinquishment of forest land for agricultural purpose. In the new policy, the indiscriminate extension of agriculture and consequent destruction of forests were stopped.

The policy realised the vital functions of the forest in fulfilling the paramount needs of the country and based on functions, the forests were classified as protection forests, national forests, village forests and tree-lands. Protective forests were to be preserved for physical and climatic considerations. They should be created on hill slopes, river banks, seashores or other erodable localities. In such sites, the need for forest cover was dictated by purely protective physical considerations, such as prevention of erosion, conservation of moisture and control of rushing torrents and floods. The scientific management of such protection forests should include the production and exploitation of timber within the limits of safety. National forests constituted the basis of India's strength and wealth, for they comprised valuable timber which was indispensable for defence, communications and vital industries. They had to be managed chiefly in the interest of the nation. The basic policy must be to attain national self-sufficiency in these vital supplies. Cultivation should not be permitted to encroach upon these valuable timber-bearing tracts. The policy stated that "the solution of the food problem of an ever-increasing population must be sought primarily in intensive cultivation and not in weakening the very basis of national existence by encroaching upon such forests." Village forests were to be maintained to provide firewood, small timber and so on to the rural population living adjacent to the forests. Tree lands, which though outside the scope of the ordinary forest management, were essential for the amelioration of the physical condition of the country. The policy emphasised expansion of tree cover in lands owned by Government and public as well as private institutions. The policy stated that "Defence, Railways, Public Works Department, Universities and Colleges, District Boards, Municipalities and other local authorities, associations and institutions can lend a helping hand by converting the lands at their disposal into tree lands". 'Tree consciousness' among the masses can alone pave way for expanding rapid tree cover in public and private lands. It should be noted that the forest departments of States were assigned important tasks in the expansion of tree lands. Thus, the classification of 1952 aimed to attract proper attention for due management of each type of forest and every kind of forest was considered significant for the country.

Control of private forests by individuals must be regulated in the national interests so that the indiscriminate exercise of individual rights might not prejudice or endanger general welfare. According to the policy of 1952 regulations and control of private forests by the State were imperative on economic, physical and climatic considerations. India as a whole should aim at maintaining one-third of its total land area under forests. As an insurance against denudation, 60 per cent of the area should be kept under forests in mountainous tracts for their protective functions and in plains the proportion should be 20 per cent. Forest area, in excess of the indicated proportion, should not be sacrificed. It was a landmark in the developmental history of Indian forestry. The policy did not fix a time-bound programme; hence, a serious shortcoming. For affording protection to the animal kingdom and particularly to rare species, laws should be enacted and sanctuaries and national parks should be set up. All grazing in forests, particularly unlimited and uncontrolled grazing was incompatible with scientific forestry. Hence, grazing should be regulated as regards the time and place and also the number of cattle admitted. Large restriction on sheep grazing and total exclusion of goats was recommended. It was suggested that a reasonable fee was to be charged from the users. Grazing should not be allowed in regeneration areas and young plantations. Grazing incidents should be kept at the minimum in protection forests. Shifting cultivation caused 'serious damage' to the forests. So, it should be guarded and co-operation of cultivators should be sought for this purpose. The policy noted that "it requires persuasion, not coercion; a missionary not an authoritarian approach."

The policy recommended proper forest legislation and it can alone provide proper legal support for the promotion of forestry. The policy stated that "the efficiency of forest administration depends directly on the adequacy of the forest laws, the training and calibre of the professional forest services and the progress of research on both the biological and the utilisation aspects of forestry." While forest legislation, forest education and research constituted the basis for sound forest management, the goodwill of the people in the neighbourhood of forests alone could provide the firm ground for the promotion of forestry. There were numerous cases of exploitation by intermediaries and hence, forest co-operative societies should be formed to solve the problem of exploitation.

Thus, the forest policy of 1952 was more towards scientific management of forests with better clarity on various aspects like the area of forests which are to be preserved. It also spelt out management strategies for various types of forests. It did lay more emphasis on the management objectives of forest resource management.

III. Highlights of National Forest Policy, 1988 (7th Dec, 1988)

The aim of forest policy is to ensure environmental stability and maintenance of ecological balance for the sustenance of all life forms, humans, animal and plants.

This national forest policy is enunciated due to the following needs:

1. To meet the increasing energy demands of the population.
2. To obey the new directive principles and duties given in the Indian constitution.
3. Constitutional amendments of 1976 and its stress on environment.
4. Marked growth of forest based industries in this era.
5. Need for the guidelines on conservation of wildlife.

Basic objectives

1. To maintain the environmental stability and ecological restoration through preservation.
2. To check soil erosion and denudation in the catchment areas and mitigation of floods.
3. To check the sanddune extension in desert and coastal lands.
4. To increase the forest and tree cover in the denuded and degraded lands.
5. To meet the requirements of the tribal people.
6. To conserve the natural heritage.
7. To increase the productivity of the forest to meet the various needs.
8. To encourage the substitution of wood and reduction of wood usage.
9. To create a massive people movement and minimize the pressure on existing forest.

Essentials of forest management

1. Existing forests should be protected and its productivity improved.
2. Diversion of agricultural lands to forestry should be discouraged.

3. Conservation of biodiversity should be strengthened through national park, sanctuary and biosphere reserve.
4. Afforestation programmes should be encouraged to meet the local requirement of fuel wood.
5. MFP production is encouraged to augment tribal employment and income.

Management strategy

1. The area under forests should be a minimum of $^{1}/_{3}{}^{rd}$ of total geographical area, in which hills and mountainous region should have $^{2}/_{3}{}^{rd}$ cover.
2. Afforestation, social forestry and farm forestry programme are encouraged.
3. Rights and concessions of the local people are suitably addressed.
4. Diversion of forest lands for non-forestry purposes is discouraged.
5. Wildlife conservation is given more importance.
6. Shifting cultivation practices are discouraged and cultivation of perennial crops through horticulture and tree farming is encouraged.
7. Fire and grazing management is given special consideration.
8. Forest based industries are advised to meet their raw material requirements from outside the forests.
9. Forest extension, research and personnel management.

Summary of the National Forest Policy of 1988

The national forest policy which was enunciated on 7 December, 1988, is the most important policy document in the recent times. It has a far-reaching impact on forest resource management. Numerous outstanding changes occurred in Indian economy between 1952 and 1988. Rapid growth of population had been the cause of huge additional requirements of food, fuel wood, fodder, timber and other products of forestry. As a result, over the years forests had suffered "serious depletion". Inadequacy of protection measures, diversion of forest lands to non-forest uses and the tendency to look upon forests as revenue earning resources were other important causes of depletion. Forestry which was in 'State List' was brought under 'Concurrent List' after the Forty-Second Amendment of the Indian Constitution in 1976. Moreover, ten fundamental duties were included in the Constitution and the seventh one is "to protect and improve natural environment including forests, lakes, rivers, wildlife and to have compassion for living creatures." Again three new directive principles were added and one is related to the promotion of natural environment including forests, lakes, rivers, wildlife by the State. The constitutional amendments were considered a landmark because they enabled the Central Government to issue guidelines for the management of forests. Subsequently, in order to consolidate depleted forest areas, the Government of India passed the Forest Conservation Act of 1980, making it mandatory to get prior concurrence of the Government of India for diversion of any forest land for non-forest use. The National Commission on Agriculture, constituted in 1972, gave its final recommendations in 1976. It gave a new thrust and meaning to forest management in India.

The Commission studied the forestry sector in toot and gave wide ranging recommendations touching all aspects of forestry. Recommendations included all aspects like forest policy, forest protection, production forestry, social forestry, wildlife management, forest-based industries and so on. So, the need to review the situation and to evolve a new strategy of forest conservation including preservation, maintenance, sustainable utilisation, restoration and enhancement of the natural environment had become imperative. Thus, a new national forest policy was formulated in 1988. The new policy envisaged the basic objectives for preservation, protection and development of forests with the principal aim to ensure environmental stability and maintenance of ecological balance including atmospheric equilibrium. Direct economic benefits derived from forests were given secondary importance in the new policy. Conservation of total biological diversity was considered gainful for national welfare. For the conservation of total biological diversity, the network of national parks, sanctuaries, biosphere reserves and other protected areas should be strengthened and extended adequately. Indian forests were put under pressure and depleted due to inadequate supply of fuel wood, fodder and small timber, particularly in the vicinity of human habitation. It was observed in the policy that firewood was the only source of energy in rural areas and hence, rapid afforestation of species to augment the supply of firewood was an urgent necessity. The guidelines in the policy regarding the adoption of need-based and time-bound programme of afforestation and tree planting on all degraded and denuded lands must be considered a landmark in the developmental history of Indian forest. The demand for forest products was increasing in India on account of rapidly rising population. The 1988 policy recommended to enhance forest cover that is, a minimum of one-third of the total area of the country as well as to increase productivity of forests by applying latest scientific and technological methods so that growing requirements of the country could be fulfilled. Moreover, the policy emphasized the creation of a massive people's movement with the involvement of rural women for achieving these objectives and minimising pressure on existing forests. The problem of wildlife conservation was analysed in the policy. It was accepted in the policy that forest management must include prescriptions for the conservation of wildlife. No doubt, the setting up of the Central Wildlife Board in 1952 and the enactment of the Central Wildlife Act in 1972, promoted development programmes for wildlife conservation in India. Maintenance of genetic continuity was considered essential for balanced wildlife conservation. It is stated that "it is specially essential to provide for 'corridors' linking the protected areas in order to maintain genetic continuity between artificially separated subsections of migrant wildlife."

The National Forest Policy of 1988 paid special attention towards the problems of forest-based industries. The forest-based industries were classified as : wood-based industries, forest plantations and tree-based industries and forest-based miscellaneous industries. The forest-based industries should raise the raw material, needed for meeting their own requirements. They were to establish direct relationship with individual growers of raw material by providing the individuals with inputs including credit, constant technical advice and finally harvesting and transport services. The practice of supplying forest produce to industry at concessional price would cease and the industry should be encouraged to use alternative raw materials and also to liberalise the import of wood and wood products in a phased manner. The forest-based industries should provide employment to local people on priority and involve them fully in raising trees and producing raw material.

Financial support for forestry was examined in the forest policy of 1988. The objectives of this policy "could not be achieved without the investment of financial and other resources on a substantial scale". Such investment was fully justified "considering the contribution of forests in maintaining essential ecological processes and life-support systems and in preserving genetic diversity. Forests should not be looked upon as a source of revenue.... They are a national asset to be protected and enhanced for the well-being of the people and the nation."

Broad comparison of National Forest Policies (NFPs)

Parameter	NFP, 1894	NFP, 1952	NFP, 1988
1. Objective	Improvement of agriculture and public interest and rights	Balanced and complementary use of forest produce	Conservation of natural heritage, biodiversity and genetic resources.
2. Forest classification	1. Commercial Forest (Forest for timber production). 2. Minor Forests 3. Preservation Forest 4. Pasture Lands	1. Protection Forests 2. National Forests 3. Village Forests 4. Tree Lands	No classification
3. Tribal people and forests	No guidelines	Not much guidelines	Symbiotic relationship between forest department and tribal
4. Scope for increasing tree cover	No guidelines	Increasing vegetative cover through planting on railways, PWD lands.	Massive afforestation programme emphasized through measures
5. Control of private forests	No guidelines	Few guidelines given	Detailed guidelines given
6. Proportion of forest area	No guidelines	1/3rd of the area, 60% in hills and 20% in plains	33% under forests cover and 66% tree cover in hills.
7. Protection to wildlife	No guidelines	Protection of rare and endangered species only	Network of protection measures strengthened.
8. Grazing	No guidelines	Grazing is allowed with nominal fee	Grazing is allowed according to carrying capacity.
9. Shifting cultivation	No guidelines	No coercive measures to stop Shifting cultivation.	Discourage Shifting cultivation
10. Sustainable yield	No guidelines	Limited scope	Detailed measures are given
11. Forest administration	No guidelines	Trained foresters are recommended	Personal management for professional foresters.
12.Forestry legislation	No guidelines	Enactment of forest acts	Appropriate legislation is given
13. Forestry training education and research	No guidelines	Few guidelines given through rangers college and Universities.	Detailed guidelines on training and scientific forestry research is given for increasing productivity, afforestation, wildlife and wood substitution.
14. Good will of local people	No guidelines	Instructions need for peoples co-operation	Focus on people's participation in forest management.

National Forest Policy, 2018

[Approved Draft version / F. No. 1-1/2012-FP (Vol.4) / Govt. of India / Ministry of Environment, Forest and Climate Change / Forest Policy Division]

As a result of the implementation of the 1988 policy prescriptions, there has been an increase in forest and tree cover and reduction in the diversion of forest land for other land uses despite compelling demands from the increasing population, industrialization and rapid economic growth. However, the low quality and low productivity of our natural forests, impacts of climate change, human-wildlife conflict, intensifying water crisis, increasing air and water pollution and deteriorating environment have been the issues of serious concern. The increased concerns for biodiversity conservation and the need to enhance forest ecosystem services, through new technological advancements and the continuously declining investments in the sector present new challenges for forest management in the country.

Hence, there is a need to revise the National Forest Policy, 1988 in order to integrate the vision of sustainable forest management by incorporating elements of ecosystem security, climate change mitigation and adaptation, forest hydrology, participatory forest management, urban forestry, robust monitoring and evaluation framework and establishment of mechanisms to oversee multi-stakeholder convergence in forest management, while building on our rich cultural heritage of co-existence and relying on our rich and diverse forest resources.

Goal and Objectives

The following objectives shall be guiding the National Forest Policy:

1. Maintenance of environmental stability and conservation of biodiversity through preservation and conservation of natural forests.
2. Reverse the degradation of forest by taking up rehabilitation without compromising its natural profile.
3. Improvement in livelihoods for people based on sustainable use of ecosystem services.
4. Contribute towards achieving forestry related Nationally Determined Contribution Targets (NDC's) of the country.

5. Checking denudation and soil erosion in the catchments of rivers and the wetlands through integrated watershed management techniques and practices.
6. Maintenance of the health of forest vegetation and forest soils for augmenting water supplies through recharge of underground aquifers and regulation of surface water flows.
7. Safeguard forest land by exercising strict restraint on diversion for non-forestry purposes, and strict oversight on compliance of the conditions.
8. Increasing substantially the forest/tree cover in the country through Afforestation & reforestation programmes, especially on all denuded and degraded forest lands and area outside forests.
9. Manage protected areas and other wildlife rich areas with the primary objective of biodiversity conservation and for enriching other ecosystem services.
10. Conserve and sustainably manage mountain forests to ensure continuous flow of ecosystem services, including watershed, biodiversity, cultural and spiritual services to both upstream and downstream population.
11. Factor green accounting, valuation of ecosystem services and climate change concerns adequately into the planning and management of all forests, protected areas and other ecosystems.
12. Increase substantially the tree cover outside forests by incentivizing agro-forestry and farm forestry, facilitating assured returns, with enabling regulations and by promoting use of wood products.
13. Integrate climate change mitigation and adaptation measures in forest management through the mechanism of REDD+ (Reducing Emissions from Deforestation and Forest Degradation plus) so that the impacts of the climate change is minimised.
14. Incentivize sustainability in community managed, community owned private forests and creating a sustained peoples' movement for achieving these objectives.
15. Managing and expanding green spaces in urban and peri-urban areas to enhance citizens' well-being.

16. Ensure effective translation of this policy into action by establishing credible measuring, monitoring and evaluation framework, ensuring good governance, providing commensurate financial support and developing an implementation framework with periodic review.

Essential Principles of Forest Management

The following essential management principles will be pursued in this policy:

1. Existing natural forests should be fully protected and their productivity improved. Adequate measures will be taken to increase rapidly the forest cover on hill slopes, in catchment areas of rivers, lakes and reservoirs and ocean shores and, on semi-arid, and desert tracts.
2. Productivity of the forest plantations will be increased through scientific and technological interventions so as to encourage usage of more timber so that the dependency on other high carbon footprint wood substitutes is reduced.
3. Management of the natural biodiversity rich forests for maximising the ecosystem services for ecological security of the nation.
4. For conservation of flora, fauna and total biodiversity, the network of national parks, sanctuaries, conservation reserves, community reserves, biosphere reserves and important wildlife corridors and biodiversity heritage sites will be strengthened and extended adequately.
5. Afforestation with suitable species will be intensified so as to cater to the needs of the rural population for fuel wood and small timber. Further alternative sources of energy like LPG, etc. will be promoted in rural areas to reduce dependency on forests.
6. Non-Timber Forest Produce (NTFP), such as medicinal and aromatic plants, oil seeds, resins, wild edibles, fibre, bamboo and grass, etc. will be sustainably managed for improving the income of the tribals & other forest dependent populations.
7. Promotion of trees outside forests & urban greens will be taken upon a mission mode for attaining the national goal of bringing one third of the area under Forests & trees cover and also for achieving the Nationally Determined Contribution (NDC's) targets of the country.

Strategy: The following strategies will be adopted to achieve the objectives of this policy :

Sustainable Management of Forests

a) Reducing Threats to Forests
b) Forest fire prevention
c) Enhance Quality and Productivity of natural forests
d) Increase the productivity of forest plantations
e) Protecting & enriching the Catchments
g) Management of forests to be as per the approved Working Plan
h) Strengthen participatory forest management
i) Management of Non-Timber Forest Produce.

- Management of trees outside forests
  a) Promote agro-forestry and farm forestry
  b) Promoting urban greens.
- New Thrust Areas in forest & tree cover Management
  a) Production Forestry
  b) Economic valuation of the forests
  c) Forest management for water recycling
  d) Forest Certification
  e) Integrate climate change concerns & REDD+ strategies in forest management
  f) Develop a national forest ecosystems management information system.
- Strengthen Wildlife Management
- Facilitate forest industry interface
- Research and Education
- Extension and awareness
- Management of North-Eastern Forests
- Legal and institutional frameworks
- Training and Skill development
- Financial support

- Harmonization with other policies and laws
- Assimilation of International Commitment and foster regional Co-operation
- Good governance
- Implementation framework and way forward.

Periodic review

The National and State Boards of Forestry will review implementation of this policy periodically. The achievements and progress made in implementing this policy will be monitored to ensure smooth and time-bound translation of this policy into action.

❑❑❑

Chapter 4

Forest Law and Legislation

(Forest Law, Legal Definition and Objectives, Legal Aspects of Forest Protection)

Introduction

Law

- Every society has a system of rules promulgated by the ruling groups for regulating the behaviour of its member.
- Law is a command (of a sovereign) which obliges a person or persons to a course of conduct.
- The right way of doing things are termed as "Norms" by sociologists.
- Individuals was conform to norms are reworded and those who deviate are punished.
- Social norms become legal norms through enactment and enforcement.
- To define law is more difficult task due to various reasons. Various schools of law have defines law from different angles on the basis of nature source and some on the effect on society.

Hooker

Law is kind of rule or cannon wave by actions are framed.

Austin

Law is command of the sovereign.

Maciver and Page

Law is the body of rules which are recognized, interpreted, and applied to particular situations by the courts of the state. It is clear that law is a rule of conduct.

Purpose of law

- To maintain law and order
- To maintain status in society
- To make an individual to have maximum freedom
- To give maximum satisfaction of the needs of the people

i) Basis of law

Whatever relationship that is envisaged by the sovereign authority between person and things on one hand and persons and persons on the other hand forms the basis of law.

ii) The concept of law

Dr. Sethna defines law as follows: "Civil law may be defined as all that body of statutes or ordinances, rules made by the Government by virtue of powers given to it by the legislature and judicial decisions based on positive morality, public opinions, customs and conventions, enforced through the machinery of judicial process and meant for regulating the rights and duties of citizens interest and the state and citizens - so as to secure the greatest good of the greatest number".

iii) The evolution of law

Law is evolved from precedent, custom, statute and these the courts apply to the exclusion of their private judgements.

iv) The characteristics of law

a) Law is a command set by a sovereign authority, backed by requisite force so as to claim habitual obedience from the bulk of the community.

b) Law is not justice in itself but is an instrument for achieving justice

c) Law is uniform and is applicable to all without any distinction

d) Law is administered by courts functioning as a limb of the state

v) Forest protection and law

The legal concept of a forest does not take the nature of vegetational growth into account. Even an area devoid of any vegetation can be a forest in a legal sense, if such an area has been decaled as one or the other category of forests according to prescribed procedure. In case of dispute, courts rely on dictionary for enlightenment.

a) The value of forest

There are three important roles played by forests; they are protective, productive and accessory. Protective means the conservation of soil and water, the production of wood and other forest produce refer to productive function, recreation, improvement of environment contribute towards aesthetic role.

b) Abuses against which forests need protection

For the protection of valuable renewable resources like forest, the aid of law is necessary.

vi) The scope of forest law

In order to secure effective protection of the forests, the law has to :

a) Define the limits of forest property

b) Classify them into different categories, requiring different degrees of protection

c) Provide for the regulation and settlement of rights of regular users

d) Incorporate suitable provisions for preventing the commission of forest offences and punishing the offenders, when they are actually committed

e) Invest public authorities with necessary powers to enforce the above provisions

f) To prescribe such other measures as would be necessary for the protection of forest generally.

Legal aspects of forest protection

Forest protection pertains to all activities concerned with protecting the forest for various influences, such as:

a) Human activity
b) Climatic factor
c) Insects and diseases
d) Wild and domestic animals

Forest law needs to protect forests from influences of human beings and their animals This includes:

a) Lopping
b) Illicit felling
c) Theft of forest produce
d) Encroachment of forest land
e) Grazing
f) Hunting of wild animals
g) Diversion of forest land for non-forestry purposes

Constitutional provisions

The Indian constitution is one of the few in the world in which there are specific provisions regarding forests and environment. **Forests, environment and wildlife are now in the concurrent list** and both Parliament and State legislatures have power to make laws in this regard. **The constitutional provisions with regard to the protection and conservation of forests are:**

1. **Article 48 A:** The state shall endeavour to protect and improve the environment and to safeguard the forests and wildlife of the country.

2. **Article 51 (A):** It shall be the duty of every citizen of India to protect and improve the natural environment including forests, lakes, rivers and wildlife and to have compassion for living creatures.

The Scheduled Tribes and other Traditional Forest Dwellers (Recognition of Forest Rights) Act, 2006.

- This forest legislation is passed in India on 18th Dec, 2006.
- This is also called as **Forest Right Act, Tribal Right Act, Tribal Bill and Tribal Land Act.**

- The law concerns with rights of forest dwelling communities of land and other resources, denied to them over decades as a result of the continuance of colonial forest laws in India.

Forest Legislation

Law: *"Law is a body of principle recognized and applied by a state in the administration of justice"*. It is a command laid by a sovereign and backed by adequate firms. This acts as an instrument for achieving justice in a social system and is applicable to all common people in the country without distinction. Court functions as limb of the state to enforce the law.

General Law: These laws are uniformly applicable to all citizens. It regulates and affects the day to day activities of citizens. People have very good general awareness of these laws.

e.g. Penal Code, Criminal Procedure Code, Traffic Code and Civil Code.

Special Law: This is made for specific purposes in special field. It may or may not be known to all. *e.g. Forest Law, International Law and Salt Law.*

There are two kinds of law in a social system :

Civil Laws: The Civil laws pertains to the enforcement of rights of the citizen in a country.

Criminal Law: Criminal laws are pertaining to the punishment for wrong offences.

Forest Law

Forest Laws: Forest Laws are the laws pertaining to forest and all other forest related activities.

The main scope of the forest laws are as follows :

1. Forest law defines the limit of forestry
2. It helps in classifying forest into distinct categories
3. Forest law deals with the provision on rights (conversion and suspension)
4. Forest law has provision for preventing abuse and offense
5. It defines the public authorities involved in and their empowerment

Necessity of Forest Laws

In India, there are number of forest laws available for the protection of forest. Forest laws are inevitable in a country in order to manage the forest property in a sustained manner :

1. Forest laws are needed to deal the misconception of common people that forest that forest can be exploited at their will.
2. The exercise of rights and concession by the people should be controlled.
3. Forests are larger in extent and are located in remote area, hence it is difficult to protect from the adverse agents.
4. Forests are subjected to varieties of injuries and damage from diverse factors.
5. Forests products are more vulnerable to threat.
6. Special power is needed to shift the forest officials, who work in remote areas.
7. Protection of wildlife from hunting and poaching is the immense need of the hour.

History of Forest Legislation

The history of forest legislation dates back to 1865, during which the first Indian Forest Act was enacted.

A chronological account of forest legislation is given below :

1865	The first Indian Forest Act (IFA) was enacted.
1918	Indian Forest Act (IFA) was amended.
1927	The Indian Forest Act, 1927 was enacted.
1972	Wildlife (Protection) Act, 1972 was passed.
1976	Tree Protection Act, 1976 was enacted for protection of trees.
1980	Forests Conservation Act, 1980 was passed.
1991	Wildlife Protection Act, 1972 was amended.
2001	Indian Forest Act (IFA), 1927 was amended in many states.
2002	Biological Diversity Act was signed by India (UN Convention on biodiversity).
2006	Scheduled Tribes (Recognition of Forest Rights) bill was introduced.

❑❑❑

Chapter 5

Important Acts Enacted in India to Conserve Forests, Wildlife and Biodiversity

A. Indian Forest Act, 1927, State Forest Acts and Rules
B. Wildlife Protection Act, 1972
C. Forest Conservation Act, 1980
D. Tribal Act, 2006
E. Biological Diversity Act, 2002
F. The Karnataka Preservation of Trees Act, 1976

A. The Indian Forest Act, 1927

Salient Features of Indian Forest Act, 1927

Objective: To consolidate the law relating to forests, the transit of forest-produce and the duty leviable on timber and other forest produce.

Salient Features

a) Does not define forest but demarcate forest areas.
b) The definition of forest produce include some produce not found in the forests e.g. timber, mahua seeds, natural varnish, bark, lac, resin, wood-oil, catechu, etc.
c) Control over the forest is divided into Govt. and Non-Govt. land:
   i) Forest under Govt. is classified as reserved, village and protected forests.
   ii) Reserved forest is created by a State Notification and is administered by a Forest Officer. The system excludes free from human interference. State Govt. had earlier power to denotify the reserve forests but is now subject to Central Govt. approval.

iii) A village forest is, through notification, is a reserve forest assigned to the village community, vesting in them some rights.

iv) Protected forests, again through notification, covers area not covered under reserve forest. However, access to and use of this forest area is quite flexible.

v) The State Govt. has power to regulate or prohibit certain activities in forest area that is not under its control for certain specific reasons.

d) The State Govt. is empowered to regulate the duty levied on timber and other forest produce.

e) Penalty for non-compliance and lies over forest produce.

f) Exploitation is the goal of the Act rather than conservation and the State Govt. has absolute control.

The Indian Forest Act, 1927

It was amended in 1948 and is the main legislation dealing with forest in India. **This Act has 13 chapters and 86 sections.**

The **Indian Forest Act, 1927** was largely based on previous Indian Forest Acts implemented under the British. The first and most famous was the Indian Forest Act of 1878. Both the 1878 Act and the 1927 one sought to consolidate and reserve the areas having forest cover, or significant wildlife, to regulate movement and transit of forest produce, and duty leviable on timber and other forest produce. It also defines the procedure to be followed for declaring an area to be a **Reserved Forest**, a **Protected Forest** or a **Village Forest**. It defines what is a forest offence, what are the Acts prohibited inside a Reserved Forest, and penalties leviable on violation of the provisions of the Act.

Reserved Forest

Reserved Forest is an area mass of land duly notified under the provisions of India Forest Act or the State Forest Acts having full degree of protection. In Reserved Forests all activities are prohibited unless permitted. Reserved Forest is notified under section 20 of the Indian Forest Act, 1927 [Act 16 of 1927] or under the reservation provisions of the Forest Acts of the State Governments of the Indian Union. The manner in which a Reserved Forest, shortly written as RF, has to be constituted is described in section 3 to 20 of the Act. It is within power of a State Government to issue a preliminary notification under section 4 of the Act declaring that it has been decided to constitute such land, as specified in a Schedule with details of its location, area and boundary description, into a Reserved Forest. Such a notification also appoints an officer of the State Government, normally the Deputy Commissioner of the concerned district, as Forest Settlement Officer. The Forest Settlement Officer fixes a period not less than three months, to hear the claims and objections of every person having or claiming any rights over the land which is so notified to be reserved. He conducts inquiries into the claims of rights, and may reject or accept the same. He is empowered even to acquire land over which right is claimed. For rights other than that of right of way, right of pasture, right to forest produce, or right to a water course, the Forest Settlement Officer may exclude such land in whole or in part, or come to an agreement with the owner for surrender of his rights, or proceed to acquire such land in the manner prescribed under the **Land Acquisition Act, 1894 [Act 1 of 1894]**. Once the Forest Settlement Officer settles all the rights either by admitting them or rejecting them, as per the provisions of the Act, and has heard appeals, if any, and settled the same, all the rights with the said piece of land [boundaries of which might have been altered or modified during the settlement process] vest with the State Government. Thereafter, the State Government issues notification under section 20 of the Indian Forest Act, 1927 declaring that piece of land to be a Reserved Forest.

Protected Forest

Protected Forest an area or mass of land notified under the provisions of India Forest Act or the State Forest Acts having limited degree of protection. In Protected Forests, all activities are permitted unless prohibited. Protected Forest is an area or mass of land, which is a reserved forest, and over which the Government has property rights, declared to be so by a State Government under the provisions of the section 29 of the Indian Forest Act, 1927. It does not require the long and tedious process of settlement, as in case of declaration of a reserved forest. However, if such a declaration infringes upon a person's rights, the Government may cause an inquiry into the same; but pending such inquiries, the declaration cannot abridge or affect such rights of persons or communities. Further, in a protected forest, the Government may issue notifications declaring certain trees to be reserved, or suspend private rights, if any, for a period not exceeding 30 years, or prohibit quarrying, removal of any forest produce, or breaking of land, etc. Indian forest Act was established in 1972 for the protection of all the flora and fauna.

Village Forest

Village Forest is constituted under section 28 of the Indian Forest Act, 1927. The Government may assign to any village community the rights over a land, which may not be a part of a reserved forest for use of the community. Usually, forested community lands are constituted into **Village Grazing Reserve [VGR]**. Parcels of land are so notified and marked on the settlement revenue maps of the villages.

The Indian Forest Act, 1927

Constitution of Reserve Forest (*Chapter II – Section 3 -27*)

The state government may notify any forestland or wasteland as a reserve forest (Section 3). The effects of this declaration are as follows:

a) It declares particular land as a Reserve Forest (RF).

b) The situation and limits of the land are specified.

c) A Forest Settlement Officer (FSO) is appointed to inquire and settle the disputes regarding claims and rights.

Section-5: After notification, no further acquisition of forest rights is allowed.

Section-6: A proclamation regarding extent of RF and rights is published by the FSO. After this the right holders can apply to the FSO for getting their rights.

Section-11: The FSO can take following action, if the claim is admitted :

a) Excluded that land form the limits of the proposed RF.

b) Enter into an agreement with the owner for the surrender of rights.

c) Acquire the land under the land acquisition Act with proper compensation.

Section-19: There is a provision for appeal against the order of the FSO regarding constitution of RF or rights related conflicts.

Section-20: After all, appeals are amicably settled, the orders of the FSO are disposed off. Thereafter a notification is published by the state government which specifies the exact limit of the boundaries of the RF.

Constitution of Protected Forest (*Chapter IV – Section 29 -34*)

The state government may notify any forestland or wasteland as a protected forest [Sec. 29(1). No notification is issued unless the nature and extent of the rights in and over the area have been inquired. After the notification, the effects of this Act are issued by the state government. The effects of this declaration are as follows :

a) Declare any tree or class of trees as a protected forest from the date of notification.

b) Declare that any specified portion of forest in the notification will be closed for a period of not more than 30 years.

c) The rights of private persons are suspended, provided alternate sources are available.

Section-31: The collector shall cause a translation of above in the local vernacular.

Section-32: The state government empowered to regulate the followings:

1. Breaking up or clearing of land for cultivation.
2. Pasturing cattle inside the Protected Forest (PF).
3. Firing or clearing of the vegetation.
4. Cutting, sawing, conversion and removal of trees and timber.
5. Collection and removal of forest produce from PF.
6. Granting permits to the people in PF to take the timber and MFP for own use.
7. Checking of MFP and passing out form PF.
8. Protecting reserved trees and timber form fires.
9. Cutting of grasses.
10. Hosting, shooting, fishing, poisoning water and setting traps in PF.
11. Protection and management of a closed forest.

Section-33: The following offences are punishable inside the PF:

a) Felling, girdling, lopping, tapping, burning, stripping of bark or leaves from a reserved tree.

b) Quarrying stone, burning lime, collection or removal of stone, collection or removal of MFP from a closed forest.

c) Breaking up of land for cultivation or clearing land in any PF.

d) Causing fire.

e) Permitting cattle to damage a reserved tree.

Section-34: The state government empowered to suspend the right of pasture for a fixed period, whenever a fire is caused willfully or by gross negligence.

Control on forest produce in transit (*Chapter VII – Section 41 -44*)

The state government controls all rivers and their banks with regard to the floating on water [Sec. 41(1)]. The rules for control of timber and other forest produce in transit may include the following provisions:

a) Provisions regarding the routes along which forest produces can be imported or exported or moved in or out from a forest.

b) Regulate the movement of forest produce without transit permit.

c) Provision for stoppage, reporting, examination and making of all forest produces in transit.

d) Provision for the establishment and regulation of depots.

e) Prohibition of any Act which may cause the river or channel to be closed or obstructed for the transit of timber or other forest produce.

f) Regulation of the use of the property marks on timber and registration of such marks.

The state government is empowered to notify that any provision of the transit rules will not apply to a specific area or a class of timber **[Sec. 41(3)]**. Offences under the transit rules are punishable **[Sec. 42]**. The government shall be responsible for any loss or damage, which may occur in respect of any forest produce at depot **[Sec. 43]**. In case of any accident or emergency, every person employed shall assist in averting such danger to secure such property from damage or loss **[Sec. 44]**.

B. Wildlife Protection Act, 1972 (details)

Summary of the Act: The Wildlife Protection Act, 1972 is a Central Act of Parliament providing for the protection of wild animals, birds and plants and for matters connected therewith or ancillary or incidental thereto with the view to ensuring the ecological and environmental securities of the country. It extends to the whole of India except the state of Jammu and Kashmir. The Act provides for the constitution of a National Board for Wildlife with the Prime Minister as the Chairperson. The National Board shall promote the conservation and development of wildlife and forests by such measures as it thinks fit. The Act also provides for the constitution of a State Board for Wildlife to advise the state government in matters connected with the protection of wildlife. The Act regulates the hunting of wild animals and protection of specified plants. It also empowers the State Government to notify Sanctuaries, National Parks, and Game Reserves. It has also setup a National Tiger Conservation Authority and regulates trade or commerce in wild animals, animal articles and trophies. Contravention of provision of the Act are punishable with imprisonment from 1 to 7 years and/with fine upto Rs. 50 lakhs depending on the nature of offence.

The **Wildlife Protection Act, 1972** is an Indian legislation enacted by the Parliament of India for protection of plants and animal species. Before 1972, India only had five designated national parks. Among other reforms, the Act established schedules of protected plant and animal species; hunting or harvesting these species was largely outlawed.

The Act provides for the protection of wild animals, birds and plants; and for matters connected therewith or ancillary or incidental thereto. It extends to the whole of India, except the State of Jammu and Kashmir which has its own wildlife Act. It has six schedules which give varying degrees of protection. **Schedule I** and part II of **Schedule II** provide absolute protection - offences under these are prescribed the highest penalties. Species listed in **Schedule III** and **Schedule IV** are also protected, but the penalties are much lower. **Schedule V** includes the animals which may be hunted. The plants in **Schedule VI** are prohibited from cultivation and planting. The hunting to the Enforcement authorities have the power to compound offences under this Schedule (i.e. they impose fines on the offenders). Upto April 2010, there have been 16 convictions under this Act relating to the death of tigers.

Definitions under the Act (Section 2)

1. **"Animal"** includes amphibians, birds, mammals, and reptiles, and their young, and also includes, in the cases of birds and reptiles, their eggs.
2. **"Animal article"** means an article made from any captive or wild animal, other than vermin, and includes an article or object in which the whole or any part of such animal has been used and an article made there from.
3. **"Hunting"** includes :
   a) Capturing, killing, poisoning, snaring, or trapping any wild animal, and every attempt to do so
   b) Driving any wild animal for any of the purposes specified in sub-clause
   c) Injuring, destroying or taking any body part of any such animal, or in the case of wild birds or reptiles, disturbing or damaging the eggs or nests of such birds or reptiles.
4. **"Taxidermy"** means the curing, preparation or preservation of trophies.
5. **"Trophy"** means the whole or any part of any captive or wild animal (other than vermin) which has been kept or preserved by any means, whether artificial or natural. This includes:
   a) Rugs, skins, and specimens of such animals mounted in whole or in part through a process of taxidermy
   b) Antler, horn, rhinoceros horn, feather, nail, tooth, musk, eggs, and nests.
6. **"Uncured trophy"** means the whole or any part of any captive animal (other than vermin) which has not undergone a process of taxidermy. This includes a freshly killed wild animal, ambergris, musk and other animal products.
7. **"Vermin"** means any wild animal specified in Schedule V.
8. **"Wildlife"** includes any animal, bees, butterflies, crustacean, fish and moths; and aquatic or land vegetation which forms part of any habitat.

Hunting (Section 9): This section describes what constitutes hunting and the intent to hunt. Hunting of wild animals is prohibited.

Ownership (Section 40 & 42): Regarding ownership issues and trade licences.

Penalties (Section 51): Penalties are prescribed in section 51. Enforcement can be performed by agencies, such as the Forest Department, the Police, the Customs and the **Central Bureau of Investigation (CBI).** Charge sheets can be filed directly by the Forest Department. Other enforcement agencies, often due to the lack of technical expertise, hand over cases to the Forest Department.

Wildlife Protection Act-1972 (chapter wise)

It is promulgated in 1972 and it is the basic law governing wildlife in India. It comprises of 6 chapters, 66 sections and 6 schedules.

Chapter I : Define the Act, terms and boundaries applicable

Chapter II : Authorities to be appointed

Chapter III : Hunting of wildlife (removed under 1991 amendment)

Chapter IV : Declaration of National Park, Game Reserve and Closed areas

Chapter V : Trade or commerce in wildlife (Section 39-49)

Chapter VI : Prevention and detection of offence

The chapter wise important sections are described below:

Chapter I: Define the Act, terms and boundaries applicable

Sec. 1: It extends to whole of India except Jammu and Kashmir

Sec. 2: It defines the animal, animal article and other terms explained in the Act.

Chapter II: This deals with the authorities to be appointed / approved under this Act.

Sec. 3: Authorities to be appointed by Central Government for the purpose of this Act.

a) Director of wildlife preservation

b) Assistant Director of wildlife preservation

c) Any officers, if necessary

Sec. 4: Authorities to be appointed by State Government for the purpose of this Act are:

a) Chief Wildlife Warden (CWW)

b) Wildlife warden

c) Any officers, if necessary

Sec. 5: It deals with the power of declaration by the director of Chief Wildlife Warden

Sec. 6: Constitution of wildlife board by the state government

Sec. 7: Procedures for setting up a wildlife advisory board.

Sec. 8: Advisory power of wildlife advisory board of state.

Chapter III: Hunting of wildlife (removed under 1991amendment)

This chapter deals with hunting of animals, issue of licenses and permits, capturing of animals and prevention of collection of specific plants. No person shall, unless authorized by a license, hunt the wild animals other than vermin (Sec. 15).

Hunting of wild animals

This Act prohibits hunting of any wild animals specified in schedule I to IV expect provide under Sec. 11 and Sec. 12. But *under special conditions the CWW can permit hunting of scheduled I animals* (Sec. 11).

Special conditions necessitating animal killing :

1. If the animal is dangerous to human life
2. If the animal is disabled or injured one
3. If the animal is diseased which is beyond the recovery stage

The killing of animals in good faith in defense shall not be considered as an offense. The animals killed or wounded under this condition is a government property.

Collection or capturing of wild animals

The CWW with the permission of Central Government can permit collection or capturing of schedule I animals under special conditions, which are as follows (Sec. 12):

1. Education
2. Scientific research
3. Scientific management (Translocation and population)
4. Collection of specimen for zoological gardens

Protection of specified plants (Chapter-IIIA, Sec, 17)

This Act prohibits picking, uprooting, damaging, destroying and acquiring of specified plants from forests. This prohibits collection of specified plants from any forest land. Possession, transforming and sale of these plants are prohibited except bonafide personal use by the scheduled tribes.

The CWW by the prior approval of state government can permit collection of these plants under specific conditions. Cultivation of specified plants without license is also prohibited. The dealing of these specified plants requires specific license from the forest department.

Specified plants are those plants that are denoted in schedule VI :

a) *Cycas beddomei*
b) *Renanthera imschootiana* (Red vanda)
c) *Vanda coerulea* (Blue vanda)
d) *Nepenthes distillatoria* (Pitcher plant)
e) *Paphiopedilum* sp. (Ladies slipper orchid)

a) ***Cycas beddomei:*** *Cycas beddomei* was originally listed as Vulnerable in the Indian Red Data Book (Nayar and Shastry, 1987) and later re-evaluated as Endangered by Rao *et al.* (2003). This species is known only from the Tirupati-Kadapa Hills in Andhra Pradesh State, north-west of Madras in eastern Peninsular India.

b) ***Renanthera imschootiana*** (Red vanda; *Orchidaceae*-orchid family): Red Vanda is restricted to the State of Manipur and neighbouring areas in NE India. It grows on small shrubs and trees at elevations of 300-500 m flowering during spring.

c) ***Vanda coerulea*** (*Blue vanda): Vanda coerulea* was formally described by John Lindley in 1847 from the description of a blue orchid found in the Khasia Hills of Assam by William Griffiths. In the wild, *Vanda coerulea* grows on exposed deciduous trees (primarily oak) at elevations of 900–1500 m.

d) ***Nepenthes distillatoria* (Pitcher plant):** *Saussurea lappa is* annual herb of the eastern Himalayas (Kashmir) having purple florets and a fragrant root that yields a volatile oil used in perfumery.

e) ***Ladies slipper orchid*:** An orchid of the genus *Paphiopedilum*

Chapter IV (Sanctuary, National Park, Game reserve and Closed area)

Sanctuary

The state government may by notification, declare any area to be a sanctuary, if it considers that area has adequate ecological, faunal, floral, geomorphologic, natural or zoological significance for the purpose of protecting, propagating or development of wildlife of its environment **(Sec. 18)**.

Sanctuary is an area declared under section 18 or 38 or deemed under sub-section 3 of section 36 to be declared as Wildlife Sanctuary. If the central government is satisfied that the conditions specified under section 18 are fulfilled, the area by notification is declared as sanctuary **[Sec. 28 (1)]**.

Before declaration, the collector publishes a proclamation regarding the sanctuary limits and claiming of rights. The collector shall determine the rights of any person in or over the land with in the sanctuary **(Sec. 19).** After notification a bar is placed on rights **(Sec. 21).** The collector shall pass an order admitting or rejects the right in whole or in part. In case of acquisition of rights or land, the collector with the previous sanctions of the state government may provide an alternative to the right holders. *e.g.* In case of stoppage of public way, an alternative public way should be given. After settling all rights and issues, the specified area is declared as sanctuary **(Sec. 26)**.

The following are restricted inside the sanctuary. Entry inside the sanctuary is restricted one. Damage to boundary work is restricted **(Sec. 27).** But the CWW can permit the entry inside the sanctuary for the purpose of photography, scientific research, tourism and transaction of any useful business with person residing inside the sanctuary **(Sec. 28)**. Destruction of forest property **(Sec. 29)**, causing fire **(Sec. 30)**, use of rigorous substances **(Sec. 32)**, grazing **(Sec. 33)** and possession of arms **(Sec. 34)** inside the sanctuary is prohibited. All livestock in and around the sanctuary region should be properly immunized **(Sec. 33A).**

National Parks

National Park is an area declared under section 35 or 38 or deemed under sub-section 3 of section 36 to be declared as National Park. If the central government is satisfied that the conditions specified under section 35 are fulfilled, the area by notification is declared as national park **[Sec. 28(1)].**

Under **Sec. 35(1)**, the state government may declare any area as a national park with the importance of its ecological, faunal, floral or geomorphologic association for the purpose of protecting, propagating or developing wildlife in its environment. The provisions of **sec. 19-26** are applicable in declaring a national park.

No alteration of the boundaries of a national park shall be made except on a resolution passed by the state legislature. No person shall destroy, exploit or remove wildlife or its habitat from the national park. No grazing of any cattle shall be permitted inside the national park.

Game Reserve

The state government may by notification, declare any area to be a game reserve **(Sec.36).** Hunting of any wild animal shall be permitted inside the game reserve.

Closed Area

The state government may by notification, declare any area to be closed for hunting for a certain period **(Sec.37).** No hunting of any wild animal shall be permitted in closed area.

Chapter IV A

This chapter deals with the constitution of ***Central Zoo Authority (CZA)*** **(Sec.38 A).** It specifies ***the minimum standards for zoo construction*** **(Sec.38 C)** and is as follows:

i) Housing, keeping and veterinary care of animals kept in zoo

ii) Recognition or de-recognition of zoo

iii) Breeding of endangered species of wild animals

iv) Coordination of acquisition and exchange of animals for breeding programme

v) Provide technical guidance for zoo management

vi) No zoo shall be operated without being recognized by the CZA. The management authority should apply for getting permit with in 6 months from the date of commencement of zoo.

vii) No person shall acquire or transfer any wild animal specified is schedule I and II except with previous permission of the CZA.

viii) No person shall be teased, molested or feed any animal or cause disturbance to animals.

Chapter V: Trade or commerce of wild animals, it articles and trophies

Wild animal other than vermin is covered under this Act **[Sec. 35(1)]**. Animal article, trophy or meat derived from any wild animal obtained under any offense of this Act shall be treated as the property of state government or central government, if it is collected from sanctuary or national park respectively.

Any person a government property shall report to the nearest police station with in 48 hours. No person shall without permission to (a) acquire or keep in possession, custody, control of wild articles, (b) transfer by gift or sale of wild articles, and/or (c) destroy or damage to wild articles.

Every person having control, custody or possession of any captive animal specified in schedule I or part II of schedule II, or any uncured trophy, salted skin, muscle of musk deer, horn of rhinoceros, shall declare to CWW within 30 days. No person shall acquire, control, custody, sell or transport of wildlife articles without permission of CWW. This is not applicable to zoo or museum **(Sec. 40)**. The CWW may issue certificate of ownership for favour of possessions of any wild animal or any animal article trophy or uncured trophy **(Sec. 42)**.

Person does not possess a certificate of ownership shall not (a) sale or gift of any wild animal specified in schedule I or part II of schedule II. When a person transfers wildlife articles to outside the state, shall report to the CWW within 30 days. This is not applicable to feathers of peacock and articles made from them **(Sec. 43)**.

Dealing in trophy and animals article without license is prohibited **(Sec. 44)**. It prohibits the commerce, such as (i) a manufacture in any animal article, (ii) a taxidermist, (iii) a dealer in trophy or uncured trophy or captive animals or meat, etc.

The **Sec. 45-49** deals with all license related issues, such as (i) suspension of any license by CWW, (ii) appeal against the cancellation of license and (iii) keeping of records by the license owner.

Chapter VI: Prevention and detection of offenses

The sections 50 to 66 deals clearly all the offenses related to wildlife.

Amendments to Wildlife Protection Act

Amendments

The Code has been amended several times.

S.No.	Short title of Amending Legislation	Year
1.	Wild Life (Protection) Amendment Act, 1982	1982
2.	Wild Life (Protection) Amendment Act, 1986	1986
3.	Wild Life (Protection) Amendment Act, 1991	1991
4.	Wild Life (Protection) Amendment Act, 1993	1993
5.	Wild Life (Protection) Amendment Act, 2002	2002
6.	Wild Life (Protection) Amendment Act, 2006	2006

Amendment to Wildlife Protection Act

Wildlife Protection Act Amendments – 1991

1. Need of appropriate representation of tribal in the state advisory board.
2. Separate chapter (III) is introduced to regulate exploitation of threatened species.
3. No alteration in the change of boundary lines of sanctuary and national park.
4. More stringent laws on the protection of sanctuary.
5. It is mandatory to immunize the livestock around 5 km^2 from a sanctuary.
6. Destruction of exploitation of any wildlife including the vegetation forming part of the habitat has been banned.
7. No new armed license would be granted in 10 km of a sanctuary without prior concurrence of CWW.
8. Molesting, teasing and littering of ground is considered as an offence.

9. Provision for setting up of the Central Zoo Authority.
10. Rewards to persons who helps in the prevention of poaching.
11. The vehicles, weapons, traps and tools used for offense shall be the property of the state and these shall not be returned to the offenders.
12. Any person could file a case against the offenders after giving a notice in the prescribed manner to the state or central government.

Wildlife Protection Act Amendments – 2002

1. Setting up of National Board of Wildlife (NBWL) with Prime Minister as chairman.
2. State governments have to act according to NBWL.
3. State Board of Wildlife (SBWL) at each state with Chief Minister as its chairman.
4. The state has to get approval from NBWL to declare national parks or sanctuaries.
5. In addition to national park and sanctuaries, the protected areas additionally include ***community reserves** and **conservation reserves.***
6. Participation of people living within and around the sanctuary to be promoted.
7. Permit from the CWW and the satisfaction of the state government is needed before a destructive action of wildlife is permitted in a sanctuary or national park.
8. The constitution of national park or sanctuary is to be completed within two years from a date of initial declaration.
9. It allows conditional resource extraction from national or sanctuaries.
10. Army personals can find place in NBWL and SBWL.
11. Assistant Conservator of Forests (ACF) can clear encroachment in the protected areas.
12. Forfeiture of property on the lines of narcotics Act is introduced.
13. Enhanced penalties for infringement of Act is a minimum three year imprisonment with fine or imprisonment upto 7 years with fine of not less than Rs. 10,000.

The Wildlife (Protection) Amendment Act, 2006

- The Wildlife (Protection) Amendment Act, 2006 (No. 39 of 2006) has come into force on 4 September, 2006. The Act provides for creating the National Tiger Conservation Authority and the Tiger and Other Endangered Species Crime Control Bureau (Wildlife Crime Control Bureau).
- The implementation over the years has highlighted the need for a statutory authority with legal backing to ensure tiger conservation. On the basis of the recommendations of National Board for Wildlife, a Task Force was set up to look into the problems of tiger conservation in the country. The recommendations of the Task Force, inter alia include strengthening of Project Tiger by giving it statutory and administrative powers, apart from creating the Wildlife Crime Control Bureau. It has also recommended that an annual report should be submitted to the Central Government for laying in Parliament, so that commitment to Project Tiger is reviewed from time to time, in addition to addressing the concerns of local people.
- The National Tiger Conservation Authority would facilitate MoU with States within our federal set up for tiger conservation. It will provide for an oversight by Parliament as well. Further, it will address livelihood interests of local people in areas surrounding Tiger Reserves, apart from ensuring that the rights of Scheduled Tribes and such other people living nearby are not interfered or adversely affected. The core (critical) and buffer (peripheral) areas have been defined, while safeguarding the interests of Scheduled Tribes and such other forest dwellers.
- The functions and powers of the Authority, inter alia include : approval of Tiger Conservation Plan prepared by States, laying down normative standards for tiger conservation, providing information on several aspects which include protection, tiger estimation, patrolling, etc., ensuring measures for addressing man-wild animal conflicts and fostering co-existence with local people, preparing annual report for laying before Parliament, constitution of Steering Committee by States, preparation of tiger protection and conservation plans by States, ensuring agricultural, livelihood interests of people living in and around Tiger Reserves, establishing the tiger conservation foundation by States for supporting their development.

- The Notification of the National Tiger Conservation Authority has been issued on 4 September, 2006, for a period of three years, with the Minister for Environment and Forests as its Chairperson and the Minister of State for Environment and Forests as the Vice-chairperson. The official members include Secretary, Ministry of Environment and Forests, Director General of Forests and Special Secretary, Ministry of Environment and Forests, Secretary, Ministry of Tribal Affairs, Secretary, Ministry of Social Justice and Empowerment, Chairperson, National Commission for the Scheduled Tribes, Chairperson National Commission for the Scheduled Castes, Secretary, Ministry of Panchayati Raj, Director, Wildlife Preservation, Ministry of Environment and Forests and six Chief Wildlife Wardens (in rotation from Tiger Reserve States) (Arunachal Pradesh, Madhya Pradesh, Odisha, Rajasthan, Tamil Nadu and Uttaranchal). Three Members of Parliament would be nominated by the Parliament. The Ministry of Law and Justice would also be nominating an officer. The Ministry of Environment and Forests is in the process of selecting the eight non-official experts or professionals having prescribed qualifications and experience, of which at least two shall be from the field of tribal development. The Inspector General of Forests in-charge of Project Tiger shall be the Member Secretary of the Authority.
- The Ministry is in the process of creating the Wildlife Crime Control Bureau, invoking the provisions created after the recent amendment. The Bureau would collate intelligence relating to wildlife crime, ensure coordination with State Governments and other Authorities through its set up, apart from developing infrastructure and capacity building for scientific and professional investigation into wildlife crimes and assist the State Governments in successful prosecution of such crimes.
- The penalty for an offence relating to the core area of a tiger reserve or hunting in the reserve has been increased. The first conviction in such offence shall be punishable with imprisonment not less than three years but may extend to seven years, and also with fine not less than fifty thousand rupees but may extend to two lakh rupees. The second or subsequent conviction would lead to imprisonment not less than seven years, and also with fine not less than five lakh rupees, which may extend to fifty lakh rupees.

Highlights of Wildlife Protection (Act) Amendment Bill, 2013

Amendment Bill, 2013 Wildlife Protection

The Government has introduced the Wildlife (Protection) Amendment Bill, 2013 in the Rajya Sabha for stricter enforcement of laws to protect wildlife. The bill seeks to further amend the Wildlife (Protection) Act, 1972.

Highlights of the Bill

- The Bill seeks to further amend the Wildlife Protection Act.
- The Bill seeks to confer power of entry, search, arrest and detention on any officer authorized by the Management Authority or any customs officer not below the rank of an inspector or any officer of the coastguard not below the rank of an Assistant Commandant.
- The Bill seeks to deal with the serious wildlife crime, such as the offence related to any animal specified in Schedule I or Part II of Schedule II or the meat of such animal or animal article, trophy, or uncured trophy derived from such animal.
- It provides for prohibition on use of animal traps except under certain circumstances.It provides for protection of hunting rights of the Scheduled Tribes in Andaman and Nicobar Islands.
- The Bill seeks to deal with the serious wildlife crime, such as the offence related to any animal specified in Schedule I or Part II of Schedule II or the meat of such animal or animal article, trophy, or uncured trophy derived from such animal.
- The Bill seeks to deal with the serious wildlife crime, such as the offence related to any animal specified in Schedule I or Part II of Schedule II or the meat of such animal or animal article, trophy, or uncured trophy derived from such animal. If a crime of this sort is committed, the bill seeks to punish the culprits with imprisonment for a term which shall not be less than five years, but may extend to seven years and also with fine which shall not be less than 1 lakh rupees but may extend to 25 lakhs rupees.
- The bill also has the provisions for the Convention on International Trade in Endangered Species of Wild Fauna and Flora (CITES).
- In the case of a second or subsequent offence of the same nature, the terms of imprisonment shall not be less than 7 years and also

with fine which shall not be less than 5 lakhs rupees but may extend to 50 lakhs rupees.

Activists have for long demanded stringent penalties for poaching but ground realities call for better implementation and higher conviction rates in the absence of which poaching will continue to thrive. If the criminals knows he will get away, they will be ready to tough it out and the cycle continues. The problem with stringent penalties is that the judiciary needs more evidence to grant stricter punishment. The primary issue here is to increase conviction rates and implement the provisions of the Act. Inclusion of provisions of CITES and Gram Sabha consultation is a positive step.

Conservation Projects

1. Project Tiger

Project Tiger launched in 1973 which aims at tiger conservation in a specially constituted tiger reserves within our country. The various tiger reserves were created in the country on a core buffer strategy. The core areas were freed from all sorts of human activities and the buffer areas were subjected to conservation oriented land use. The habitat management is only to repair the damages done to the ecosystem by human and other interferences, so as to facilitate recovery of the ecosystem to its natural state. In addition, monitoring of faunal and floral changes over time is done besides carrying out research about wildlife.

2. Project Lion

The Asiatic lion is localized in the Gir forests of Gujarat. The Gir lion project was launched in 1972. This looks mainly on the conservation of lions in their habitat. It also facilitates the social upliftment of maldhari tribes.

3. Crocodile Breeding Project

The crocodile population in India was declined considerably due to unabated persecution of these animals for their skin. Hence, this project was implemented from the 1st of April, 1975 from all the three crocodilian species found in our country. This project looks on the protection of crocodiles in its natural habitat and conservation and augmentation of its population through artificial measures.

4. Project Elephant

Elephant is an animal included in Schedule-I of the Wildlife (Protection) Act, 1972. Project Elephant (PE) was launched by the Government of India in the year 1992 as a centrally sponsored scheme to conserve the elephants and its habitat.

The project seeks to address **(a)** the threats to the survival of elephant in our country on account of loss of its habitat, migration path and poaching for tusks and **(b)** issues arising out of elephant depredation in villages. Project Elephant also seeks **(i)** to maintain an appropriate size of the population in any habitat to safeguard it against extinction and **(ii)** to maintain genetic continuity of isolated populations, which are otherwise susceptible to inbreeding.

5. Project Snow Leopard

The Indian government launched "**Project Snow Leopard**" on January, 2009 to safeguard and conserve India's unique natural heritage of high altitude wildlife populations and their habitats by promoting conservation through participatory policies and actions. This project covers Jammu and Kashmir, Himachal Pradesh, Uttarakhand, Arunachal Pradesh and Sikkim. It aims at promoting a knowledge based and adaptive conservation framework that fully involves the local community.

With nearly 750 snow leopards in the country, this project will facilitate a landscape level approach to wildlife conservation by developing scientific frameworks for comprehensive surveys, rationalizing the existing protected area network and improving protected area management. It will develop a framework for wildlife conservation outside protected areas and promote ecologically responsible development.

A number of Wildlife Acts have been made from time to time by the Union and the state governments.

Important among them are :

i) Madras Wild Elephant Preservation Act, 1873

ii) All India Elephant Preservation Act, 1879

iii) The Wild Birds and Animals Prohibition Act, 1912

iv) Bengal Rhinoceros Preservation Act, 1932

v) Assam Rhinoceros Preservation Act, 1954
vi) Indian Board for Wildlife (IBWL) Act, 1952
vii) Prevention of Cruelty to Animal Act, 1960
viii) Wildlife (Protection) Act, 1972.

Broad comparison of different protected areas

S.No.	National Park	Sanctuary	Biosphere Reserves
1.	NP is hitched to the habitat of particular animal like tiger, lion, hangul, rhino, etc.	This is generally species oriented (pitcher plant, great Indian Bustard)	BR considers the whole ecosystem (all life forms)
2.	The size range is 0.04 to 3162 km^2. Most common size is 100 to 500 km^2.	The size range is 0.61 to 7818 km^2. Most common size is 100 to 500 km^2.	Size range over 5670 km^2
3.	Boundaries are circumscribed by the legislation	Boundaries are not sacrosanct (sacred)	Boundaries are circumscribed by the legislation
4.	Except buffer zone, no biotic interference	Limited biotic interference	Except buffer zone, no biotic interference
5.	Tourism is permissible	Tourism is permissible	Tourism is normally not permissible
6.	Research and scientific management is lacking.	Research and scientific management is lacking.	Research and scientific management is available.
7.	No attention is given for gene pool conservation.	No attention is given for gene pool conservation.	Attention is given for gene pool conservation.

C. Forest Conservation Act, 1980

Salient features of Forest Conservation Act, 1980

Objective: To provide for the conservation of forests and for matters inclusive of ancillary and incidental ones.

Salient Features

1. It was enacted for preventing and regulating the diversion of forestland for non-forestry purposes.
2. According to the enactment of this Act, prior approval of central Government is mandatory and essential for dereserving a forest area for non forestry purposes.
3. The Central Government can make rules under this Act, which are laid before both houses of Parliament, if need arises.
4. Constitution of Advisory Committee to grant approval and also advice the Govt. on any other matter.

5. Penalty for any contravention is 15 days which is very obscure and no course of action is provided to remedy any contravention.

This Act is applicable to whole of India except Jammu and Kashmir and came into force on 25th Oct, 1980 (**Sec. 1**). Prior approval of Central Government is necessary, if (i) any reserve forest or any portion of forest to be reserved for non forestry purposes (**Sec. 2**). In this concern, the government may constitute an advisory committee with regard to grant of approval (**Sec. 3**).

Amendments of Forest Conservation Act (1988)

1. Penalty prescribed for violation of the provision of this Act.
2. Detailed guidelines given for the diversion of land.
3. Rules framed for diversion of land for non-forestry purposes.
4. For this prior approval from central government is necessary.

The ministry of Environment and Forest is dealing with this matter in all spheres. Regional central conservator of forest will process in this line. Central Government staff can make field inspections. Based on the recommendation, compensatory afforestation measures can be suggested.

The prior approval is required for reservation of forest lands for the following non-forestry projects, viz.:

a) Mining
b) Raising commercial crops
c) Transmission lines
d) Hydroelectric projects
e) Irrigation schemes
f) Road and railway lines
g) Pipes for drinking water supply
h) Exploratory drillings

Forest Conservation Act, 1980 (Summary)

The Forest Conservation Act was passed in 1980 to provide for the conservation of forests and for matters connected therewith. The Act extends in whole of India except the State of Jammu & Kashmir and is in force from 25th October, 1980.

The Act which was subsequently amended in 1988 (69 of 1988) have the following sections:

1. Extent and commencement.
2. Restriction on the conservation of forests of use of forest land for non-forest purpose.
3. Constitution of advisory committee :
   a) Penalty for conservation of Act.
   b) Offences by authorities and government departments.
4. Power to make rules.
5. Repeal and saving.

Sections 3 (A) and 3 (B) were added through the amendments of 1988, which deal with penalty for conservation of the provisions of the Act and offences by authorities and Government Department, respectively.

Salient Features of the Act: The Forest Conservation Act was enacted with a view to check further deforestation, which ultimately results in ecological imbalances, accordingly the provisions made therewith must apply to all forest irrespective of the nature of ownership for classification thereof.

The world forest covers all statutorily recognized forests whether designated as reserved, protected or otherwise for Section 2(i) of the Act. The term 'forest land' included any area recorded as forest in the Government record irrespective of the ownership.

The salient features of the Act are as follows :

1. The act places restrictions on the power of the State Government concerning preservation of forests or use of forest land for non-forest purposes. Section 2 of the Act provides that the State Government shall not make amendments except with the prior

approval of the Central Government or any order directing thereon:

i) That any reserved forest or any portion thereof, shall cease to be reserved.

ii) That any forest land or any portion thereof may be used for any non-forest purpose.

iii) That any forest land or any portion thereof may be assigned by way of lease of otherwise to any private person or non-Government body.

iv) That any forest or any portion thereof may be cleared of trees which have grown naturally in that land for the purpose of using it for reforestation.

2. The Act provides for the constitution of advisory committee to advise the Government with regard to the grant of approved by the Central Government (Sec. 2) or any other matter connected with conservation of forests which may be referred to it by the Central Government (Sec. 3)

3. As per Section 2 of the Act, all ongoing non-forest activities within any forest, in any State throughout the country, without prior approval of the Centre, must cease forthwith.

4. On violation of the provision of Section 2, the offender shall be punishable with imprisonment for a period extending to 15 days (Section 3-A). Any government department or any authority deemed to be guilty of the offence shall be liable to be proceeded against and punished accordingly.

5. The amendment of 1988 shattered all the expectations of tribal communities and many voluntary agencies placed all the forest land under the jurisdiction of the forest department.

For the purpose of section 2 of the Act, non-forest purpose means the breaking up or clearing of any forest land or portion thereof for:

a) The cultivation of tea, coffee, spices, rubber, palms, oil-bearing plant, horticulture crops or medicinal plants.

b) Any purpose other than reforestation, but does not include any work relating to ancillary conservation, development and management of forest and wildlife, namely the establishment of check posts, fire-lines, wireless communication and construction of fencing, bridges and culverts, dams, waterholes, trench marks, boundary marks, pipelines or other like purposes.

In conclusion the forest should be looked upon as a source of revenue. Forests are renewable natural sources.

These are national assets to be protected and enhanced for the well-being of the people and Nation.

D. Tribal Act, 2006

The tribal enjoyed full privileges inside the forest in pre-independence era. Then British people prevented few rights from them in the form of forest management. After independence, most of their rights were taken away in the name of forest conservation. In recent years, many social activists appreciated the tribal rights. As a result of the continuance of these efforts, Indian government on December 18, 2006 passed tribal Act, 2006 that is referred as ***"Scheduled Tribes and other Traditional Forest Dwellers (Recognition of Forest Rights) Act, 2006".*** This Act deals with the rights of the forest dwelling communities to land and other forest resources. This is also referred as "**Forest Right Act**", "**Tribal Right Act**", "**Tribal Bill**" and "**Tribal Land Act**". This Act is applicable to whole of India except Jammu and Kashmir.

Tribal Rights

The section 3(1) of the Tribal Act recognizes following rights:

1. Rights to hold and live in the forest land under the individual or common occupation for habitation or for self-cultivation for livelihood by a member or members of a forest dwelling scheduled Tribe or other traditional forest dwellers.
2. Community rights, such as nistar, by whatever name called, including those used in erstwhile Princely states, Zamindari, or such intermediary regimes.
3. Rights of ownership, access to collect, use and dispose off minor forest produce which has been traditionally collected within or outside village boundaries.
4. Other community rights of uses or entitlements, such as fish and other products of water bodies, grazing (both settled or transhumant) and traditional seasonal resource access of nomadic or pastoralist communities.

5. Rights including community tenures of habitat and habitation for primitive tribal groups and pre-agriculture communities.
6. Rights for conversion of *Pattas* or leases or grants issued by any local authority or any State Govt. on forest lands to titles.
7. Rights of settlements and conversion of all forest villages, old habitation, un-surveyed villages and other villages in forest, whether recorded, notified or into revenue villages.
8. Rights to protect, regenerate or conserve or manage any community forest resource for sustainable use.
9. Rights which are not recognized under any state law or laws of any Autonomous District Council or Autonomous Regional Council or which are accepted as rights of tribal's under any traditional or customary law of the concerned tribes of any state.
10. Rights of access to biodiversity and community right to intellectual property and traditional knowledge related to biodiversity and cultural diversity.
11. Any other traditional rights customarily enjoyed by the forest dwelling Scheduled Tribes or other traditional forest dwellers, as the case may be, which are not mentioned in clause -1 to 11, but excluding the traditional right of hunting or trapping extracting a part of the body of any species of wild animal.

Above all rights are grouped into four categories :

i) ***Title Rights*** gave ownership to land that is being framed by tribal or forest dwellers as on **December 13, 2005,** subject to a maximum of 4 hectares. This ownership is only for land that is actually being cultivated by the concerned family as on that date, meaning that no new lands are granted.

ii) ***Use Rights*** of tribal define the use of minor forest produce, grazing and pastoralist routes.

iii) ***Relief and Development Rights*** deals with rehabilitation in case of illegal eviction or forced displacement and to basic amenities, subject to restrictions for forest protection.

iv) ***Forest Management Rights*** confines to role of tribal in protection of forest and wildlife.

Eligibility

The person/families who primarily reside in forests and who depend on forests and forestland for a livelihood is/are alone eligible. Further, the claimant (petitioner) must be a member of the scheduled tribes notified in that area or must have been residing in the forest for 75 years.

Process of Rights Recognition

The **Gram Sabha** or **Village Assembly** will pass a resolution recommending eligible right holders with specification of which lands belong to whom and how much land was under the cultivation of each person as on Dec. 13, 2005. This resolution is screened and approved at sub-division level and followed by district level. For this purposes, one **screening committee** is constituted composed of **three government officials** from ***Forest, Revenue*** and ***Tribal Welfare Departments*** and **three elected members of local body.** This committee looks over the various appeals made by the discrepant too.

The forest rights recognized in this Act may subsequently be modified or re-settled in case of critical wildlife habitats such as national park, sanctuaries, etc. This is very specific for the purpose of wildlife conservation (section 4). The relocation of tribal is to be considered when no other alternatives are available and it has to be scientifically proved. The public consultation is needed for arriving conclusion. Most importantly, the local community must consent to the resettlement must provide not only compensation but a secure livelihood. This assures the tribal safety well. According to the Act, no re-settlement shall take place until new facilities and land allocation at the new settlement area is complete.

The most common misconception is that the purpose of the law is to distribute forest land to tribal at the rate of 4 hectares per family. But in real this Act is applicable to forest lands that are already under cultivation as on December 13, 2005 and it does not grant title to any new forest lands. Due to this misconception, many environmentalists opposed to this Act initially. Wildlife conservationists fear that the human interference creates big problem to wildlife conservation and also believes that peaceful resettlement of tribal is questionable for the purpose of wildlife conservation.

E. Biological Diversity Act, 2002

An Act to provide for conservation of biological diversity, sustainable use of its components and fair and equitable sharing of the benefits arising out of the use of biological resources, knowledge and for matters connected therewith or incidental thereto.

The **Biological Diversity Act, 2002** is a federal legislation enacted by the Parliament of India for preservation of biological diversity in India, and provides mechanism for equitable sharing of benefits arising out use of traditional biological resources and knowledge. The Act was enacted to meet the obligations under Convention on Biological Diversity (CBD), to which India is a party.

Biodiversity and biological resource

Biodiversity has been defined under Section 2(b) of the Act as "the variability among living organisms from all sources and the ecological complexes of which they are part, and includes diversity within species or between species and of eco-systems". The Act also defines, Biological resources as "plants, animals and micro-organisms or parts thereof, their genetic material and by-products (excluding value added products) with actual or potential use or value, but does not include human genetic material.

National Biodiversity Authority and State Biodiversity Boards

Main article: National Biodiversity Authority

The National Biodiversity Authority (NBA)is a statutory autonomous body, headquartered in Chennai, under the Ministry of Environment and Forests, Government of India established in 2003 to implement the provisions under the Act. State Biodiversity Boards (SBB) has been created in 28 States along with 31,574 Biological management committees (for each local body) across India.

Functions

- Regulation of Acts prohibited under the Act
- Advise the Government on conservation of biodiversity
- Advise the Government on selection of biological heritage sites
- Take appropriate steps to oppose grant of intellectual property rights in foreign countries, arising from the use of biological resources or associated traditional knowledge.

Regulations

A foreigner, non-resident Indian as defined in clause (30) of section 2 of The Income-tax Act, 1961 or a foreign company or body corporate need to take permission from the NBA before obtaining any biological resources or associated knowledge from India for research, survey, commercial utilization. Indian citizens or body corporates need to take permission from the concerned State Biodiversity Board.

Result of research using biological resources from India cannot be transferred to a non-citizen or a foreign company without the permission of NBA. However, no such permission is needed for publication of the research in a journal or seminar, or in case of a collaborative research made by institutions approved by Central Government.

No person should apply for patent or other form of intellectual property protection based on the research arising out of biological resources without the permission of the NBA. The NBA while granting such permission may make an order for benefit sharing or royalty based on utilization of such protection.

Benefit sharing

Benefit sharing out of usage of biological resources can be done in following manner:

- Joint ownership of intellectual property rights
- Transfer of technology
- Location of production, research development units in the area of source
- Payment of monetary and non-monetary compensation
- Setting up of venture capital fund for aiding the cause of benefit claimers

Penalties

If a person, violates the regulatory provisions he will be "punishable with imprisonment for a term which may extend to five years, or with fine which may extend to ten lakhs rupees and where the damage caused exceeds ten lakhs rupees such fine may commensurate with the damage caused, or with both."

Any offence under this Act is non-bailable and cognizable.

Convention on Biological Diversity

The Convention on Biological Diversity (CBD) is a comprehensive, binding agreement covering the use and conservation of biodiversity.

History

It was created and adopted by governments at the 1992 Earth Summit in Rio de Janeiro, when world leaders agreed on a comprehensive strategy for "sustainable development" - to meet current needs while ensuring a living planet for future generations.

Signed by 193 governments the CBD sets out commitments for maintaining the world's biodiversity which directly supports the livelihoods of billions and underpins global economic development.

The Convention has 3 main goals :

1. The conservation of biological diversity,
2. The sustainable use of its components, and
3. The fair and equitable sharing of the benefits from the use of genetic resources.

How does the CBD work?

The Conference of the Parties (COP) meets every 2 years to look at new issues and adopt targets and work programmes to address biodiversity loss.

Signatory governments to the CBD are required to develop national strategies and action plans based on COP decisions and report back on implementation 2020 Target.

In 2010, governments gathered in Japan at the 10th Conference of the Parties to CBD and set a new strategy to save the world's valuable nature. A 20-point plan was adopted, to be implemented by governments in the next 10 years, to help tackle the mass extinction of species and the loss of vital habitats around the world. As part of the biodiversity rescue plan, governments agreed to boost the area of protected land in the world to 17%, and strive for marine protected areas covering 10% of our oceans by 2020.

WWF and the CBD

WWF supported the development of the CBD in the 1980s and works at global and national level to advocate the adoption of strong targets and work plans by the COP and their implementation by national governments.

International Conventions / Obligations

1. **The Convention on wetlands, 1971 (Ramsar Convention):** The Convention on Wetlands of International Importance, called the **Ramsar Convention**, is an inter-governmental treaty that provides the framework for national action and international co-operation for the conservation and wise use of wetlands and their resources. The Ramsar Convention is the only global environmental treaty that deals with a particular ecosystem. **The treaty was adopted in the Iranian city of Ramsar in 1971** and the Convention's member countries cover all geographic regions of the planet.
2. **The Convention Relative to the Preservation of Fauna and Flora in their Natural State, 1936:** This is also known as London Convention enacted in 1933 at London and entered into force in 1936.
3. **The International Convention for the Regulation of Whaling, 1946:** This is an international environmental agreement signed in 1946, in order to "provide for the proper conservation of whale stocks and thus make possible the orderly development of the whaling industry".
4. **The International Plant Protection Convention, 1951 : IPPC** is a **Multilateral Treaty** overseen by the Food and Agriculture Organization that aims to secure coordinated, effective action to prevent and to control the introduction and spread of pests of plants and plant products. The Convention created an organization known as the **Commission on Phytosanitary Measures.**
5. **The Antarctic Treaty, 1959 :** The Antarctic Treaty was signed in Washington on 1st December, 1959 by the twelve countries whose scientists had been active in and around Antarctica during the International Geophysical Year (IGY) of 1957-58. It entered into force in 1961 and has since been acceded to by many other nations. **The total number of Parties to the Treaty is now 50.**

6. **The Convention on International Trade in Endangered Species (CITES) of Wild Fauna and Flora, 1973:** CITES is an international treaty drawn up in 1973 to protect wildlife against over-exploitation, and to prevent international trade from threatening species.

7. **The Convention on the Conservation of Migratory Species of Wild Animals, 1979 (Bonn Convention)**: The Convention was signed in 1979, in Bonn (Germany) and entered into force in 1983.This aims to conserve terrestrial, marine and avian migratory species concerned with the conservation of wildlife and habitats on a global scale.

8. **The Convention on the Conservation of Antarctic Marine Living Resources (CCAMLR), 1980:** This is also known as **Commission on the Conservation of Antarctic Marine Living Resources**. The Convention was opened for signature on 1 August, 1980 and entered into force on 7 April, 1982 by the Commission for the Conservation of Antarctic Marine Living Resources, headquartered in Tasmania, Australia. The goal is to preserve marine life and environmental integrity in and near Antarctica.

9. The **International Tropical Timber Agreement (ITTA, 1983, 1994 and 2006):** ITTA is an agreement to provide an effective framework for co-operation between tropical timber producers and consumers and to encourage the development of national policies aimed at sustainable utilization and conservation of tropical forests and their genetic resources. The International Tropical Timber Organization was established under this agreement.

The *International Tropical Timber Organization* **(ITTO)** was *established* under the support of the United Nations in 1986. **ITTO** is an inter-governmental organization promoting the conservation and sustainable management, use and trade of tropical forest resources. Its members represent about 80% of the world's tropical forests and 90% of the global tropical timber trade.

10. ***International Convention on Biological Diversity, 1992:*** The Convention on Biological Diversity (CBD) was signed in 1992 at the 1992 UN Conference on Environment and Development (UNCED).

F. The Karnataka Preservation of Trees Act, 1976

Chapter I	**Short title**, extent, commencement and Definitions
Chapter II	**Tree Authority** - Establishment of the Tree Authority and Meetings of the Tree Authority
Chapter III	**Officers and Servants** - Appointment of Tree Officer, Appointment of other officers.
Chapter IV	**Duties of Tree Authority** - Duties of Tree Authority
Chapter V	**Restriction on felling of Trees and Liability for Preservation of Trees** Restriction on felling of trees Planting of adequate number of trees Planting in place of fallen or destroyed trees Preservation of trees Adoption of trees Recovery of expenditure on failure to comply with order for planting treesAppeal
Chapter VI	**Penalties and Procedure** Seizure of Property Power to release property seized under Section Power to arrest without warrant Power to release a person arrested Power to prevent commission of offence Operation of other laws not barred Power to compound offences Penalty.
Chapter VII	**Miscellaneous** Rules Indemnity Investing Tree officer with certain powers Transit of felled materials Power of State Government and the Tree Authority to give directions Schedule.

The Karnataka Preservation of Trees Act, 1976

(First published in the Karnataka Gazette Extraordinary on the fourth day of December 1976)

(Received the assent of the governor on the first day of December 1976)

An Act to make better provision for preservation of trees in the state. Whereas, with the growing pace of urbanization, industrialization and increasing population, there has been indiscriminate felling of a large number of tree in the rural and urban areas of the state of Karnataka leading to erratic to rainfall, famines and floods, soil erosion and consequent ecological disturbances; Whereas, it is expedient to provide for the preservation of trees in the state by regulating the felling of trees and for the planting of adequate number of trees to restore ecological balance and for matters connected therewith; Be it enacted by the Karnataka State Legislature in the twenty-seventh year of the Republic of India as follows:

CHAPTER-1

1. Short title, extent and commencement

1. This Act may be called the Karnataka Preservation of Trees Act, 1976.
2. It extends to the whole of the State of Karnataka.
3. This section shall be deemed to have come into force on the seventeenth day of July 1976 and other provisions shall come into force on such date as the state government may by notification appoint and different dates may be appointed for different provisions of this Act and this Act for different urban areas or rural areas or parts thereof.

2. Definitions

1. In this Act, unless the context otherwise requires:
   a) 'Appointed day' in relation to any area means the date notified under sub- section (3) of Section 1;
   b) 'Local authority' means a Municipal Corporation or a Municipal Council or a Notified Area Committee or a Taluk Development Board;
   c) 'Preservation of trees' means, maintenance and protection of tree to encourage normal growth and prevent damage or cutting of felling and includes planting of new trees and transplanting trees;
   d) 'Relevant Act' means the enactment under which a local authority is constituted;
   e) 'Rural area' means an area and of the kind specified in Schedules I and II;
   f) 'To fell a tree' means severing the trunk from the roots, uprooting the tree and includes burning or cutting or girdling or applying arboricides to a tree to cause substantial damage thereto or destruction thereof;

g) 'Tree' means any woody plant whose branches springs from and are supported upon a trunk or body and which trunk or body is not less than five and a half centimetres in diameter and not less than one metre in height from the ground level and includes palms, bamboos, stumps, brushwood canes and seedlings of such tree but does not include sandal and rosewood trees;

h) 'Tree officer' means a forest officer appointed as such by the Chief Conservator of Forests (General) for the purposes of this Act;

i) 'Urban area' means an area comprising a Municipal Corporation, a Municipality or a Notified Area Committees;

j) 'Wood lot' means any piece of land of which trees from the main crop, the average number of such tree in each hectare being not less than twenty-five.

2. Words and expressions used herein but not defined shall have the meanings assigned to them in the relevant Act.

CHAPTER-II

Tree Authority

3. Establishment of the tree authority

1. The State Government shall, by notification, constitutes a Tree Authority for each area and for rural area.
2. Such Authority shall consist of five members as follows:

   a) For an urban area :

      i) The Mayor President of the Municipal corporation, the Municipal council or the Notified Area Committee, as the case may be;

      ii) The Divisional Forest Officer or his nominee;

      iii) The District Horticultural Officer having jurisdiction;

      iv) The Municipal Commissioner or the Chief Executive Officer, as the case may be; and

      v) one member of the Municipal Corporation, the Municipal Council or the Notified Area Committee, as may be, nominated by the Mayor or the President, as the case may be:

Provided that where the Corporation or the Municipal Council or the Notified Area Committee is superseded, such person as the State Government may nominate shall be the member.

b) For a rural area specified in Schedule I :

i) The concerned Conservator of Forests having jurisdiction;

ii) The Special Deputy Commissioner and where there is no Special Deputy Commissioner, the Deputy Commissioner of the district;

iii) The Superintending Engineer, Communication and buildings having jurisdiction; and

iv) Two non-official members appointed by the State Government

c) For a rural area specified in Schedule II :

i) The President of the Taluk Development Board;

ii) The Block Development Officer having jurisdiction;

iii) The Assistant Conservator of Forests nominated by the Divisional Forest Officer;

iv) The district horticultural officer having jurisdiction;

v) One member of the Taluk Development Board nominated by the President;

Provided that where a Taluk Development Board is superseded, such person as the State Government may nominate.

3. The State Government shall appoint one of the members to be the Chairman.

4. The Tree Authority may co-opt in such manner and for such period, as it may determine not more than three representatives of non-official organisations having special knowledge or practical experience in the preservation of trees.

4. Meetings of the Tree Authority

1. The Tree Authority shall meet at least once in three months at such place and time as the Chairman may decide and shall conduct its business in such manner, as may be prescribed.

2. The quorum to constitute a meeting of the Tree Authority shall be one-third of the total number of its members.

CHAPTER III

Officers and Servants

5. Appointment of tree officer

1. The chief conservator of forests (General) may, subject to sub-section (2) appoint for each urban area and rural area one or more Forest Officers as Tree Officers for the purpose of this Act.
2. Such tree Officer shall :
   i) In an urban area comprising of a Municipality Corporation, be not below the rank of an Assistant Conservator for the Forests;
   ii) In an urban area comprising of a Municipality or Notified Area Committee, be not below the rank of a Range Forest Officer;
   iii) In a rural area of the kind specified in Schedule II, be not below the rank of a Range Forest Officer;
   iv) In a rural area of the kind specified in Schedule I, be not below the rank of Divisional Forest Officer.

6. **Appointment of other officers :** The Chief Conservator of Forests (General) may from time to time, appoint such other officers and servants to assist the Tree Officer, as he may consider necessary be subordinate to the Tree Officer.

CHAPTER IV

Duties of Tree Authority

7. **Duties of tree authority:** Notwithstanding anything in the relevant Act any other law for the time being in force, the Tree Authority shall, subject to any general or special orders of the State Government, be responsible for :

a) The preservation of all trees within its jurisdiction;

b) Carrying out a census of the existing trees and obtaining, whenever considered necessary, declarations from all owners or occupants about the numbers of trees in their lands;

c) Specifying the standards regarding the number and kind of trees which each locality, type of land and premises shall have and which shall be planted subject to a minimum of five trees per hectare in the case of rural areas;

d) Development and maintenance of nurseries, supply of seeds, saplings and trees to persons who desire or are required to plant new trees or to replace trees which have been felled;

e) Planting and transplanting of trees necessitated by construction of new roads or widening of existing roads or replacement of trees which have failed to come up along roads or for safeguarding danger to life and property;

f) Organisation of demonstration and extension services for the purposes of this Act and assisting private and public institutions connected with planting and preservation of trees;

g) Planting and maintaining such number of trees, as may be considered necessary according to the prescribed standards on roads, in public parks and gardens and on the banks of rivers or lakes or seashores; and

h) Undertaking such schemes or measures as may be directed from time by the state government for achieving the objects of the Act.

CHAPTER-V

Restriction on Felling of Trees and Liability for Preservation of Trees

8. Restriction on felling of tree

1. With effect on and from the appointed day, notwithstanding any custom, usage contract or law for the time-being in force, no person shall fell any tree or cause any tree to be felled in any land, whether in his ownership or occupancy or otherwise, except with the previous permission of the Tree Officer.

2. Any person desiring to fell, a tree shall apply in writing to the concerned Tree Officer for permission in that behalf. A site plan or survey sketch specifying clearly the site or survey number shall accompany the application, the number, kind and girth of the tree sought to be cut and the reasons, therefore, along with the consent of the owner or occupant.

3. On receipt of the application, the Tree Officer may, after inspecting the tree and holding such inquiry, as he deems necessary, either grant permission in whole or in part or refuse permission.

Provided that permission shall not be refused, if the tree :

i) Is dead, diseased or wind-fallen; or
ii) Has silviculturally matured; or
iii) Constitutes a danger to life or property; or
iv) Constitutes obstruction to traffic; or
v) Is substantially damaged or destroyed by fire, lightning, rain or other natural causes; or
vi) Is required in rural areas to be removed either for extension of the cultivation in areas specified in schedule II or for the bona fide use of the applicant.

4. If the Tree Officer fails to inform the applicant of his decision :
   i) In the case of an application in respect of a tree in an urban area and in rural area of the kind specified in Schedule II, within sixty days; and
   ii) In the case of an application in respect of a tree in a rural area of the kind specified in schedule I, within one year from the date of receipt of the application by him or, if the receipt of the application has been acknowledged by him from the date of such acknowledgment, such permission shall be deemed to have been granted.
5. Where permission to fell a tree is granted, the Tree Officer may grant it subject to the condition that the applicant shall plant another tree or trees of the same or any other suitable species on the same site or other suitable place within thirty days from the date, the tree is felled or within such extended time as the Tree Officer may allow.
6. Notwithstanding anything contained in sub-sections- (1) to (5) but subject to such conditions and restrictions, as may be prescribed, for bonafide domestic use of a family, one or more members of such family may, if they are otherwise entitled to do so, would fetch 1[not more than 2.8 cubic metres of timber and five tonnes of firewood].

2[(7) Nothing in this section shall apply to felling of 3[Casuarina, Coconut, Erythrina, Fucalyptus, Glyrecidia, Hopea, Wightina, Prosipis, Rubber, Sesbania, Silver Oack and Subabul trees]

1. Substituted by Act, 21 of 1977, S, 2 (29th July, 1977)
2. Inserted by Act, 21 of 1977, s, 2 (29th July, 1977)
3. Substituted by Act No. 39 of 1987 Dt. (1-12-1987)

9. Planting of adequate number of trees

1. Every owner or occupant of a land shall, within a period of five years from the appointed day or within such extended period as the Tree Authority may specify, plant trees so to conform to the standards prescribed by the tree authority under clause © of Section 7.
2. If in the opinion of the Tree Officer the number of tree in any land is not adequate according to the standards referred to in sub-section (1), the Tree Officer may by order giving a reasonable opportunity to the owner or occupier of the land of making representation, require him to plant such trees, or additional trees, as the case may be, and at such places in the land, as may be specified in the order.
3. The owner or occupier of the land shall comply with such order within thirty days from the receipt thereof or such extended time, as the tree officer may allow on this behalf.

10. Planting in place of fallen or destroyed trees

1. Where any tree has fallen or is destroyed by wind, fire lightning, torrential rain or such other natural causes, the tree office may suo moto or on information given to him, after holding such enquiry as he deems fit, by order, require such owner or occupier to plant a tree in place of the tree so or destroyed, of the same or other species at the same or other suitable place as may be specified in the order.
2. The owner of the occupier of the land shall comply with such order within thirty days from the receipt thereof or such extended time as the tree officer may allow.

11. Preservation of trees

Subject to the provisions of section 12, it shall be the duty of the owner or occupier of the land who is required by an order under section 8, 9 or 10 to plant a tree or tees to ensure that they grow properly and are well-preserved.

12. Adoption of trees

Notwithstanding anything contained in this Act or in any other law for the time-being in force, the tree authority may, subject to such terms and conditions as it may specify in that behalf, permit any individual, body corporate or institution to adopt any tree for such period, as may be specified therein and during such period the said individual, body corporate or institution shall be responsible for the maintenance and preservation of the said tree.

13. Recovery of expenditure on failure to comply with order for planting trees

Where the owner or occupier fails to comply with an order made by the Tree Officer under section 8, 9 or 10, the tree officer may, after giving a reasonable opportunity to such owner or occupier of making representation and without prejudice to any other action which may be taken against the defaulter under this Act, take necessary action himself and recover the expenditure incurred therefor from the owner or the occupier, as the case may be. If such expenditure is not paid within the time specified by the Tree Officer, the amount along with interest at six per cent annum and other expense, if any, shall be recovered, as if it were an a arrear of land revenue.

14. Appeal

1. Against the order of the Tree Officer under section 8, 9 or 10, an appeal shall lie to the Tree Authority.
2. Such appeals shall be filed within thirty days from the date the decision is communicated to the owner or occupier of the land and shall be accompanied by a fee of one hundred rupees.
3. The Tree Authority shall decide the appeal after giving to the appellant a reasonable opportunity of being heard. The decision of the Tree Authority shall be final.

4. Where an appeal is made in time, the period for compliance specified in the order of the Tree Officer shall be reckoned from the date on which the appeal is decided against the appellant and where the appeal is allowed the fee paid under subsection (2) shall be refunded to the appellant.

5. Every appeal shall be heard by not less than three members of the Tree Authority.

CHAPTER VI

Penalities and Procedure

15. Seizure of property

Where the tree officer has reason to believe than an offence under this act is committed in respect of any tree, he may seize the tools and any boats, vehicles or other conveyances or animals used for the commission of the said offence along with the tree or part thereof which has been severed from the ground or the trunk, as the case may be.

16. Power to release property seized under section 15

The Tree Officer may release the properties seized under Section 15, if the owner or occupier executes a bond for their production, whenever required.

17. Power to arrest without warrant

1. Any Tree Officer may arrest without warrant any person reasonably suspected of having been concerned in any offence under this Act, if such person refuses to give his name and residence or gives a name or residence which the Tree Officer has reason to believed is false, if he has reasons it believes that person will abscond.

2. Any person arrested under this section shall be informed, as soon as may be, of the grounds for such arrest and shall be produced before the nearest magistrate having jurisdiction in the case within a period of twenty-four hours of such arrest, excluding the time necessary for the journey from the place of arrest to the court of the magistrate and no such person shall be detained in custody beyond in the said period without the authority of a magistrate.

18. Power to release a person arrested

Any tree officer who has arrested any person any person under the provisions of section 17 may release such person on his executing a bond with proper surety to appear, if and when so required, before the magistrate having jurisdiction in the case, or before the police or the Tree Officer concerned.

19. Power to prevent commission not barred

Every Tree Officer or his subordinates or any forest, revenue or police officer shall prevent and may interfere for the purpose of preventing, the commission of any offence under the Act.

20. Operation of other laws not barred

Nothing in this Act shall be deemed to prevent any person from being prosecuted under any other law for any Act or omission which constitutes an offence under this Act or from being liable under such other law to any higher punishment or penalty than that provided by this Act or the rules made thereunder: Provided that no person shall be punished twice for the some offence.

21. Power to compound offences

1. The State Government may, by order, empower a Tree Officer.
   a) To compound on payment of a sum not exceeding five thousand rupees any offence under this Act;
   b) To release any propriety seized or liable to confiscation, on payment of the value thereof, as estimated by such officer.
2. On the payment of such sum or such value or both, as the case may be, to such officer, the offender, if in custody, shall be released. The property, if any, seized shall be released and no further proceedings shall be taken against such offender or property.

22. Penalty

Any person who contravenes any of the provisions of this Act or orders made thereunder shall, on conviction be punishable with imprisonment which may extend to three months or with fine which may extend to one thousand rupees or with both. Upon such conviction the court may order any property in respect of which the offence is committed to be forfeited to the State Government.

CHAPTER VII

Miscellaneous

23. Rules

1. The State Government may, by notification, make rules to carry out the purposes of this Act.
2. Every rule made under this Act shall be laid, as soon as may be after it is made, before each house of the state legislature, while it is in session for a total period of thirty days which may be comprised in one session or in two or more successive sessions, and if before the expiry of the session immediately following the session or the successive sessions aforesaid, both Houses agree in making any modification in the rule or both Houses agree that the rule should not be made, the rule shall from the date on which the modification or annulment is notified by the Government in the Official Gazette have effect only in such modified from on be of no effect, as the case may be, so, however, that any such modification or annulment shall be without prejudice to the validity of anything previously done under such rule.

24. Indemnity

No suit, prosecution or other legal proceedings shall lie against any officer for anything done or omitted to be done by him in good faith under this Act or the rules or orders made thereunder.

25. Investing tree officer with certain powers

1. The State Government may, by notification, invest the Tree Officers and other officers with all or any of the following powers, namely:
    a) Power to enter upon any land and to survey, demarcate and make a map of the same;
    b) Powers of a Civil Court to compel the attendance of witnesses and the production of documents and material objects;

c) Power to issue a search warrant under the Code of Criminal Procedure, 1973;

d) Power to hold inquiries into offences under the Act and in the course of such inquiry to receive and record evidence;

e) power to take possession of property under the Act;

f) power to direct release of property or withdrawal of charges;

g) power to insist any person to plant tree or trees of suitable species in adequate numbers on any land owned or occupied by him.

2. Any evidence recorded under clause (d) of sub-section (1) shall be admissible in any subsequent trial before a magistrate, if such evidence has been taken in the presence of the accused person and recorded in the manner provided by section 355, section 356 or section 367 of the Code of Criminal Procedure, 1973.

26. Transit of felled materials

The provisions of section 50 of the Karnataka Forest Act, 1963 (Karnataka Act 5 of 1964) and Chapter XVI of the Karnataka Forest Rules shall, mutatis mutandis, apply to the transit of the felled trees under this Act.

27. Power of state government and the tree authority to give directions

The state government may from time to time give to the Tree Authority any Tree Officer and officers subordinate to him and the Tree Authority may give to the Tree Officer or officers subordinate to him, such general or special directions regarding the discharge of their functions and for carrying out effectively the purposes of this Act and such Tree Authority or Tree Officers shall comply with the directions issued.

Guidelines for liberalizing felling and transit regime for tree species grown on non-forest / private land

"The guidelines for felling and transit regulations for tree species grown on Non-Forest Private Lands" was issued to all State/Union Territory (UT) Governments vide this Ministry's letter No. 8-14/2004-

FP dated 15.12.2004 for augmenting the pace of tree plantation on private land. It was expected that the respective State/UT Governments would take necessary steps for the implementation of the guidelines in order to achieve the target of National Forest Policy, 1988 to promote partnership of industry, voluntary organizations, institutions and individuals, *etc.* in tree plantations. However, it is felt that required degree of simplification in felling and transit rules has not taken place".

Guidelines

1. Preferred Tree and bamboo species under agro-forestry by farmers and not naturally available in neighbouring forests are to be invariably exempted from the transit permit and felling rules :

   i) As the regulatory mechanism is not uniform across various States/UTs, there is a need for a simple uniform mechanism/procedure to regulate the transit rules of forest produce within the State, and also across various States. An indicative list (List-A), which is not exhaustive, is enclosed. The State/UT Governments may include other such species as required, based on their own local conditions.

   ii) There should not be any requirement of permission for felling of trees and transit permits in case of important timber species like Teak (*Tectona grandis*), Shisham *(Dalbergia sissoo),* Padauk *(Pterocarpus dalbergioides)* and Pines, etc. in the States and Union Territories where these species are not found in natural forests, but farmers and private land owners raise plantations of such species. These species should be included in List A by all such States and Union Territories, which have no natural forests/forest plantations of these species. Similar exemptions should be applicable in those districts of a State,where there are no natural forests of such species.

   iii) The Revenue and other State Acts/Regulations/Rules which inhibit tree felling and free movement of timber within and across the States also need to be suitably amended and liberalized by the concerned States.

   iv) In respect of preferred trees spp. grown on private lands in urban/metropolitan areas, the respective Tree Preservation Act(s), wherever applicable, will continue to apply. But the

State/UT Governments should see that the provisions of such Act(s) do not discourage private efforts in tree planting.

2. i) Preferred Tree and bamboo species in areas, where they are found in the neighbouring forests may be brought under the limited restrictive provisions for felling and transit to safeguard trees from such forests. The concerned Gram Sabha or equivalent institution at the village level, may be authorized to regulate felling and transit of trees/timber grown under agro-farm forestry on private or community lands, by whatever name called, in the village in respect of such species. A Special/Standing Committee of Gram Sabha or the Joint Forest Management Committee or other such committees by whatever name called (as the case may be) to be constituted for the purpose, which may authorize at least two office bearers to certify the origin of timber from trees felled in private non-forest lands for utilization of timber/such produce within the District. This may accordingly be recognized under the existing transit rules of the State.

ii) The Forest Department should issue permits based on the certificate of origin issued by authorized representative of such Committees of Gram Sabha/JFMC or other such committees for movement across Districts or States. The Forest Department should also initially guide the committee in technical matters and maintain an oversight mechanism. An indicative list (List-B), which is not exhaustive, is enclosed for this purpose. The State/UT Governments may include other such species as required, based on their own local conditions.

iii) In respect of trees grown on non-forest lands/private lands in urban/peri-urban areas, the permission for felling of trees will be issued by concerned DFO/ Tree Officer or any/ such other Authorised Officer as per the provisions of relevant Act(s) and/or Rules. However, the process needs to be simplified and well-publicized to encourage private initiative in greening of cities and surrounding areas.

iv) The Government of States and UTs may decide the limit for neighbourhood forests as per their circumstances and may review from time to time. The neigbourhood limit should take into account the practical considerations.

3. i) The permission for felling and transit, wherever required, may be given in a time bound manner and this provision should be well-publicized. The permission involving the forest officials should be disposed off through transparent and time bound process. Such measures need to be continuously reviewed.

   ii) Reviewing and streamlining the Transit Pass system in light of above recommendations is necessary to balance the need for reducing discretion and complexity, at the same time in maintaining the utility of the document which will be an important link in the chain of custody process. Use of Information Technology should be encouraged in streamlining the process and making it more authentic and verifiable.

4. Facilitation of Interstate movement and setting up of regional coordination mechanism:

   i) Inter-state movement of timber derived from agroforestry plantations or trees from non-forest lands/private lands needs to be facilitated for benefitting tree growers to get best market price. Felling and transit permits may not be required for exempted species (List A) grown on non-forest/private/ farm lands and logs/ timber/ pulpwood of these species, so that the same can be transported within and across all States and Union Territories without any timber transit permits. This will help growers to get not only the best possible price for timber produced by them without any difficulty but also develop our full potential of agroforestry.

   ii) The mechanism of lieu TP or other similar arrangements may be simplified by the Regional Coordination Committee of the States concerned, which should meet at regular intervals to facilitate inter-state movement and resolve issues, if any. The produce/timber obtained from non-forest lands/private lands, which is to be transported from a State to other States may be covered under an appropriate mechanism through mutual consultation, such as Nationally Valid Permit for such consignments. A database should be maintained by the agencies which are issuing such permits as well as by those who are finally receiving it in the respective state.

   iii) There is an urgent need to move towards one simple and uniform nationally adopted transit permit system on electronic format. Regional Offices of the Ministry should facilitate such coordination among the States/ UTs within their jurisdiction.

5. Recording of Agro-forestry plantations:

   i) There is no mechanism for recording of tree plantations outside forests. Transparent and simple methodology for maintenance of records of tree plantation on private land needs to be worked out by the state government or through its authorized agencies. This is important for creating and maintaining a dynamic resource inventory. Such records will help in de-centralizing issuing of transit permits and facilitate harvesting of trees planted subsequently at village level. Information Technology should be used for creation of registers/database and regular updating at the time of verification of felling requests and re-planting. Registration of plantations should also be encouraged. Such database should be linked to existing forest and revenue recording system of the respective states. Online submission of tree plantation form to a designated nodal office, preferably at the district/division level, may be tried to create plantation database.

   ii) Maintenance of Records: All the records in respect of planting of trees, felling and transit of timber may be placed on website or other such computerized public record system including revenue and forest records.

6. Preparing Manuals on Agroforestry in local and official languages of the States for public awareness:

   i) Manuals/brochures on growing preferred tree species along with relevant information on procedure for harvesting, transporting and marketing in simple local language may be prepared and made available to farmers/peoples in meeting, such as Gram Sabha meetings, and also through website.

   ii) The State Forest Departments should bring out a list of all the trees exempted from the requirements of felling and transit permission in the concerned State at the beginning of planting season for public information and publicise it through appropriate media. This should have the concurrence of the MoEF, especially to confirm that such species are not threatened or come under the threatened list of any national statute including, Wildlife Protection Act, National Biodiversity Act or EXIM policy or under any International Convention or Treaty, such as CITES, ITTO, etc.

7. Other Measures:

   i) State/Union Territories Governments are encouraged to have more simplified procedures than suggested above to further encourage people to take up farm/agroforestry and send a copy of rules/norms applicable within their jurisdiction, particularly after the simplification.

   ii) State/Union Territories Governments must give effective publicity to the simplified procedures felling of trees and transit of forest produce thereof in vernacular/local languages.

   iii) State/Union Territories Governments should facilitate felling and marketing of Teak, Shisham and other valuable timber species trees grown on the private lands of poorer sections of society including scheduled tribes and scheduled castes and encourage them to plant more Teak and other such valuable species which they will be permitted to fell and market the produce without difficulty.

   iv) State/Union Territories Governments should strengthen technical extension services for promoting Agroforestry plantations by using powerful electronics media, such as television and radio as is the case for agricultural crops.

   v) State/Union Territories Governments should make appropriate rules or norms for registration of nurseries and certification of seed and seedlings and clonal planting stock so that farmers get best quality planting stock of tree species to be planted in their private lands/non-forest lands.

   vi) The forest officers should reach out to persons and provide technical guidance in tree planting and maintenance through suitable extension programmes including creation and strengthening of Van Vigyan Kendras.

   vii) States/UTs should take initiatives in Research, Development and Extension and Education with involvement of Indian Council of Forestry Research & Education (ICFRE) and other Central and State Forestry Research Institutions in following areas:

a) Preparation/refinement of volume tables for preferred tree species both in irrigated/non-irrigated plantations for different bio-geographic regions;

b) Preparation of suitable Agroforestry models appropriate to various biogeographic regions with forecasting of yield(s) of various preferred species at harvestable period and likely income prospects from such planting models including study of carbon sequestration potential;

c) Assisting persons/farmers in raising quality planting material and standardizing nursery stock;

d) Coordinate to create viable partnerships with landowners/farmers/tree growers, wood based industries and financial institutions for expansion of trees outside forest areas/forest land. For providing good prices for privately grown timber under Agroforestry/ farm forestry, it is necessary to promote Wood based Industries which primarily depend on such produce and these Wood based industries should be encouraged to tie up with the farmers for growing of raw materials and have a medium to long-term forecast of their demand;

e) Setting up of modern timber markets or upgrade existing timber markets in selected important towns to facilitate transparent timber trade so that farmers get competitive prices for the farm grown timber;

f) Promote plantations of high value trees and other plants such as Teak, Red Sanders, Sandalwood, Shisham, Agarwood, etc. and plants of high medicinal values with active involvement of people, especially local communities for creating better livelihood opportunities, income generation and helping in conservation of such species and keeping in mind national and international laws in place. A robust registration mechanism should be put in place for such high values tree species to conform to national and international laws and norms;

g) Suitable incentives for promoting tree planting may be considered.

8. List of Preferred Agro-Forestry Species :

List 'A' Tree species, when exclusively grown on agriculture/ farm land and not naturally available in neighbouring forests:

a) Khair (*Acacia catechu*), Babool (*Acacia nilotica*) Eucalyptus spp., Poplar spp., Subabul (*Leucaena* spp.), Casuarina spp., Ailanthus spp.; Gamari (*Gmelina arborea),* Silver Oak *(Grevillea robusta),* Mulberry (*Morus alba),*Sissoo (*Dalbergia sisso*), Kadam *(Anthocephalus cadamba/Anthocephalus chinensis) Acacia mangium; Acacia lenticularis, Sirris (Albizzia spp.), Neem (Azadirachta indica),* Rubber *(Hevea brasiliensis),* Toon*(Cedrela toona),* Imli (*Tamarindus indica), Grewia oppositifolia,* Meliadubia, Jamun, (*Syzigium cumini*), Teak (*Tectona grandis*), Khejri (*Prosopis cineraria*), Arjun (*Terminalia arjuna*), Indian willow*(Salix alba)*. This list may be revised from time to time and in accordance with the suggestion by the States.

b) Horticultural tree species like Mango, Guava, Coconut, Cashew nut, Citrus, Areca nut, Kathal (*Artocarpus spp.), Zyiphus spp.* This list may be revised from time to time and in accordance with the suggestion by the States.

c) NTFPs including Bamboo species.

List 'B' Tree species grown on non-forest landwhere they are found in the neighbouring forests

Teak (*Tectona grandis), Terminalia spp.,*Jamun (*Syzigium cumini), Khair (Acacia catechu),* Pines, Semal*(Bombax ceiba), Schima wallichii,* Rosewood (*Dalbergia latifolia),* Shisham (*Dalbergia sissoo),* Padauk (*Pterocarpus dalbergioides*).This list may be revised from time to time and in accordance with the suggestion by the States.

Government Notification (dated 07.12.2016) regarding the exemption of certain species from obtaining transit permits

Government has notified exemption for the following tree species for obtaining transit permit from the operation of Chapter XVI of the sub-rule (f) of rule 144 of the Karnataka Forest Rules, 1969 in the State of Karnataka :

S.No.	Botanical Name	Common English Name
1	*Acacia hybrid*	Acacia hybrid
2	*Acacia mangium*	Acacia mangium
3	*Ailanthus excels*	Tree of heaven
4	*Albizia saman (Samanea saman)*	Rain tree
5	All bamboos except *Bambusa arundinacea, Dandrocalamus strictus* and those of genus Ochlandra	*All bamboos except Bambusa arundinacea, Dandrocalamus strictus and those of genus Ochlandra*
6	All Cassia species except *Cassia fistula*	All Cassias species except Golden Rain Tree
7	All exotic ornamental/ oil palms	All exotic ornamental/oil palms
8	*Anacardium occidentale*	Cashsew
9	*Araucaria heterophylla* (*Araucaria excelsa*)	Christmas tree
10	*Areca catechu*	Arecanut
11	*Casuarina Species*	Casuarina, Indian Beef wood
12	Citrus x limon	Lemon
13	Citrus species generally sinensis	Orange
14	*Cocus nucifera*	Coconut tree
15	*Coffee species*	Coffee
16	*Delonix regia*	Mayflower
17	*Erythrina indica*	Indian coral tree
18	*Eryrhtina variegata*	Indian coral tree
19	*Eucalyptus species*	Eucalyptus
20	*Gliricidia sepium*	Glyricidia, Quick stick
21	*Grevillea robusta*	Silver oak
22	*Hevea brasilensis*	Rubber
23	*Jacaranda mimosifolia*	Jacaranda
24	*Kigelia africana*	Sausage tree
25	*Leucaena leucocephala*	Subabul
26	*Maesopsis eminii*	Umbrella tree
27	*Manilkara zapota*	Sapota, chikoo fruit
28	*Melia dubia*	Mela
29	*MIllintonia hortensis*	Indian cork tree
30	*Moringa oleifera*	Drumstick

31	*Morus alba*	Mulberry
32	*Murraya koenigii*	Curry leaf tree
33	*Peltophorum pterocarpum*	Peltoform
34	*Phanera purpurea (Bauhinia purpurea)*	Purple bauhinia
35	*Plumeria species*	Pagoda tree
36	*Polyalthia longifolia*	False ashoka
37	*Psidium guajava*	Guava
38	*Sesbania grandiflora*	Sesbania, Hummingbird tree
39	*Simarouba glauca*	Paradise tree
40	*Spathodea compunulata*	African tulip
41	*Tabebuia species*	Tabebuia
42	*Tecoma species*	Trumpet tree

❏❏❏

Chapter 6

Legal Rights, Types of Legal Rights, Law of Evidence, Admission, Confession, Punishments

Rights and Property

Rights

- "Rights has been defined as the interest recognized and protected by the rule of law" (Shetty, 1980).
- It is an interest respect for which is duty and disregard of which is wrong (Salmond).

Legal Rights

- Legal rights are those which are enforceable legally or with the help of law. Legal rights are possessed by persons while, animals don not have any legal rights.

Therefore legal rights require :

a) Recognition

b) Protection

c) Possession

Legal Rights includes :

a) Right of the state to own and protect the trees growing in a forest.

b) Right of the state to manage and extract produce from the forest.

c) Legal right to prevent encroachments in the forest.

The principal characteristics of legal rights are :

1. It is vested in a particular person or organization or the state who may be distinguished as the owner.
2. A right is availed against a person who is obliged to agree to the right of the holder.
3. A person is legally obliged to act in accordance to the right of the holder.
4. Right may also be a title which may be vested in its owner or holder.

Moral Rights

Moral right is usually unwritten and includes the right of parents to expect their children to obey them. However, this right cannot be enforced by law and there can be no punishment for violation of moral right. This is the basic distinction between moral and legal right.

Rights and Obligations

Duties and obligations are born out of rights. Moral duties and moral obligations arise from moral rights while, legal rights give rise to legal rights and obligations. It is not possible to have moral and or legal right without corresponding duties and obligations. These go together and may be bond together.

Sources of Rights

Rights are born and supported from the following sources:

a) Law of the land

b) Legislation

c) Precedents

d) Customs

Types of Legal Rights

Legal rights are of the following types or kinds :

I. Perfect and Imperfect Rights

II. Positive and Negative Rights

III. Personal and Proprietary Rights

IV. Private and Public Rights

V. Rights in rem and personam

VI. Rights in reporia and realiena

VII. Liberties, Powers and Immunities of Rights

I. Perfect and Imperfect Rights

Perfect rights can readily be enforced by court of law. On the other hand, imperfect right cannot be enforced by court of law.

Some examples of imperfect rights are:

a) A debt that is time barred

b) A right conceded in a document which has insufficient stamp duty on it.

II. Positive and Negative Rights

a) Positive rights give rise to positive duties

e.g. The right of a creditor to receive money from his debtor.

b) Negative rights give rise to negative duties

III. Personal and Proprietary Rights

Personal rights have little or no values on purely economic terms.

Some examples of personal rights are :

a) Citizenship rights

b) Right to follow the religion of one's choice

c) Right of speech

Proprietary rights have direct monetary and economic value. Examples of such rights are :

a) Right to land

b) Rights to a building

c) Copyright

IV. Private and Public Rights

Private rights are those which belong to a person as a private individual. In this case, infringement of private rights is taken cognizance of by courts, when the right holder approaches the court as a person.

Members of the general public hold the public right. In this case any infringement is taken cognizance of under a public appeal. Examples of public rights are:

a) Right to use public roads

b) Right to use public parks and gardens

c) Right to vote or elect representatives to legislative bodies.

V. Rights in rem and personam (Rem - world)

The right in "**rem**" is available against the all world at large. Examples of such rights are:

a) Copyright protection

b) Right to occupy one's premises

On the other hand, right in "personam" is available against a particular person or group of persons. Some examples are:

a) Right for payment of debt

b) Right to receive rent from the tenant of a premises owned by a particular person.

Differences between Rights in Rem and Rights in Personam are as follows:

Rights in Rem

1. A right in rem is available against the world at large. (Rem = world).
2. Example: I have a house. The people of the world have a duty not to interfere with my possession. Nobody has right to disturb my possession and enjoyment.
3. I have money in my pocket. I can use my money as like. The world at large has no right to interfere with my possession.

4. It is called "real right". Converse this right; there is a duty upon every person of the world not to interfere with other's rights.
5. This right protects interest against the world at large.
6. Patent right, copy right, etc. are the best examples for the rights in rem.
7. All rights in rem are negative.
8. It is available against an open or indefinite class of persons.
9. The freedoms given in Article 19 of the Indian constitution with its restrictions are the rights in rem.
10. All "general offers" are "rights in rem".

Rights in Personam

1. A right in personam is available only against a particular person.
2. Example: I let my house to Z-tenant. I have a right to receive rent from my tenant. This right to receive rent from my tenant. This right to receive rent is a right in personam. The rest of the world is not concerned with this right.
3. y-debtor has to give me Rs. 5,000/-, who had taken from me as a hand-loan. I have the right in personam to receive back the sum of Rs. 5,000/- from X.
4. It is also called as "personal right". Converse this right, there is a duty imposed upon determinate individuals.
5. This right protects an interest solely against determinate individuals.
6. Purchase of good-will of business is the best example for the right in personam.
7. All rights in personam are positive.
8. It is available only against a specific person or persons.
9. All easements are the rights in personam.
10. All "specific offers" are "rights in personam".

VI. Right in reporia and realiena

A **right in reporia** pertains to the real right and is vested in the owner of the property or premises.

A **Right in realiena** limits or derogates (detract) a right from the more general rights. These are also known as encumbrance (hindrance) and include the following:

a) Leases

b) Servitudes (slavery)

c) Securities

d) Trusts

VII. Liberties, Powers and Immunities of Rights

a) **Liberties:** This pertains the liberty or ability of a person to do something or act in accordance to the law. This includes:

   i) Freedom of speech and expression

   ii) Freedom of choosing a particular religion

b) **Powers**: Power or authority may be:

   i) **Private** - This is exercised by a person for his own purpose. This may also be referred to as capacity.

   ii) **Public** - This is vested in a person acting on behalf of the state.

c) **Immunities:** This refers to the advantage conferred by the absence of legal power in others or disability of others. Some examples are :

   i) Immunity of a judge acting on behalf of the state;

   ii) Immunity of specific public servants acting for the state or private.

❏❏❏

Chapter 7

Indian Penal Code (IPC)

Criminal Law: In India, the criminal law is manifested or codified in the following two codes:

I. Indian Penal Code (IPC)

II. Criminal Procedure Code (CrPC)

Before the enactment of the IPC, the criminal laws in India were not uniform. **Macaulay** was entrusted with framing uniform criminal law and then IPC came into operation from 1862. It is now the substantative criminal law of the country.

The CRPC is primarily an adjective law of procedure which provides the mechanism for the punishment of offenders. Its scope is outlined in the following points :

a) Creating different grades/levels of courts and defining their powers.

b) Laying down the duties of the police in investigation of offences, arresting offenders and producing them before the court of law.

c) Framing rules of procedure for production of documents and other matters.

Terms used in Criminal Law

1. **Crime**: This is an act of commission or omission that is harmful to society. It is punishable by a criminal law.

2. **Wrongful gain and Wrongful loss: Gain** of property by unlawful means to which the person gaining is not legally entitled is **wrongful gain**.

Loss: By unlawful means of property to which the person losing is legally entitled to is wrongful loss.

3. **Mens Rea**: (In Latin- guilty mind-As an element of criminal responsibility, a guilty mind, a guilty or wrongful purpose, a criminal intent).

This refers to the guilty intent in an act of commission or omission which otherwise constitutes an offence. It implies that an accused should not be found guilty of an offence unless he has a guilty mind. However, this principle is not universally applicable in all statutes.

4. **Accident**: Any act done by accident or misfortune and without any criminal intention or knowledge in the doing of a lawful Act in a lawful manner and with proper care and caution, which is not an offfence.

Punishment

Objects: The main objects of punishment are:

a) **Deterrent (discourage):** To deter people from committing crimes
b) **Prevention:** To prevent the occurrence of crimes, particularly when more than one offence are involved.
c) **Retributive (Recompense)**: To give the offender retribution for what he has done or what crime has been committed by him.
d) **Reformative**: To reform the offender so that he does not commit any more crimes.

Kinds of punishments

Various kinds of punishments are listed below :

1. Death
2. Imprisonment for life
3. Simple or rigorous imprisonment for a fixed period of time
4. Solitary confinement
5. For feiture of penalty
6. Fine
7. Imprisonment in lieu (instead of) of fine

Punishments under forest laws

Various punishments under forest laws are :

1. Imprisonment for a specific time period

2. Fine
3. Confiscation (to seize) of property (an act of seizing)
4. Confiscation of seizures made in respect of forest offences
5. For feiture - A right as a penalty for a fault or mistake
6. Levy (fine) of compensation by courts
7. Compounding of offences

Indian Penal Code (IPC)

The Indian Penal Code (IPC) is a comprehensive criminal law effective since 1862. It was drafted by Macaulay who presided over the first Indian law commission. The IPC is considered to be one of the most detailed criminal laws in the world.

Its coverage includes :

1. Criminal conspiracy
2. Abetment - encourage or assist someone to do something wrong in particular to commit a crime
3. False evidence
4. Offences against public justice
5. Wrongful confinement
6. Harbouring offender
7. Unlawful assembly
8. Theft
9. Murder
10. Receiving stolen property
11. Voluntarily causing hurt
12. House breaking
13. Criminal trespass
14. Extortion by threat (Illegally grabbing)
15. Criminal breach of trust (violation of law)
16. Attempt to murder
17. Mischief
18. Counterfeiting (forgering)
19. Selling Counterfeit goods
20. Offences by and against the authority of public servants.

Applicability of Indian Penal Code (IPC) in forest laws / offences

The Indian Forest Act and Wildlife (Protection) Acts are fairly comprehensive and cover most types of offences in connection with forests and wildlife, the IPC is also applicable both directly and indirectly to forest offences/laws and forest administration. This includes the following offences where the provisions of the IPC are attracted.

The IPC is applicable both directly and indirectly to forest offences that are listed below :

1. Theft of timber from government sale depots outside the limits of the forest.
2. Receiving of stolen timber
3. Thefts of forest department property (other than forest produces)
4. Criminal breach of trust
5. Assault on the staff of the forest department
6. Unlawful assembly inside the forest
7. Omitting to give the information about a forest offence
8. Giving false information to forest officials
9. Usage of false property marks
10. Tampering of property marks
11. Marking or possession of instruments for counterfeiting property marks
12. Counterfeiting property marks.

Indian Penal Code (IPC) is the main criminal code of India. It is a comprehensive code, intended to cover all substantive aspects of criminal law. It was drafted in 1860 and came into force in colonial India during the British Raj in 1862. It has since been amended several times and is now supplemented by other criminal provisions. In the state of Jammu and Kashmir, the IPC is known as Ranbir Penal Code (RPC).

After independence, Indian Penal Code was inherited by Pakistan (now called Pakistan Penal Code) and Bangladesh, formerly part of

British India. It was also adopted wholesale by the British colonial authorities in Burma, Sri Lanka, Malaysia, Singapore and Brunei, and remains the basis of the criminal codes in those countries.

History

During the Moghul rule courts administered the "Sharia" to the exclusion of Hindu law. Islamic law gave way to English criminal law with the increase of British influence in the Indian subcontinent. Before 1860, The English criminal law, as modified by several Acts was administered in the Presidency-Towns of Bombay, Calcutta and Madras.

The draft of the Indian Penal Code was prepared by the First Law Commission, chaired by Thomas Babington Macaulay. Its basis is the law of England freed from superfluities, technicalities and local peculiarities. Elements were also derived from the Napoleonic Code and from Edward Livingston's Louisiana Civil Code of 1825. The first final draft of the Indian Penal Code was submitted to the Governor-General of India in Council in 1837, but the draft was again revised. The drafting was completed in 1850 and it was presented to the Legislative Council in 1856 but it did not take its place on the Indian statute book until a generation later, following the Indian Rebellion of 1857. The draft then underwent a very careful revision at the hands of Barnes Peacock, who later became the first Chief Justice of Calcutta High Court, and the future puisne judges of the Calcutta High Court, who were members of the Legislative Council, and was passed into law on 6 October, 1860. The Code came into operation on 1 January, 1862. Unfortunately, Macaulay did not survive to see his masterpiece come into force, having died near the end of 1859.

Objective

The objective of this Act is to provide a general penal code for India. Though not an initial objective, the Act does not repeal the penal laws which were in force at the time of coming into force in India. This was so because the Code does not contain all the offences and it was possible that some offences might have still been left out of the Code, which were not intended to be exempted from penal consequences. Though this Code consolidates the whole of the law on the subject and is exhaustive on the matters in respect of which it declares the law, many more penal statutes governing various offences have been created in addition to the code.

Structure

Indian Penal Code, 1860, sub-divided into **23 chapters, comprises 511 sections**. The code starts with an introduction, provides explanations and exceptions used in the code, and covers a wide range of offences.

Indian Penal Code, 1960

Objective of the Indian Penal Code

The objective of this Act is to provide a general Penal Code for India. Though this Code consolidates the whole of the law on the subject and is exhaustive on the matters in respect of which it declares the law, many more penal statutes governing various offences have been created in addition to this code.

The Indian security system has been one that has gone through a lot of tests and examinations throughout the time. This is due to the political as well as the social situation of the country. India is a land of diverse cultures and traditions and it is a place where people from various religions as well as ethnic backgrounds live together.

"Indian penal code is the skeleton of the Indian criminal justice system".

1. What exactly Indian Penal code is?
2. How and when did it originate?
3. What is its applicability?
4. How does it work?
5. To what extend it helps the law enforcement agencies?
6. What is modus operandi of judges while applying the relevant sections?

Indian Penal Code is a document that has been formulated to counter crimes of various natures and breach of law. IPC traces its roots to the British colonial rule in India.IPC covers any Indian citizen or a person of Indian origin with the exceptions to any kind of military or the armed forces crimes, which are handled by a dedicated list of armed force Acts.

The most important feature of the Indian Penal Code is the impartial nature of judgements promoted by the document. The Indian

Penal Code does not include any special favors for any special person at some position. Thus, the Indian Penal Code stands alike for government employees, as for a common man, and even for a judicial officer. This builds up the faith of the common citizens in the law making and enforcing bodies in the country and prevents any sort of corruption or misuse of power on the part of the people in power.

All in all, the Indian Penal Code of the present day has done away with almost all its flaws and has evolved into a modern law enforcing document that takes into consideration the humane side of the personalities of culprits as well. This has escalated and improved the Indian system of Law to greater heights and has led to a firm respect for it in every citizen of the country.

Importance of the Penal Code

Indian Penal Code is a very important set of regulation which is very important for the system to be operated in a proper way. It is the main criminal code of India. They are various offences that are made under this law. The Indian Penal Code includes all the relevant criminal offences dealing with offences against the state, offenses for public, offences for armed forces, kidnapping, murder, and rape. It deals with offense related to religion, offences against property and it has an important section for offences for marriage, cruelty from husband or relatives, defamation and so on so forth. This was an general over view of the structure of Indian Penal Code. It is not only important for India but also every country should have a Penal Code in order for its system to be operated in a systematic way. This document majorly covers all the basic offences which are highlighted in the society.

❑❑❑

Chapter 8

Criminal Procedure Code (CrPC)

The **Criminal Procedure Code** lays down the mechanism for investigation, prosecution and punishment in crimes including forest/ wildlife offences. It lays down the procedure for the investigation and trials in connection with various offences under the forest and wildlife laws.

In cases where the procedure is laid down in the forest laws, this code supplements those and provides the strength to the relevant law.

Types / classes of criminal courts

The following types/classes of criminal courts have been provided for in the code:

1. Courts of session
2. Chief Judicial Magistrate
3. Judicial Magistrates of the first class or Metropolitan Magistrate in Metropolitan areas
4. Judicial Magistrates of the second class
5. Special Judicial Magistrates
6. Executive Magistrates

Powers of Courts

On the basis of the powers of courts to take cognizance of them, offences may be divided into two:

a) Offences under the Indian Penal Code

b) Offences under any other law

The powers of various courts with regard to the passing of sentences of punishment are clearly stated in the Criminal Procedure Code (CrPC).

Law of Evidence

Evidence is required for proving in a court of law whether a particular offence has been committed or not by a specific person. This is dealt with by the Indian Evidence Act of 1872, which lays down the mechanism for proving in a court that an offence has been committed. **It was authorized by Stephen and came into operation on the first day of September, 1872.**

Objects and Scope

According to Stephen (Shetty, 1981), the Law of Evidence aims to provide answer to the following :

a) What sort of facts may or may not be proved?

b) What sort of evidence is to be given of such facts which may be proved?

c) By whom is such evidence given?

d) In what manner should the evidence be produced for proving a fact?

Terms used in Law of Evidence

1. **Fact:** Fact means (a) Anything, the state of things, relation to things, capable of being perceived by the senses.

   (b) Any mental condition of which any person is conscious.

Facts in issue : This pertains to any and all facts from which the existence/non-existence nature or extent of any right, liability or disability is asserted or denied either by the fact itself or in a combination/connection with other facts.

The facts in issue may pertain to matters that are affirmed by one party while they could be denied by the opposing party.

Relevant facts: This refers to condition wherein one fact is relevant to the other, Relevant facts are connected with each other in a way that may prove or disprove the facts in issue.

2. **Document**: This pertains to any matter expressed or described upon any substance by means of :

   a) Letters or figures

   b) Marks

   c) A combination of the above

3. **Evidence**: Broadly speaking, evidence covers all matters of facts which may be produced in a court of law for proving or disproving certain matters. It includes:
   a) Oral evidence
   b) Documentary evidence: Primary evidence and Secondary evidence
   c) Circumstantial evidence
   d) Real evidence
4. Proved/Disproved/Not proved:
   a) **Proved:** A fact may be proved, when it is accepted by the court of law to be correct.
   b) **Disproved:** A fact may be disproved, when it is regarded as not correct by a court of law.
   c) **Not proved:** A fact may be termed as not proved, when it is neither proved nor disproved.
5. **Motive**: Refers to an ulterior (known) object for which a crime is committed.
6. **Attest:** Attest means to bear witness to a fact. Attesting witness is a person who witnesses the execution of a deed or affixing of signature on a document. Thereafter, the attesting person affixes his signature on the document to this effect.
7. **Collusion** (conspiracy secret agreement): Pertains to a secret agreement or contract between two persons or parties for illegal purposes, such as :
   a) For deceiving and
   b) For improper use
8. **Admission:** This refers to an oral or written statement admitting a fact in issue or relevant fact. According to the evidence act, the following persons are competent to make admissions:
   a) Party to civil or criminal proceedings or their legal/ authorized representatives.
   b) Persons with proprietary or pecuniary (economic) interest in the proceedings.
   c) Persons from whom the parties to the suit have derived their interest.

d) Persons who have explicit information in a suit or proceedings.

1. **Confession:** This refers to an admission of crime or acknowledgement of guilt made by a person who has committed a crime. These may be:
   a) Judicial confession which is made before a magistrate or a court in due course of proceedings
   b) Extra judicial confession which are made other than those made before a magistrate or court.

   Confessions are not admissible under the following conditions:

i) Made before a police officer in the absence of a magistrate
ii) Made under threat or inducement (encouragement) from a person in authority.

Criminal Procedure Code

The **Code of Criminal Procedure** is the main legislation on procedure for administration of substantive criminal law in India. It was enacted in 1973 and came into force on 1 April, 1974. It provides the machinery for the investigation of crime, apprehension of suspected criminals, collection of evidence, determination of guilt or innocence of the accused person and the determination of punishment of the guilty. Additionally, it also deals with public nuisance, prevention of offences and maintenance of wife, child and parents.

The Act consists of 484 sections, 2 schedules and 56 forms. The sections are divided into 38 chapters.

History

In mediaeval India, subsequent to the conquest by the Muslims, the Mohammedan Criminal Law came into prevalence. The British rulers passed the Regulating Act of 1773 under which a Supreme Court was established in Calcutta and later on, at Madras and in Bombay. The Supreme Court was to apply British procedural law while deciding the cases of the Crown's subjects.

After the Rebellion of 1857, the crown took over the administration in India. The Criminal Procedure Code, 1861 was passed by the British parliament. The 1861 code continued after independence and was amended in 1969. It was finally replaced in 1972.

Classification of offences under the code

Cognizable and non-cognizable offences

Cognisable offences are those offences for which a police officer may arrest without court mandated warrant in accordance with the first schedule of the code. For non-cognisable cases, the police officer may arrest only after being duly authorised by a warrant. Non-cognisable offences are, generally, relatively less serious offences than cognisable ones.

Summons case and warrant case

Under Section 204 of the code, a Magistrate taking cognisance of an offence is to issue summons for the attendance of the accused, if the case is a summons case. If the case appears to be a warrant case, he may issue a warrant or a summons as he sees fit. According to the section 2(w), those case are not warrant case or summon case and warrant case are those which lies to imprisonment of death,life and for more than two-years according to section 2(x).

Bailable and non-bailable

According to Section 2(a), bailable offence are offences listed under the First Schedule as bailable or made bailable under any other law for the time being in force. All other offences are non-bailable.

Territorial extent, scope and applicability

The Criminal Procedure Code is applicable in the whole of India except in the State of Jammu and Kashmir. The Parliament's power to legislate in respect of Jammu & Kashmir is curtailed by Article 370 of the Constitution of India.

Provisions under Chapters VIII, X and XI of the code do not apply to the State of Nagaland and some tribal areas in Assam. However, the concerned State Government may, by notification apply any or all of these provisions in these areas. Morever, the Supreme Court of India has also ruled that even in these areas, the authorities are to be governed by the substance of these rules.

Functionaries under the code

1. Magistrates and judges of the Supreme Court and High Court
2. Police

3. Public prosecutors
4. Defence Counsels
5. Correctional services personnel

Bail

There is no definition of the term "bail" under the code though the terms "bailable" and "non-bailable" have been defined. It has, however, been defined by the Black's Law Lexicon as security for the appearance of the accused person on giving which he is released pending trial or investigation

The First Schedule to the code refers to all offences under the Indian Penal Code and classifies them into bailable and non-bailable. There is no test or criteria for determining which offence is bailable and which is non-bailable. However, generally speaking, less serious offences are usually bailable, whereas more serious ones are non-bailable.

Summary trials

Section 260 Clause 2 of the Code lists certain offences which may be summarily tried by any Chief Judicial Magistrate, any Metropolitan Magistrate or any Judicial Magistrate First Class. A First Class Magistrate must first be authorized by the respective High Court to that effect before he may try cases summarily under this Section.

The offences that may be tried summarily under this Section are:

1. Offences not punishable with death, life imprisonment, or imprisonment for a term exceeding two years.
2. Theft under Section 379, 380 and 381 of the Indian Penal Code provided that the value of the stolen property is below Rs. 2,000.
3. Receiving or retaining stolen property under Section 411 of the penal code, where the value of the stolen property is below Rs. 2,000.
4. Assisting in the concealment or disposal of stolen property, under Section 414 of the penal code, the value of the stolen property being below 2,000.
5. Lurking house-trespass (Section 454 of the Indian Penal Code) and house-breaking (Section 456 of the Penal Code) at night.

6. Insult with an intent to provoke a breach of peace under Section 504 and criminal intimidation under Section 506 of the penal code.
7. Abetting of any of the above mentioned offences.
8. Attempt to commit any of the above mentioned offences.
9. Offences with respect to which complaints may be made under Section 20 of Cattle Trespass Act, 1871.

Apart from the above, a Second Class Magistrate may, if so empowered by the High Court, summarily try an offence punishable with fine or with imprisonment not exceeding six months or the abetment or attempt to commit such an offence.

A summary trial tried by a magistrate without being empowered to do so is void. The procedure for a summon case is to be followed, subject to special provisions made in this behalf. The maximum sentence that may be awarded by way of a summary trial is three months with or without fine.

The Magistrate may give up the summary trial in favour of the regular trial, if he finds it undesirable to try the case summarily. The judgement is to be delivered in abridged form.

Judgement

Judgement is the final reasoned decision of the Court as to the guilt or innocence of the accused. Where the accused is found guilty, the judgement must also contain an order requiring the accused to undergo punishment or treatment.

Every court must deliver the judgement in the language of that court as determined by the State Government. It must contain the points that lead to the determination of guilt or innocence. It usually commences with facts and must indicate careful analysis of evidence. It must also specify the offence under the penal code or such other specific law as well as the punishment sentenced. If acquitted the offence of which the accused is so acquitted, must be specified along with a direction that the accused be set at liberty.

Judgements in abridged form

According to Section 355 of the Code, a Metropolitan Magistrate may deliver judgements in abridged form and should contain:

1. Serial number of the case
2. Date of commission of the offence
3. Name of the complainant (if any)
4. Name of the accused person, his parentage and residence
5. Offence complained of (or proved, as the case may be)
6. Plea of the accused and his examination (if any)
7. Final order
8. Date of the order
9. In cases where appeal lies from the final order, a brief statement of reasons for the decision.

Compensation and costs

The functions of a civil court may be performed by a criminal court by virtue of Section 357, 358 and 359. This has been done to provide just, speedy and less expensive redress to the victim. The court is empowered to levy a fine from the offender. Such fine may, wholly or in part, be used for the purpose of compensating the victim.

Post-conviction orders

Having regads to the age, character and antecedents of the offender, and the circumstances in which the offence was committed, if the Court convicting the accused considers it expedient to release the offender, it may do so either on probation of good conduct or after due admonishment. This provision is contained in Section 360 of the Code.

Thus, the court may direct that the offender be released on his entering into a bond, with or without surities. The offender is further required to keep peace and be of good behaviour as well as appear thereafter before the court, when called upon during such period as the court may decide. This period should not exceed three years. The following conditions have to be satisfied:

- There is no previous conviction proved against the offender.
- In case the person convicted is a woman of any age, or a man aged below twenty-one years, the offence committed is not punishable with life imprisonment or death penalty.

- In case the person is a man above twenty-one years of age, the offence of which he is convicted is punishable with fine.

Alternatively, the offender may be released after due admonition, if the following conditions are satisfied:

- There is no previous conviction proved against the offender.
- The offence of which the accused is convicted is any of the following:
  1. Theft,
  2. Theft in a building,
  3. Dishonest misappropriation,
  4. Any offence punishable under the Indian Penal Code with no more than two years of imprisonment,
  5. Any offence punishable only by fine.

No Magistrate of Second Class may release an offender under in such manner without being empowered to do so. He may transfer the case to a Magistrate for consideration.

Section 361 narrows down the discretion of the Court to sentence an offender without taking into consideration the provisions of Section 360 and similar provisions contained in the Probation of Offenders Act or any other law for treatment, training and rehabilitation of youthful offenders. It requires that when such provisions are applicable, the Court must record in writing, the reason for not allowing the benefit of the same to the offender.

Section 30 provides the Court of a Magistrate with the power to award imprisonment for additional terms over the substantive period awarded.

Appeal

The Code and the Constitution of India together provide for multiple ranges of appellate remedy. A person convicted by the High Court exercising original criminal jurisdiction may appeal before the Supreme Court. Where the High Court has, on appeal reversed an order of acquittal and sentenced him to death and imprisonment for a term of ten years or more, the accused may appeal to the Supreme Court. The Constitution provides that an appeal shall lie to the

Supreme Court against the direction of Supreme Court if the High Court certifies that the case involves substantial questions of law as to the interpretation of the Constitution.[8]

Judgements and orders arising from petty cases are not appealable unless the sentences are combined with other sentences. There cannot be an appeal when the accused pleads guilty and is convicted on such plea by the High Court. If the conviction from a plea of guilt is by a Sessions Court, Metropolitan Magistrate or a Magistrate of First or Second Class, only the legality of the sentence may be brought into question in an appeal.

What are the differences between Indian Penal Code and Criminal Procedure Code?

Indian Penal Code provides the details of the various penal offences, punishment applicable to these offences & definitions of various terms used in the penal code, etc, whereas the **Criminal Procedure Code provides the procedure of getting the penal offences prosecuted & punished** by the criminal courts as well details regarding the arrest, investigation, bail, jurisdiction, appeals, revisions & compounding of offence, etc. with regards to the various offences. In short you can say, whereas the penal code defines the punishable offences, the criminal code provides method to get them punished. Both these are enactment to check the crime in the society.

❑❑❑

Chapter 9

Constitution of Criminal Courts and Offices, Power of Courts

Classes of Criminal Courts

Section 6 of the Code of Criminal Procedure (Cr. P.C.): Besides the High Courts and the Courts constituted under any law, other than this Code, there shall be, in every State, the following classes of Criminal Courts, namely :

1. Courts of Session;
2. Judicial Magistrates of the first class and, in any metropolitan area, Metropolitan Magistrates;
3. Judicial Magistrates of the second class; and
4. Executive Magistrates.

It may be noted that the classes of Criminal Courts mentioned in this section are besides the High Courts and the Courts constituted under any law, other than this Code.

Criminal Courts are :

1. High Courts
2. Courts constituted under any Law other than this Code
3. Courts of Session
4. Judicial Magistrates of the First Class
5. Metropolitan Magistrates in any metropolitan area
6. Judicial Magistrates of the Second Class
7. Executive Magistrates
8. Special Executive Magistrate

Courts of Session (Section 9 CrPC)

1. The State Government shall establish a Court of Session for every sessions division.
2. Every Court of Session shall be presided over by a Judge, to be appointed by the High Court.
3. The High Court may also appoint Additional Sessions Judges and Assistant Sessions Judges to exercise jurisdiction in a Court of Session.

Courts of Judicial Magistrates (Section 11 CrPC)

1. In every district (not being a metropolitan area), there shall be established as many Courts of Judicial Magistrates of the first class and of the second class and at such places, as the State Government may after consultation with the High Court, by notification specify.
2. The presiding officers of such Courts shall be appointed by the High Court.

Chief Judicial Magistrate and Additional Chief Judicial Magistrate, etc. (Section 12 CrPC)

1. In every district (not being a metropolitan area), the High Court shall appoint a Judicial Magistrate of the first class to be the Chief Judicial Magistrate.
2. The High Court may appoint any Judicial Magistrate of the first class to be an Additional Chief Judicial Magistrate, and such Magistrate shall have all or any of the powers of a Chief Judicial Magistrate under this Code or under any other law for the time being in force as the High Court may direct.

Subordination of Judicial Magistrates (Section 15 CrPC)

1. Every Chief Judicial Magistrate shall be subordinate to the Sessions Judge; and every other Judicial Magistrate shall, subject to the general control of the Sessions Judge, be subordinate to the Chief Judicial Magistrate.

Courts of Metropolitan Magistrates (Section 16 CrPC)

1. In every metropolitan area, there shall be established as many Courts of Metropolitan Magistrates, and at such places, as the State Government may, after consultation with the High Courts, by notification, specify.
2. The presiding officers of such Courts shall be appointed by the High Court.
3. The jurisdiction and powers of every Metropolitan Magistrate shall extend throughout the metropolitan area.

Chief Metropolitan Magistrate and Additional Chief Metropolitan Magistrate (Section 17 CrPC)

1. The High Court, shall in relation to every metropolitan area within its local jurisdiction appoint a Metropolitan Magistrate to be the Chief Metropolitan Magistrate for such metropolitan area.
2. The High Court may appoint any Metropolitan Magistrate to be an Additional Chief Metropolitan Magistrate, and such Magistrate shall have all or any of the powers of a Chief Metropolitan Magistrate under this Code or under any other law for the time-being in force as the High Court may direct.

Subordination of Metropolitan Magistrates (Section 19 CrPC)

1. The Chief Metropolitan Magistrate shall be subordinate to the Sessions Judge; and every other Metropolitan Magistrate shall subject to the general control of the Sessions Judge, be subordinate to the Chief Metropolitan Magistrate.
2. The High Court may, for the purpose of this Code, define the extent of subordination, if any, of the Additional Chief Metropolitan Magistrates to the Chief Metropolitan Magistrate.
3. The Chief Metropolitan Magistrate may, from time to time, make rules or give special orders, consistent with this Code, as the distribution of business among the Metropolitan Magistrates and as to the allocation of business to an Additional Chief Metropolitan Magistrate.

Executive Magistrates (Section 20 CrPC)

1. In every district and in every metropolitan area, the State Government may appoint as many persons as it thinks fit to be Executive Magistrates and shall appoint one of them to be the District Magistrate.
2. The State Government may appoint any Executive Magistrate to be an Additional District Magistrate and such Magistrate shall have such of the powers of a District Magistrate under this Code or under any other law for the time being in force, as may be directed by the State Government.

Special Executive Magistrates (Section 21 CrPC)

The State Government may appoint, for such term as it may think fit, Executive Magistrates, to be known as Special Executive Magistrates, for particular areas or for the performance of particular functions and confer on such Special Executive Magistrates such of the powers as are conferrable under this Code on Executive Magistrates, as it may deem fit.

CHAPTER 3

Power of Courts

Section 26 – Courts by which offences are triable

Subject to the other provisions of this Code:

1. Any offence under the Indian Penal Code (45 of 1860) may be tried by:
    1. The High Court, or
    2. The Court of Session, or
    3. Any other Court by which such offence is shown in the First Schedule to be triable;

Provided that any offence under section 376 and sections 376A to 376D of the Indian Penal Code shall be tried as far as practicable by a Court presided over by a woman.

2. Any offence under any other law shall, when any Court is mentioned in this behalf in such law, be tried by such Court and when no Court is so mentioned, may be tried by

1. The High Court, or
2. Any other Court by which such offence is shown in the First Schedule to be triable.

Section 27 – Jurisdiction in the case of juveniles

Any offence not punishable with death or imprisonment for life, committed by any person who at the date, when he appears or is brought before the Court is under the age of sixteen years, may be tried by the Court of a Chief Judicial Magistrate, or by any Court specially empowered under the Children Act, 1960 (60 of 1960), or any other law for the time being in force providing for the treatment, training and rehabilitation of youthful offenders.

Section 28 – Sentences which High Courts and Sessions Judges may pass

1. A High Court may pass any sentence authorised by law.
2. A Sessions Judge or Additional Sessions Judge may pass any sentence authorised by law; but any sentence of death passed by any such Judge shall be subject to confirmation by the High Court.
3. An Assistant Sessions Judge may pass any sentence authorised by law except a sentence of death or of imprisonment for life or of imprisonment for a term exceeding ten years.

Section 29 – Sentences which Magistrates may pass

1. The Court of a Chief Judicial Magistrate may pass any sentence authorised by law except a sentence of death or of imprisonment for life or of imprisonment for a term exceeding seven years.
2. The Court of a Magistrate of the first class may pass a sentence of imprisonment for a term not exceeding three years, or of fine not exceeding ten thousand rupees, or both.
3. The Court of a Magistrate of the second class may pass a sentence of imprisonment for a term not exceeding one year, or of fine not exceeding five thousand rupees, or of both.
4. The Court of a Chief Metropolitan Magistrate shall have the powers of the Court of a Chief Judicial Magistrate and that of a Metropolitan Magistrate, the powers of the Court of a Magistrate of the first class.

Section 30 – Sentence of imprisonment in default of fine

1. The Court of a Magistrate may award such term of imprisonment in default of payment of fine as is authorised by law:

   Provided that the term:

   1. Is not in excess of the powers of the Magistrate under section 29;
   2. Shall not, where imprisonment has been awarded as part of the substantive sentence, exceed one-fourth of the term of imprisonment which the Magistrate is competent to inflict as punishment for the offence otherwise than as imprisonment in default of payment of the fine.

2. The imprisonment awarded under this section may be in addition to a substantive sentence of imprisonment for the maximum term awardable by the Magistrate under section 29.

Section 31 – Sentence in cases of conviction of several offences at one trial

1. When a person is convicted at one trial of two or more offences, the Court may, subject to the provisions of section 71 of the Indian Penal Code (45 of 1860), sentence him for such offences, to the several punishments, prescribed therefore which such Court is competent to inflict; such punishments when consisting of imprisonment to commence the one after the expiration of the other in such order, as the Court may direct, unless the Court directs that such punishments shall run concurrently.

2. In the case of consecutive sentences, it shall not be necessary for the Court by reason only of the aggregate punishment for the several offences being in excess of the punishment which it is competent to inflict on conviction of a single offence, to send the offender for trial before a higher Court.

Provided that

1. In no case shall such person be sentenced to imprisonment for a longer period than fourteen years;

2. The aggregate punishment shall not exceed twice the amount of punishment which the Court is competent to inflict for a single offence.

3. For the purpose of appeal by a convicted person, the aggregate of the consecutive sentences passed against him under this section shall be deemed to be a single sentence.

Section 32 – Mode of conferring powers

1. In conferring powers under this Code, the High Courts or the State Government, as the case may be, may, by order, empower persons specially by name or in virtue of their offices or classes of officials generally by their official titles.

2. Every such order shall take effect from the date on which it is communicated to the person so empowered.

Section 33 – Powers of officers appointed

Whenever any person holding an office in the service of Government who has been invested by the High Court or the State Government with any powers under this Code throughout any local area is appointed to an equal or higher office of the same nature, within a like local area under the same State Government, he shall, unless the High Court or the State Government, as the case may be, otherwise directs, or has otherwise directed, exercise the same powers in the local area in which he is so appointed.

Section 34 – Withdrawal of powers

1. The High Court or the state Government, as the case may be, may withdraw all or any of the powers conferred by it under this Code on any person or by any officer subordinate to it.

2. Any powers conferred by the Chief Judicial Magistrate or by the District Magistrate may be withdrawn by the respective Magistrate by whom such powers were conferred.

Section 35 – Powers of Judges and Magistrates exercisable by their successors-in-office

1. Subject to the other provisions of this Code, the powers and duties of a Judge or Magistrate may be exercised or performed by his successor-in-office.

2. When there is any doubt as to who is the successor-in-office of any Additional or Assistant Sessions Judge, the Sessions Judge

shall determine by order in writing the Judge who shall, for the purposes of this Code or of any proceeding or order there under, be deemed to be the successor-in-office of such Additional or Assistant Sessions Judge.

3. When there is any doubt as to who is the successor-in-office of any Magistrate, the Chief Judicial Magistrate, or the District Magistrate, as the case may be, shall determine by order in writing the Magistrate who shall, for the purposes of this Code or of any proceedings or order thereunder, be deemed to be the successor-in-office of such Magistrate.

❑❑❑

Chapter 10

Constitution of India

The Preamble reads

We, The People of India having solemnly resolved to constitute India into a **Sovereign, Socialist, Secular, Democratic, Republic** and to secure to all its citizens;

Justice, social, economic, political;

Liberty of thought, expression, belief, faith and worship;

Equality of status and opportunity; and to promote among them all;

Fraternity, assuring the dignity of the individual and the unity and integrity of the nation;

In our **Constituent Assembly** this, twenty sixth day of November, 1949 do **Hereby Adopt, Enact and Give to Ourselves this Constitution**.

The words 'Socialist 'Secular" and 'Integrity were initially not there in the Preamble. These were added by the 42nd Amendment (1976) of the Constitution.

The Constitution of India is the **supreme law of India**. It lays down the framework defining fundamental political principles, establishes the structure, procedures, powers, and duties of government institutions, and sets out fundamental rights, **directive principles,** and the duties of citizens. It is the longest written constitution of any sovereign country in the world, **containing 444 articles in 22 parts, 12 schedules and 118 amendments**. Besides the Hindi version, there is an official English translation. **Dr. Bhimrao Ramji Ambedkar is widely known as the father of the Indian Constitution.**

The Constitution follows **parliamentary system** of government and **the executive** is directly accountable to legislature. Article 74 provides that there shall be a **Prime Minister of India** as the head of government. It also states that there shall be a **President of India** and a **Vice-President of India** under **Articles 52 and 63**. Unlike the Prime Minister, the President largely performs ceremonial roles.

The Constitution is **federal** in nature. Each State and each Union territory of India have their own government. Analogues to President and Prime Minister, is the **Governor** in case of States, **Lieutenant Governor** for Union territories and the **Chief Minister. The 73rd and 74th Amendment Act** also introduced the system of **Panchayati raj** in villages and municipalities. Also, **Article 370** of the Constitution gives special status to the state of **Jammu and Kashmir**.

The Constitution was adopted by the Constituent Assembly on 26 November, 1949, and came into effect on 26 January, 1950. The date 26 January was chosen to commemorate the **Purna Swaraj declaration of independence** of 1930. With its adoption, the **Union of India** officially became the modern and contemporary **Republic of India** and it replaced the **Government of India Act, 1935** as the country's fundamental governing document. To ensure **constitutional autochthony,** the framers of constitution inserted Article 395 in the constitution and by this Article the Indian Independence Act, 1947 was repealed. The Constitution declares India to be a **sovereign, socialist, secular, democratic republic**, assuring its citizens of **justice, equality**, and **liberty,** and endeavours to promote **fraternity** among them. The words "socialist" and "secular" were added to the definition in 1976 by constitutional amendment (mini constitution). **India celebrates the adoption of the constitution on 26 January each year as Republic Day.**

Background (Main article: Indian independence movement)

The major portion of the **Indian subcontinent** was under **British colonial rule** from 1857 to 1947. The impact of economic, political and social exploitation during this period helped the gradual rise of the Indian independence movement to gain independence from foreign rule. The movement culminated in the formation of the **Dominion of India** on 15 August, 1947, along with the **Dominion of Pakistan**. The Constitution of India was adopted on 26 November, 1949 and came into effect on 26 January, 1950, proclaiming India to be a sovereign, democratic republic. It contained the founding principles of the law of the land which would govern India after its independence from British rule. On the day the constitution came into effect, India ceased to be a **dominion of the British Crown**. The Indian constitution is the world's longest constitution. At the time of commencement, the constitution had 395 articles in 22 parts and 8 schedules. It consists of almost 80,000 words and took 2 years 11 months and 18 days to build.

In the United Kingdom, the office of the **Secretary of State for India** was the authority through whom Parliament exercised its rule (along with the **Council of India)**, and established the office of **Viceroy of India** (along with an Executive Council in India, consisting of high officials of the British Government). The **Indian Councils Act, 1861** provided for a Legislative Council consisting of the members of the Executive council and non-official members. The **Indian Councils Act, 1892** established provincial legislatures and increased the powers of the Legislative Council. Although these Acts increased the representation of Indians in the government, their power still remained limited. The **Indian Councils Act, 1909** and the **Government of India Act, 1919** further expanded participation of Indians in the government.

Government of India Act, 1935 (Main article: Government of India Act, 1935)

The provisions of the Government of India Act, 1935, though never implemented fully, had a great impact on the Constitution of India. Many key features of the constitution are directly taken from this Act. The federal structure of government, provincial autonomy, a bicameral central legislature consisting of a **federal assembly** and a **Council of States** and the separation of legislative powers between the centre and states are some of the provisions of the Act, which are present in the Constitution of India.

The Cabinet Mission Plan (Main article: 1946 Cabinet Mission to India)

In 1946, **British Prime Minister Clement Attlee** formulated a **cabinet mission** to India to discuss and finalize plans for the transfer of power from the British Raj to Indian leadership as well as provide India with independence under **Dominion** status in the **Commonwealth of Nations.** The Mission discussed the framework of the constitution and laid down in some detail the procedure to be followed by the constitution drafting body. Elections for the 296 seats assigned to the British Indian provinces were completed by August 1946. The **Constituent Assembly of India** first met and began work on 26 November, 1946.

The mission consisted of Lord Pethick-Lawrence, the Secretary of State for India, Sir Stafford Cripps, President of the Board of Trade, and A. V. Alexander, the First Lord of the Admiralty. However, Lord Wavell, the Viceroy of India, did not participate.

Indian Independence Act, 1947 (Main article: Indian Independence Act, 1947)

The Indian Independence Act, passed by the British Parliament on 18 July 1947, divided British India into two new independent states, India and Pakistan, which were to be dominions under the **Commonwealth of Nations** until they had each finished drafting and enacted a new constitution. The Constituent Assembly was divided into two for the separate states, with each new Assembly having sovereign powers transferred to it for the respective dominion. The Act also terminated British **suzerainty** over the **princely states,** each of which was left to decide whether to accede to one or other of the new dominions or to continue as independent states in their own right. However, in most cases the states were so dependent on central institutions that they were widely expected to accede to a dominion.

When the Constitution of India came into force on 26 January, 1950, it repealed the Indian Independence Act. India ceased to be a dominion of the British Crown and became a sovereign democratic republic. 26 November, 1949 is also known as National Law Day.

Constituent Assembly (Main article: Constituent Assembly of India)

The Constitution was drafted by the **Constituent Assembly,** which was elected by the elected members of the provincial assemblies. **Dr B.R. Ambedkar,** Sanjay Phakey, Jawaharlal Nehru, C. Rajagopalachari, Rajendra Prasad, Sardar Vallabhbhai Patel, Kanhaiyalal Munshi, Purushottam Mavalankar, Sandipkumar Patel, Maulana Abul Kalam Azad, Shyama Prasad Mukherjee, Nalini Ranjan Ghosh, and Balwantrai Mehta were some important figures in the Assembly. There were more than **30 members of the scheduled classes**. **Frank Anthony** represented the Anglo-Indian community, and the **Parsis** were represented by H. P. Modi. The Chairman of the Minorities Committee was **Harendra Coomar Mookerjee**, a distinguished Christian who represented all Christians other than Anglo-Indians. Ari Bahadur Gururng represented the Gorkha Community. Prominent jurists like Alladi Krishnaswamy Iyer, Benegal Narsing Rau and K. M. Munshi, Ganesh Mavlankar were also members of the Assembly. Sarojini Naidu, Hansa Mehta, Durgabai Deshmukh, Rajkumari Amrit Kaur and Vijayalakshmi Pandit were important women members.

"Dr. Bhimrao Ramji Ambedkar is hailed as the prime architect of Indian Constitution".

The first temporary 2-days president of the Constituent Assembly was **Dr.Sachidanand Sinha**. Later, **Rajendra Prasad** was elected president of the Constituent Assembly. The members of the Constituent Assembly met for the first time on 9 December, 1946.

Drafting

On the 14 August, 1947 meeting of the Assembly, a proposal for forming various committees was presented.[9] Such committees included a Committee on Fundamental Rights, the Union Powers Committee and Union Constitution Committee. On 29 August, 1947, the Drafting Committee was appointed, with **Dr B. R. Ambedkar** as the Chairman along with six other members assisted by a constitutional advisor. These members were Pandit Govind Ballabh Pant **Kanhaiyalal Maneklal Munshi** (K M Munshi, Ex- Home Minister, Bombay), **Alladi Krishnaswamy Iyer** (Ex-Advocate General, Madras State), N Gopalaswami Ayengar (Ex-Prime Minister, J&K and later member of Nehru Cabinet), B L Mitter (Ex-Advocate General, India), Md. Saadullah (Ex-Chief Minister of Assam, Muslim League member) and D P Khaitan (Scion of Khaitan Business family and a renowned lawyer). The constitutional advisor was **Sir Benegal Narsing Rau** (who became First Indian Judge in International Court of Justice, 1950–54). Later B L Mitter resigned and was replaced by Madhav Rao (Legal Advisor of Maharaja of Vadodara). Owing to death of D P Khaitan, **T T Krishnamachari** was chosen to be included in the drafting committee. A Draft Constitution was prepared by the committee and submitted to the Assembly on 4 November, 1947. Draft constitution was debated and over 2000 amendments were moved over a period of two years. Finally on 26 Nov., 1949, the process was completed and Constituent assembly adopted the constitution. 284 members signed the document and the process of constitution making was complete.[10]

The Assembly met in sessions open to the public, for 166 days, spread over a period of 2 years, 11 months and 18 days before adopting the Constitution, the 308 members of the Assembly signed two copies of the document (one each in Hindi and English) on 24 January, 1950. The original Constitution of India is hand-written with beautiful calligraphy, each page beautified and decorated by artists from **Shantiniketan** including Beohar Rammanohar Sinha and **Nandalal Bose.** Two days later, on 26 January, 1950, the Constitution of India became the law of all the **States and territories of India**. Rs. 1,00,00,000 was official estimate of expenditure on constituent assembly. The Constitution has undergone **many amendments** since its enactment.

Structure

The Constitution, in its current form (September 2012), consists of a preamble, 22 parts containing 444 articles, 12 schedules, 2 appendices and 98 amendments to date.

Parts

The individual Articles of the Constitution are grouped together into the following Parts :

- Preamble
- Part I - Union and its Territory
- Part II - Citizenship.
- Part III - Fundamental Rights.
- Part IV - Directive Principles of State Policy.
- Part IVA - Fundamental Duties.
- Part V - The Union.
- Part VI - The States.
- Part VII - States in the B part of the First schedule *(Repealed)*.
- Part VIII - The Union Territories
- IX - The Panchayats.
- Part IXA - The Municipalities.
- IXB – The Co-operative Societies

- Part X - The scheduled and Tribal Areas
- Part XI - Relations between the Union and the States.
- Part XII - Finance, Property, Contracts and Suits
- Part XIII - Trade and Commerce within the territory of India
- Part XIV - Services under the Union, the States.
- Part XIVA - Tribunals.
- Part XV - Elections
- Part XVI - Special Provisions Relating to certain Classes.
- Part XVII - Languages
- Part XVIII - Emergency Provisions
- Part XIX - Miscellaneous
- Part XX - Amendment of the Constitution
- Part XXI - Temporary, Transitional and Special Provisions
- Part XXII - Short title, date of commencement, Authoritative text in Hindi and Repeals.

Schedules

Schedules are lists in the Constitution that categorize and tabulate bureaucratic activity and policy of the Government :

- First Schedule (Articles 1 and 4)- This lists the states and territories of India, lists any changes to their borders and the laws used to make that change.
- Second Schedule (Articles 59(3), 65(3), 75(6), 97, 125, 148(3), 158(3), 164(5), 186 and 221)- - This lists the salaries of officials holding public office, judges, and Comptroller and Auditor General of India.
- Third Schedule (Articles 75(4), 99, 124(6), 148(2), 164(3), 188 and 219)—Forms of Oaths - This lists the oaths of offices for elected officials and judges.
- Fourth Schedule (Articles 4(1) and 80(2)) - This details the allocation of seats in the *Rajya Sabha* (the upper house of Parliament) per State or Union Territory.

- Fifth Schedule (Article 244(1)) - This provides for the administration and control of Scheduled Areas and Scheduled Tribes (areas and tribes needing special protection due to disadvantageous conditions).
- Sixth Schedule (Articles 244(2) and 275(1))— Provisions for the administration of tribal areas in Assam, Meghalaya, Tripura, and Mizoram.
- Seventh Schedule (Article 246)—The union (central government), state, and concurrent lists of responsibilities.
- Eighth Schedule (Articles 344(1) and 351)—The official languages.
- Ninth Schedule (Article 31-B) - Originally Articles mentioned here were immune from judicial review on the ground that they violated fundamental rights. but in a landmark judgement in 2007, the Supreme Court of India held in I.R. Coelho v. State of Tamil Nadu and others that laws included in the 9th schedule can be subject to judicial review, if they violated the fundamental rights guaranteed under Article 14, 15, 19, 21 or the basic structure of the Constitution {(ambiguous)}[21]
- Tenth Schedule (Articles 102(2) and 191(2))—"Anti-defection" provisions for Members of Parliament and Members of the State Legislatures.
- Eleventh Schedule (Article 243-D)—*Panchayati Raj* (rural local government).
- Twelth Schedule (Article 243-W)—Municipalities (urban local government).

Amendment (Main article: Amendment of the Constitution of India)

The process of re writing any part of the constitution is called amendment. Amendments to the Constitution are made by the Parliament, the procedure for which is laid out in Article 368. An amendment bill must be passed by both the Houses of the Parliament by a two-thirds majority and voting. In addition to this, certain amendments which pertain to the federal nature of the Constitution must be ratified by a majority of state legislatures.

As of July 2013, there have been 118 amendment bills presented in the Parliament, out of which 98 have been passed to become Amendment Acts. Most of these amendments address issues dealt with by statute in other democracies. However, the Constitution is so specific in spelling out government powers that many of these issues must be addressed by constitutional amendment. As a result, the document is amended roughly twice a year.

In 2000, the National Commission to Review the Working of the Constitution (NCRWC) was set up to look into updating the constitution.

Limitations

The Supreme Court has ruled in **Kesavananda Bharati v. State of Kerala** case that not every constitutional amendment is permissible, the amendment must respect the "**basic structure**" of the constitution, which is immutable.

Adoptions from other constitutions

The architects of Indian constitution were most heavily influenced by the British model of **parliamentary democracy.** In addition, a number of principles were adopted from the **Constitution of the United States of America,** including the **separation of powers** among the major branches of government and the establishment of a **supreme court**. The principles adopted from **Canada** were Unitary government with strong centre and also distribution of powers between central government and state governments along with placing residuary powers with central government. From **Ireland, directive principle of state policy** was adopted. From **Germany,** the principle of suspension of **fundamental rights** during **emergency** was adopted. From **Australia,** the idea of having a Concurrent list of shared powers was used as well and some of the terminology was utilized for the preamble.

Judicial review

Judicial review is adopted in the Constitution of India from the **Constitution of the United States of America**. In the Indian constitution, Judicial review is dealt with under Article 13. Judicial Review refers that the Constitution is the supreme power of the nation and all laws are under its supremacy. Article 13 states that:

1. All pre-constitutional laws, if in part or completely in conflict with the Constitution, shall have all conflicting provisions deemed ineffective until an amendment to the Constitution ends the conflict. In such situation, the provision of that law will again come into force, if it is compatible with the constitution as amended. This is called the ***Doctrine of Eclipse***.
2. In a similar manner, laws made after adoption of the Constitution by the Constituent Assembly must be compatible with the constitution, otherwise the laws and amendments will be deemed to be void *ab initio*.
3. In such situations, the Supreme Court or High Court interprets the laws to decide, if they are in conformity with the Constitution. If such an interpretation is not possible because of inconsistency, and where a separation is possible, the provision that is inconsistent with constitution is considered to be void. In addition to article 13, articles 32, 226 and 227 provide a constitutional basis to judicial review in India.

I. Fundamental Rights and Duties

Fundamental Duties: It shall be the duty of every citizen of India:

1. To abide by the constitution and to respect ideals of constitution and institutions, the National Flag and the National Anthem.
2. To cherish and follow the noble ideals which inspired our national struggle for freedom.
3. To uphold and protect the sovereignty, unity and integrity of India.
4. To defend the country and render national service, when called upon to do so.
5. To promote harmony and the spirit of common brotherhood amongst all the people of India linguistic and regional or sectional diversities; to renounce practices derogatory to the dignity of women.
6. To value and preserve the rich heritage of our composite culture.
7. To protect and improve the natural environment including forests, lakes, rivers and wildlife, and to have compassion for living creatures.

8. To develop the scientific temper, humanism and the spirit of inquiry and reform.
9. To safeguard public property and to abjure violence.
10. To strive towards excellence in all spheres of individual and collective activity so that the nation constantly rises to higher levels of endeavour and achievement.

Fundamental Rights of an Indian Citizen

"**Rights** literally mean those freedoms which are essential for personal good as well as the good of the community".

The six fundamental rights are :

1. Right to equality
2. Right to freedom
3. Right against exploitation
4. Right to freedom of religion
5. Cultural and educational rights
6. Right to constitutional remedies

1. Right to equality Includes :

- Equality before law.
- Prohibition of discrimination on grounds of religion, race, caste, sex or place of birth.
- Equality of opportunity in matters of employment.
- Right to equality

2. Right to freedom includes

- Right to freedom and expression, which enable an individual to participate in public activities.
- Freedom to assemble peacefully without arms
- Freedom to form associations or unions
- Freedom to move freely throughout the territory of India

- Freedom to reside and settle in any part of the territory of India
- Freedom to practice any profession or to carry on any occupation, trade or business

3. Right against exploitation includes :

- Abolition of trafficking in human beings & Begar (forced labour).
- Abolition of employment of children below the age of 14 years in dangerous jobs like factories and mines.

4. Right to freedom of religion includes :

- All religions are equal before the State and no religion shall be given preference over the other.
- Citizens are free to preach, practice and propagate any religion of their choice.
- The objective of this right is to sustain the principle of secularism in India.

5. Cultural and educational rights includes :

- Any community which has a language and a script of its own has the right to conserve and develop them.
- No citizen can be discriminated against for admission in State or State aided institutions.

6. Right to constitutional remedies

- Empowers the citizens to move a court of law in case of any denial of fundamental rights

II. Constitutional Provisions of SC/ST, Minorities and Women and Child

Special Provisions for SCs, STs, BCs, Minorities & Anglo Indians

In order to realize the objectives of equality and justice as laid down in the preamble itself, the constitution makes special provisions for the scheduled castes(SCs), the scheduled Tribes(STs), the Backward Classes(BCs), the minorities and the Anglo-Indians.

Provisions for SCs and STs

Some of the articles in part XVI, Part III, part IV and others parts of the constitution contain special provisions for SCs and STs, These provisions can be classified into the following board categories :

I. Permanent and Temporary

a) Some of the provisions are permanent feature of the constitution,

b) While some others continue to operate only for a special period (Temporary feature)

II. Protective and Development

a) Provisions aim at protecting the SCs and Sts from all forms of injustice and exploitation.

b) Some provisions aim at promoting their socio- economic interests.

The various constitutional safeguards for SCs and STs are :

1. Seats are to be reserved for the SCs and STs in the Lok Sabha and the state Legislative Assemblies on the basis of population ratios (10yrs upto 1960)
2. The claims of SCs and STs are to be taken into consideration, while making appointments to the public services of the centre and the states, without sacrificing the efficiency of administration.
3. The president should set up a National commission for the SCs to investigate all matters relating to the constitutional safe guards for the SCs and to report to him(Article 338)
4. The president is required to appoint a commission to report on administration of the scheduled areas and the welfare of the STs in the states.
5. The centre should pay grants in aid to the states for meeting the costs of schemes of welfare of the STs and for raising the level of administration in the scheduled areas.
6. The Vth and VIth Schedules of the constitution envisage a special system of administration for the areas inhibited by the STs (Designated as "Scheduled areas" and Tribal Areas")
7. A minister in charge of tribal welfare should be appointed in the states of Chhattisgarh, Jharkhand, MP and Odisha.

8. The state is permitted to make any special provision for the advancement of the SCs and STs (Article 15(4))
9. The two fundamental rights (the right to move freely throughout the territory of India and right to reside and settle in any part of the territory of India) can be restricted on the ground of the protection of interests of the STs (Article 19)
10. The state is directed to promote with special care there educational and economic interests of the SCs and STs and protect them from social injustice and all forms of exploitation (Article 46).

Provisions for BCs

The expression BCs means other backward classes (OBCs) as the SCs and STs are also backward classes of citizens (as specified by the central Govt.)

The various constitutional safeguards for the BCs (OBCs) are as follows:-

1. The state is permitted to make any special provision for the advancement of any socially and educationally backward classes of citizens (Article 15(4))
2. The state can provide for the reservation of appointments or posts in favour of any backward class which is not adequately represented in the state services.
3. The state is directed to promote with special care the educational and economic interests of the weaker section of the people and protect them from social injustice and all forms of exploitation (Article 4&6)
4. The tribal welfare ministers appointed in Chhattisgarh, Jharkhand, MP and Odisha may also be put additionally in-change of the welfare of the BCs (Article 164)
5. The president may appoint a commission to investigate the conditions of socially and educationally backward classes and to recommend the steps to improve their condition. The report of the commission is to be placed before the parliament along with action taken memorandum.

The President appointed two commissions so far

1. The first Backward classes Commission was appointed in 1953 under the chairmanship of Kaka Kalelkar and report was submitted in 1955.
2. The second backward classes was appointed in 1979 with BP.Mandal as chairman and submitted in 1980.
3. A National commission for backward classes was established in 1993 as a permanent statutory body.
4. The Govt. has made reservation for SCs, STs and OBCs in services under its control. The quantum of reservation to SCs, STs and OBCs in direct recruitment on all India basis by open competition is 15%, 7.5% and 27% respectively.

Provisions for Minorities

The term Minority has not been defined anywhere in the constitution. The central government has notified five communities, namely Muslims, Sikhs, Christians, Buddhists and Zoroastrians as religious minorities at the national level.

a) **Religious and Linguistic Minorities**

1. Any section of the citizens having a distinct language, script or culture of its own has the Fundamental Right to conserve the same (Article 29).
2. No citizen is to be denied admission into any educational institution maintained by the state or aided by the state on grounds of religion, race, caste or language (Article 29).
3. All minorities, whether based on religion or language, have the Fundamental Right to establish and administer educational institutions of their choice (Article 30).
4. The compensation amount fixed by the state for the compulsory acquisition of any property of a minority educational institution should not restrict or abrogate the fundamental right guaranteed to the minorities, whether based on religion or language (Article 30).
5. In granting aid to educational institutions, the state should not discriminate against any educational institution on the ground that it is under the management of a minority, whether based on religion or language (Article 30).

Linguistic minorities

1. When the president (on a demand being made) is satisfied that a substantial proportion of the population of a state desire the use of any language spoken by them to be recognized by that state, Then he may direct that such language should also be officially recognized in that state.
2. Every aggrieved (Injured) person has the light to submit a representation for the redress of any grievance to any officer or authority of the union or a state in any of the languages used in the Union or in the state, as the case may be.
3. Every state and local authority in the state should provide adequate facilities for instruction in the mother tongue at the primary stage of education to children belonging to linguistic minority groups.
4. The president should appoint a special officer for linguistic minorities to investigate all matters relating to the report to him. The president should place all such reports before the parliament and send to the state government concerned.

State Council of Ministers

Constitutional Provisions

Article 163: Deals with the states of the council of ministers.

Article 164: Deals with the appointment, tenure, responsibility, qualifications, oath and salaries and allowances of the ministers.

Article 163: Council of ministers to aid and advise the governor.

1. They shall be a council of ministers with the chief Minister as the head to aid and advise the Governor in the exercise of his functions.
2. The decision of the Governor shall be final, if any question arises whether a matter falls within the governors discretion or not
3. The advice tendered by ministers to the Governor shall not be inquired into in any court.

Article 164: Other provisions as to Ministers.

1. The CM shall be appointed by the Governor and the other Ministers shall be appointed by the Governor on the advice of the CM.

2. The total number of ministers including the CM in the council of ministers in a state shall not exceed 15% of the total strength of the legislative assembly of that state (91st Amendment Act of 2003).
3. A member of either House of state legislature belonging to any political party who is disqualified on the ground of defection shall also be disqualified to be appointed as a minister (91st Amendment Act of 2003).
4. The ministers shall hold office during the pleasure of the Governor.
5. The council of ministers shall be collectivity responsible to the state legislative assembly.
6. The governor shall administer the oaths of office and secrecy to a minister.
7. A minister who is not a member of the state legislature for any period of six consecutive months shall cease to be a minister.
8. The salaries and allowance of minister shall be determined by the State Legislature.

Responsibility of Ministers

a) Collective Responsibility

Article 164 clearly states that the council of ministers is collectively responsible to the legislative assembly of the state. This means that all the ministers own joint responsibility to the legislative assembly for all their Acts of omission and commission,.

b) Individual Responsibility

Article 164 contains the principle of individual responsibility. It states that the ministers hold office during the pleasure of the governor. This means that the governor can remove a minister at a time, when the council of ministers enjoys the confidence of the legislative assembly.

c) No legal Responsibility

There is no provision in the constitution for the system of legal responsibility of the minister in the states (As in the Centre).

Cabinet

A smaller body called "Cabinet" is the nucleus of the council of ministers. It is the real centre of authority in the state government.

Role of cabinet

Cabinet performs the following role :

1. It is the highest decision-making authority in the politico-administrative system of a state.
2. It is the chief policy formulating body of the State govt.
3. It is the supreme executive authority of the State govt.
4. It is the chief coordinator of state administration.
5. It is an advisory body to the governor.
6. It is the chief crisis manager and thus deals with all emergency situations.
7. It deals with all major legislative and financial matters.
8. It exercises control over higher appointments like constitutional authorities and senior secretariat administrators.

❑❑❑

Chapter 11

Union Executive-President, Vice President, Pro-Council of Ministers

Part V - The Union

Chapter I —The Executive

The President and Vice-President

The President of India — There shall be a President of India.

Executive power of the Union

1. The executive power of the Union shall be vested in the President and shall be exercised by him either directly or through officers subordinate to him in accordance with this Constitution.
2. Without prejudice to the generality of the foregoing provision, the supreme command of the Defence Forces of the Union shall be vested in the President and the exercise thereof shall be regulated by law.
3. Nothing in this article shall :
   a) Be deemed to transfer to the President any functions conferred by any existing law on the Government of any State or other authority; or
   b) Prevent Parliament from conferring by law functions on authorities other than the President.

Election of President—The President shall be elected by the members of an electoral college consisting of :

a) The elected members of both Houses of Parliament; and

b) The elected members of the Legislative Assemblies of the States.

Explanation – In this article and in article 55, "State" includes the National Capital Territory of Delhi and the Union territory of Pondicherry.

Manner of election of President

1. As far as practicable, there shall be uniformity in the scale of representation of the different States at the election of the President.
2. For the purpose of securing such uniformity among the States *inter se* as well as parity between the States as a whole and the Union, the number of votes which each elected member of Parliament and of the Legislative Assembly of each State is entitled to cast at such election shall be determined in the following manner:
    a) Every elected member of the Legislative Assembly of a State shall have as many votes as there are multiples of one thousand in the quotient obtained by dividing the population of the State by the total number of the elected members of the Assembly;
    b) If, after taking the said multiples of one thousand, the remainder is not less than five hundred, then the vote of each member referred to in sub-clause *(a)* shall be further increased by one;
    c) Each elected member of either House of Parliament shall have such number of votes, as may be obtained by dividing the total number of votes assigned to the members of the Legislative Assemblies of the States under sub-clauses (a) and (b) by the total number of the elected members of both Houses of Parliament, fractions exceeding one-half being counted as one and other fractions being disregarded.
3. The election of the President shall be held in accordance with the system of proportional representation by means of the single transferable vote and the voting at such election shall be by secret ballot.

Explanation – In this article, the expression "population" means the population as ascertained at the last preceding census of which the relevant figures have been published:

Provided that the reference in this *Explanation* to the last preceding census of which the relevant figures have been published shall, until the relevant figures for the first census taken after the year 2026 have been published, be construed as a reference to the 1971 census.

Term of office of President

1. The President shall hold office for a term of five years from the date on which he enters upon his office.

   Provided that:

   a) The President may, by writing under his hand addressed to the Vice-President, resign his office;

   b) The President may, for violation of the Constitution, be removed from office by impeachment in the manner provided in Article 61;

   c) The President shall, notwithstanding the expiration of his term, continue to hold office until his successor enters upon his office.

2. Any resignation addressed to the Vice-President under clause *(a)* of the proviso to clause (1) shall forthwith be communicated by him to the Speaker of the House of the People.

Eligibility for re-election – A person who holds, or who has held, office as President shall, subject to the other provisions of this Constitution, be eligible for re-election to that office.

Qualifications for election as President

1. No person shall be eligible for election as President unless he:

   a) Is a citizen of India,

   b) Has completed the age of thirty-five years, and

   c) Is qualified for election as a member of the House of the People.

2. A person shall not be eligible for election as President if he holds any office of profit under the Government of India or the Government of any State or under any local or other authority subject to the control of any of the said Governments.

Explanation – For the purposes of this article, a person shall not be deemed to hold any office of profit by reason only that he is the President or Vice- President of the Union or the Governor of any State or is a Minister either for the Union or for any State.

Conditions of President's office

1. The President shall not be a member of either House of Parliament or of a House of the Legislature of any State, and if a member of either House of Parliament or of a House of the Legislature of any State be elected President, he shall be deemed to have vacated his seat in that House on the date on which he enters upon his office as President.
2. The President shall not hold any other office of profit.
3. The President shall be entitled without payment of rent to the use of his official residences and shall be also entitled to such emoluments, allowances and privileges, as may be determined by Parliament by law and, until provision in that behalf is so made, such emoluments, allowances and privileges as are specified in the Second Schedule.
4. The emoluments and allowances of the President shall not be diminished during his term of office.

Oath or affirmation by the President – Every President and every person acting as President or discharging the functions of the President shall, before entering upon his office, make and subscribe in the presence of the Chief Justice of India or, in his absence, the senior-most Judge of the Supreme Court available, an oath or affirmation in the following form, that is to say:

"I, A.B., do swear in the name of God that I will faithfully execute solemnly affirm the office of President (or discharge the functions of the President) of India and will to the best of my ability preserve, protect and defend the Constitution and the law and that I will devote myself to the service and well-being of the people of India.".

Procedure for impeachment of the President

1. When a President is to be impeached for violation of the Constitution, the charge shall be preferred by either House of Parliament.

2. No such charge shall be preferred unless:

    a) The proposal to prefer such charge is contained in a resolution which has been moved after at least fourteen days' notice in writing signed by not less than one-fourth of the total number of members of the House has been given of their intention to move the resolution; and

    b) Such resolution has been passed by a majority of not less than two-thirds of the total membership of the House.

3. When a charge has been so preferred by either House of Parliament, the other House shall investigate the charge or cause the charge to be investigated and the President shall have the right to appear and to be represented at such investigation.

4. If as a result of the investigation a resolution is passed by a majority of not less than two-thirds of the total membership of the House by which the charge was investigated or caused to be investigated, declaring that the charge preferred against the President has been sustained, such resolution shall have the effect of removing the President from his office as from the date on which the resolution is so passed.

Time of holding election to fill vacancy in the office of President and the term of office of person elected to fill casual vacancy

1. An election to fill a vacancy caused by the expiration of the term of office of President shall be completed before the expiration of the term.

2. An election to fill a vacancy in the office of President occurring by reason of his death, resignation or removal, or otherwise shall be held as soon as possible after, and in no case later than six months from, the date of occurrence of the vacancy; and the person elected to fill the vacancy shall, subject to the provisions of Article 56, be entitled to hold office for the full term of five years from the date on which he enters upon his office.

The Vice-President of India

The Vice-President of India—There shall be a Vice-President of India.

The Vice-President to be *ex officio* Chairman of the Council of States—The Vice-President shall be *ex officio* Chairman of the Council of States and shall not hold any other office of profit:

Provided that during any period when the Vice-President acts as President or discharges the functions of the President under Article 65, he shall not perform the duties of the office of Chairman of the Council of States and shall not be entitled to any salary or allowance payable to the Chairman of the Council of States under Article 97.

The Vice-President to act as President or to discharge his functions during casual vacancies in the office, or during the absence of President

1. In the event of the occurrence of any vacancy in the office of the President by reason of his death, resignation or removal, or otherwise, the Vice-President shall act as President until the date on which a new President elected in accordance with the provisions of this Chapter to fill such vacancy enters upon his office.
2. When the President is unable to discharge his functions owing to absence, illness or any other cause, the Vice-President shall discharge his functions until the date on which the President resumes his duties.
3. The Vice-President shall, during, and in respect of, the period while he is so acting as, or discharging the functions of, President, have all the powers and immunities of the President and be entitled to such emoluments, allowances and privileges, as may be determined by Parliament by law and, until provision in that behalf is so made, such emoluments, allowances and privileges, as are specified in the Second Schedule.

Election of Vice-President

1. The Vice-President shall be elected by the members of an electoral college consisting of the members of both Houses of Parliament in accordance with the system of proportional representation by means of the single transferable vote and the voting at such election shall be by secret ballot.
2. The Vice-President shall not be a member of either House of Parliament or of a House of the Legislature of any State, and if a member of either House of Parliament or of a House of the

Legislature of any State be elected Vice-President, he shall be deemed to have vacated his seat in that House on the date on which he enters upon his office as Vice-President.

3. No person shall be eligible for election as Vice-President unless he:
    a) Is a citizen of India;
    b) Has completed the age of thirty-five years; and
    c) Is qualified for election as a member of the Council of States.
4. A person shall not be eligible for election as Vice-President, if he holds any office of profit under the Government of India or the Government of any State or under any local or other authority subject to the control of any of the said Governments.

Explanation. – For the purposes of this article, a person shall not be deemed to hold any office of profit by reason only that he is the President or Vice- President of the Union or the Governor of any State or is a Minister either for the Union or for any State.

Term of office of Vice-President. – The Vice-President shall hold office for a term of five years from the date on which he enters upon his office.

Provided that

a) A Vice-President may, by writing under his hand addressed to the President, resign his office;
b) A Vice-President may be removed from his office by a resolution of the Council of States passed by a majority of all the then members of the Council and agreed to by the House of the People; but no resolution for the purpose of this clause shall be moved unless at least fourteen days' notice has been given of the intention to move the resolution;
c) A Vice-President shall, notwithstanding the expiration of his term, continue to hold office until his successor enters upon his office.

Time of holding election to fill vacancy in the office of Vice-President and the term of office of person elected to fill casual vacancy

1. An election to fill a vacancy caused by the expiration of the term of office of Vice-President shall be completed before the expiration of the term.

2. An election to fill a vacancy in the office of Vice-President occurring by reason of his death, resignation or removal, or otherwise shall be held as soon as possible after the occurrence of the vacancy, and the person elected to fill the vacancy shall, subject to the provisions of article 67, be entitled to hold office for the full term of five years from the date on which he enters upon his office.

Oath or affirmation by the Vice-President—Every Vice-President shall, before entering upon his office, make and subscribe before the President, or some person appointed in that behalf by him, an oath or affirmation in the following form, that is to say:

"I, A.B., do swear in the name of God that I will bear true faith and solemnly affirm allegiance to the Constitution of India as by law established and that I will faithfully discharge the duty upon which I am about to enter."

Discharge of President's functions in other contingencies—Parliament may make such provisions, as it thinks fit for the discharge of the functions of the President in any contingency not provided for in this Chapter.

Matters relating to, or connected with, the election of a President or Vice-President

1. All doubts and disputes arising out of or in connection with the election of a President or Vice-President shall be inquired into and decided by the Supreme Court whose decision shall be final.
2. If the election of a person as President or Vice-President is declared void by the Supreme Court, acts done by him in the exercise and performance of the powers and duties of the office of President or Vice-President, as the case may be, on or before the date of the decision of the Supreme Court shall not be invalidated by reason of that declaration.
3. Subject to the provisions of this Constitution, Parliament may by law regulate any matter relating to or connected with the election of a President or Vice-President.
4. The election of a person as President or Vice-President shall not be called in question on the ground of the existence of any vacancy for whatever reason among the members of the electoral college electing him.

Power of President to grant pardons, etc., and to suspend, remit or commute sentences in certain cases

1. The President shall have the power to grant pardons, reprieves, respites or remissions of punishment or to suspend, remit or commute the sentence of any person convicted of any offence :

    a) In all cases where the punishment or sentence is by a Court Martial;

    b) In all cases where the punishment or sentence is for an offence against any law relating to a matter to which the executive power of the Union extends;

    c) In all cases where the sentence is a sentence of death.

2. Nothing in sub-clause *(a)* of clause (1) shall affect the power conferred by law on any officer of the Armed Forces of the Union to suspend, remit or commute a sentence passed by a Court Martial.

3. Nothing in sub-clause *(c)* of clause (1) shall affect the power to suspend, remit or commute a sentence of death exercisable by the Governor of a State under any law for the time being in force.

Extent of executive power of the Union

1. Subject to the provisions of this Constitution, the executive power of the Union shall extend:

a) To the matters with respect to which Parliament has power to make laws; and

b) To the exercise of such rights, authority and jurisdiction as are exercisable by the Government of India by virtue of any treaty or agreement.

Provided that the executive power referred to in sub-clause *(a)* shall not, save as expressly provided in this Constitution or in any law made by Parliament, extend in any State to matters with respect to which the Legislature of the State has also power to make laws.

2. Until otherwise provided by Parliament, a State and any officer or authority of a State may, notwithstanding anything in this article, continue to exercise in matters with respect to which Parliament has power to make laws for that State such executive

power or functions as the State or officer or authority thereof could exercise immediately before the commencement of this Constitution.

Council of Ministers

Council of Ministers to aid and advise President

1. There shall be a Council of Ministers with the Prime Minister at the head to aid and advise the President who shall, in the exercise of his functions, act in accordance with such advice:

Provided that the President may require the Council of Ministers to reconsider such advice, either generally or otherwise, and the President shall act in accordance with the advice tendered after such reconsideration.

2. The question whether any, and if so what, advice was tendered by Ministers to the President shall not be inquired into in any court.

Other provisions as to Ministers

1. The Prime Minister shall be appointed by the President and the other Ministers shall be appointed by the President on the advice of the Prime Minister :
    a) The total number of Ministers, including the Prime Minister, in the Council of Ministers shall not exceed fifteen per cent. of the total number of members of the House of the People.
    b) A member of either House of Parliament belonging to any political party who is disqualified for being a member of that House under paragraph 2 of the Tenth Schedule shall also be disqualified to be appointed as a Minister under clause (1) for duration of the period commencing from the date of his disqualification till the date on which the term of his office as such member would expire or where he contests any election to either House of Parliament before the expiry of such period, till the date on which he is declared elected, whichever is earlier.
2. The Ministers shall hold office during the pleasure of the President.
3. The Council of Ministers shall be collectively responsible to the House of the People.

4. Before a Minister enters upon his office, the President shall administer to him the oaths of office and of secrecy according to the forms set out for the purpose in the Third Schedule.

5. A Minister who for any period of six consecutive months is not a member of either House of Parliament shall at the expiration of that period cease to be a Minister.

6. The salaries and allowances of Ministers shall be, such as Parliament may from time to time by law determine and, until Parliament so determines, shall be as specified in the Second Schedule.

The Attorney-General for India

Attorney-General for India

1. The President shall appoint a person who is qualified to be appointed a Judge of the Supreme Court to be Attorney- General for India.

2. It shall be the duty of the Attorney-General to give advice to the Government of India upon such legal matters, and to perform such other duties of a legal character, as may from time to time be referred or assigned to him by the President, and to discharge the functions conferred on him by or under this Constitution or any other law for the time being in force.

3. In the performance of his duties, the Attorney-General shall have right of audience in all courts in the territory of India.

4. The Attorney-General shall hold office during the pleasure of the President, and shall receive such remuneration as the President may determine.

Conduct of Government Business

Conduct of business of the Government of India

1. All executive action of the Government of India shall be expressed to be taken in the name of the President.

2. Orders and other instruments made and executed in the name of the President shall be authenticated in such manner, as may be specified in rules to be made by the President, and the validity of an order or instrument which is so authenticated shall not be

called in question on the ground that it is not an order or instrument made or executed by the President.

3. The President shall make rules for the more convenient transaction of the business of the Government of India, and for the allocation among Ministers of the said business.

Duties of Prime Minister as respects the furnishing of information to the President, etc.—It shall be the duty of the Prime Minister:

a) To communicate to the President all decisions of the Council of Ministers relating to the administration of the affairs of the Union and proposals for legislation;

b) To furnish such information relating to the administration of the affairs of the Union and proposals for legislation as the President may call for; and

c) Of the President so requires, to submit for the consideration of the Council of Ministers any matter on which a decision has been taken by a Minister but which has not been considered by the Council.

Chapter II—Parliament

General

Constitution of Parliament—There shall be a Parliament for the Union which shall consist of the President and two Houses to be known respectively, as the Council of States and the House of the People.

Composition of the Council of States

1. The Council of States shall consist of:
   a) Twelve members to be nominated by the President in accordance with the provisions of clause (3); and
   b) Not more than two hundred and thirty-eight representatives of the States and of the Union territories.
2. The allocation of seats in the Council of States to be filled by representatives of the States and of the Union territories shall be in accordance with the provisions in that behalf contained in the Fourth Schedule.

3. The members to be nominated by the President under sub-clause *(a)* of clause (1) shall consist of persons having special knowledge or practical experience in respect of such matters as the following, namely: Literature, science, art and social service.
4. The representatives of each State in the Council of States shall be elected by the elected members of the Legislative Assembly of the State in accordance with the system of proportional representation by means of the single transferable vote.
5. The representatives of the Union territories in the Council of States shall be chosen in such manner as Parliament may by law prescribe.

Composition of the House of the People

1. Subject to the provisions of article 331, the House of the People shall consist of:
   a) Not more than five hundred and thirty members chosen by direct election from territorial constituencies in the States, and
   b) Not more than twenty members to represent the Union territories, chosen in such manner as Parliament may by law provide.
2. For the purposes of sub-clause (a) of clause (1) :
   a) There shall be allotted to each State a number of seats in the House of the People in such manner that the ratio between that number and the population of the State is, so far as practicable, the same for all States; and
   b) Each State shall be divided into territorial constituencies in such manner that the ratio between the population of each constituency and the number of seats allotted to it is, so far as practicable, the same throughout the State:

Provided that the provisions of sub-clause *(a)* of this clause shall not be applicable for the purpose of allotment of seats in the House of the People to any State so long as the population of that State does not exceed six millions.

3. In this article, the expression "population" means the population as ascertained at the last preceding census, of which the relevant figures have been published:

Provided that the reference in this clause to the last preceding census of which the relevant figures have been published shall, until the relevant figures for the first census taken after the year 2026 have been published, be construed :

i) For the purposes of sub-clause (*a*) of clause (2) and the proviso to that clause, as a reference to the 1971 census; and

ii) For the purposes of sub-clause (*b*) of clause (2) as a reference to the 2001 census.

Duration of Houses of Parliament

1. The Council of States shall not be subject to dissolution, but as nearly as possible one-third of the members thereof shall retire as soon as may be on the expiration of every second year in accordance with the provisions made in that behalf by Parliament by law.
2. The House of the People, unless sooner dissolved, shall continue for five years from the date appointed for its first meeting and no longer and the expiration of the said period of five years shall operate as a dissolution of the House:

Provided that the said period may, while a Proclamation of Emergency is in operation, be extended by Parliament by law for a period not exceeding one year at a time and not extending in any case beyond a period of six months after the Proclamation has ceased to operate.

Qualification for membership of Parliament

A person shall not be qualified to be chosen to fill a seat in Parliament unless he :

a) Is a citizen of India, and makes and subscribes before some person authorized in that behalf by the Election Commission an oath or affirmation according to the form set out for the purpose in the Third Schedule;

b) Is, in the case of a seat in the Council of States, not less than thirty years of age and, in the case of a seat in the House of the People, not less than twenty- five years of age; and

c) Possesses such other qualifications as may be prescribed in that behalf by or under any law made by Parliament.

Sessions of Parliament, prorogation and dissolution

1. The President shall from time to time summon each House of Parliament to meet at such time and place as he thinks fit, but six months shall not intervene between its last sitting in one session and the date appointed for its first sitting in the next session.
2. The President may from time to time:
   a) Prorogue the Houses or either House;
   b) Dissolve the House of the People.

Right of President to address and send messages to Houses

1. The President may address either House of Parliament or both Houses assembled together, and for that purpose require the attendance of members.
2. The President may send messages to either House of Parliament, whether with respect to a Bill then pending in Parliament or otherwise, and a House to which any message is so sent shall with all convenient despatch consider any matter required by the message to be taken into consideration.

Special address by the President

1. At the commencement of the first session after each general election to the House of the People and at the commencement of the first session of each year the President shall address both Houses of Parliament assembled together and inform Parliament of the causes of its summons.
2. Provision shall be made by the rules regulating the procedure of either House for the allotment of time for discussion of the matters referred to in such address.

The Speaker and Deputy Speaker of the House of the People.— The House of the People shall, as soon as may be, choose two members of the House to be respectively Speaker and Deputy Speaker thereof and, so often as the office of Speaker or Deputy Speaker becomes vacant, the House shall choose another member to be Speaker or Deputy Speaker, as the case may be.

Vacation and resignation of, and removal from the offices of Speaker and Deputy Speaker— A member holding office as Speaker or Deputy Speaker of the House of the People.

a) Shall vacate his office if he ceases to be a member of the House of the People;

b) May at any time, by writing under his hand addressed, if such member is the Speaker, to the Deputy Speaker, and if such member is the Deputy Speaker, to the Speaker, resign his office; and

c) May be removed from his office by a resolution of the House of the People passed by a majority of all the then members of the House:

Provided that no resolution for the purpose of clause *(c)* shall be moved unless at least fourteen days' notice has been given of the intention to move the resolution:

Provided further that, whenever the House of the People is dissolved, the Speaker shall not vacate his office until immediately before the first meeting of the House of the People after the dissolution.

Power of the Deputy Speaker or other person to perform the duties of the office of, or to act as, Speaker

1. While the office of Speaker is vacant, the duties of the office shall be performed by the Deputy Speaker or, if the office of Deputy Speaker is also vacant, by such member of the House of the People, as the President may appoint for the purpose.
2. During the absence of the Speaker from any sitting of the House of the People the Deputy Speaker or, if he is also absent, such person as may be determined by the rules of procedure of the House, or, if no such person is present, such other person as may be determined by the House, shall act as Speaker.

The Speaker or the Deputy Speaker not to preside while a resolution for his removal from office is under consideration

1. At any sitting of the House of the People, while any resolution for the removal of the Speaker from his office is under consideration, the Speaker, or while any resolution for the removal of the Deputy Speaker from his office is under consideration, the Deputy Speaker, shall not, though he is present, preside, and the provisions of clause (2) of Article 95 shall apply in relation to every such sitting as they apply in relation to a sitting from which the Speaker, or, as the case may be, the Deputy Speaker, is absent.

2. The Speaker shall have the right to speak in, and otherwise to take part in the proceedings of, the House of the People while any resolution for his removal from office is under consideration in the House and shall, notwithstanding anything in Article 100, be entitled to vote only in the first instance on such resolution or on any other matter during such proceedings but not in the case of an equality of votes.

Salaries and allowances of the Chairman and Deputy Chairman and the Speaker and Deputy Speaker.— There shall be paid to the Chairman and the Deputy Chairman of the Council of States, and to the Speaker and the Deputy Speaker of the House of the People, such salaries and allowances, as may be respectively fixed by Parliament by law and, until provision in that behalf is so made, such salaries and allowances, as are specified in the Second Schedule.

Conduct of Business

Oath or affirmation by members— Every member of either House of Parliament shall, before taking his seat, make and subscribe before the President, or some person appointed in that behalf by him, an oath or affirmation according to the form set out for the purpose in the Third Schedule.

Voting in Houses, power of Houses to act notwithstanding vacancies and quorum

1. Save as otherwise provided in this Constitution, all questions at any sitting of either House or joint sitting of the Houses shall be determined by a majority of votes of the members present and voting, other than the Speaker or person acting as Chairman or Speaker. The Chairman or Speaker, or person acting as such, shall not vote in the first instance, but shall have and exercise a casting vote in the case of an equality of votes.

2. Either House of Parliament shall have power to act notwithstanding any vacancy in the membership thereof, and any proceedings in Parliament shall be valid notwithstanding that it is discovered subsequently that some person who was not entitled so to do sat or voted or otherwise took part in the proceedings.

3. Until Parliament by law otherwise provides, the quorum to constitute a meeting of either House of Parliament shall be one-tenth of the total number of members of the House.
4. If at any time during a meeting of a House, there is no quorum, it shall be the duty of the Chairman or Speaker, or person acting as such, either to adjourn the House or to suspend the meeting until there is a quorum.

Disqualifications of Members

Vacation of seats

1. No person shall be a member of both Houses of Parliament and provision shall be made by Parliament by law for the vacation by a person, who is chosen a member of both Houses of his seat in one House or the other.
2. No person shall be a member both of Parliament and of a House of the Legislature of a State, and if a person is chosen a member both of Parliament and of a House of the Legislature of a State, then, at the expiration of such period, as may be specified in rules made by the President, that person's seat in Parliament shall become vacant, unless he has previously resigned his seat in the Legislature of the State.
3. If a member of either House of Parliament:
    a) Becomes subject to any of the disqualifications mentioned in clause (1) or clause (2) of article 102, or
    b) Resigns his seat by writing under his hand addressed to the Chairman or the Speaker, as the case may be, and his resignation is accepted by the Chairman or the Speaker, as the case may be, his seat shall there upon become vacant:

Provided that in the case of any resignation referred to in sub-clause (*b*), if from information received or otherwise and after making such inquiry as he thinks fit, the Chairman or the Speaker, as the case may be, is satisfied that such resignation is not voluntary or genuine, he shall not accept such resignation.

4. If for a period of sixty days a member of either House of Parliament is without permission of the House absent from all meetings thereof, the House may declare his seat vacant:

Provided that in computing the said period of sixty days no account shall be taken of any period during which the House is prorogued or is adjourned for more than four consecutive days.

Disqualifications for membership

1. A person shall be disqualified for being chosen as, and for being, a member of either House of Parliament:
   a) If he holds any office of profit under the Government of India or the Government of any State, other than an office declared by Parliament by law not to disqualify its holder;
   b) If he is of unsound mind and stands, so declared by a competent court;
   c) If he is an undischarged insolvent;
   d) If he is not a citizen of India, or has voluntarily acquired the citizenship of a foreign State, or is under any acknowledgement of allegiance or adherence to a foreign State;
   e) If he is so disqualified by or under any law made by Parliament.

Explanation – For the purposes of this clause a person shall not be deemed to hold an office of profit under the Government of India or the Government of any State by reason only that he is a Minister either for the Union or for such State.

2. A person shall be disqualified for being a member of either House of Parliament, if he is so disqualified under the Tenth Schedule.

Decision on questions as to disqualifications of members

1. If any question arises as to whether a member of either House of Parliament has become subject to any of the disqualifications mentioned in clause (1) of Article 102, the question shall be referred for the decision of the President and his decision shall be final.
2. Before giving any decision on any such question, the President shall obtain the opinion of the Election Commission and shall act according to such opinion.

Penalty for sitting and voting before making oath or affirmation under Article 99 or when not qualified or when disqualified. – If a person sits or votes as a member of either House of Parliament before he has complied with the requirements of Article 99, or when he knows that he is not qualified or that he is disqualified for membership thereof, or that he is prohibited from so doing by the provisions of any law made by Parliament, he shall be liable in respect of each day on which he so sits or votes to a penalty of five hundred rupees to be recovered as a debt due to the Union.

Powers, Privileges and Immunities of Parliament and its Members

Powers, privileges, etc., of the Houses of Parliament and of the members and committees thereof

1. Subject to the provisions of this Constitution and to the rules and standing orders regulating the procedure of Parliament, there shall be freedom of speech in Parliament.
2. No member of Parliament shall be liable to any proceedings in any court in respect of anything said or any vote given by him in Parliament or any committee thereof, and no person shall be so liable in respect of the publication by or under the authority of either House of Parliament of any report, paper, votes or proceedings.
3. In other respects, the powers, privileges and immunities of each House of Parliament, and of the members and the committees of each House, shall be such as may from time to time be defined by Parliament by law, and, until so defined, shall be those of that House and of its members and committees immediately before the coming into force of section 15 of the Constitution (Forty-fourth Amendment) Act, 1978.
4. The provisions of clauses (1), (2) and (3) shall apply in relation to persons who by virtue of this Constitution have the right to speak in, and otherwise to take part in the proceedings of, a House of Parliament or any committee thereof as they apply in relation to members of Parliament.

Salaries and allowances of members— Members of either House of Parliament shall be entitled to receive such salaries and allowances as may from time to time be determined by Parliament by law and, until provision in that respect is so made, allowances at such rates and upon such conditions as were immediately before the commencement of this Constitution applicable in the case of members of the Constituent Assembly of the Dominion of India.

Legislative Procedure

Provisions as to introduction and passing of Bills

1. Subject to the provisions of articles 109 and 117 with respect to Money Bills and other financial Bills, a Bill may originate in either House of Parliament.
2. Subject to the provisions of articles 108 and 109, a Bill shall not be deemed to have been passed by the Houses of Parliament unless it has been agreed to by both Houses, either without amendment or with such amendments only, as are agreed to by both Houses.
3. A Bill pending in Parliament shall not lapse by reason of the prorogation of the Houses.
4. A Bill pending in the Council of States which has not been passed by the House of the People shall not lapse on a dissolution of the House of the People.
5. A Bill which is pending in the House of the People, or which having been passed by the House of the People is pending in the Council of States, shall, subject to the provisions of Article 108, lapse on a dissolution of the House of the People.

Joint sitting of both Houses in certain cases

1. If after a Bill has been passed by one House and transmitted to the other House:
    a) The Bill is rejected by the other House; or
    b) The Houses have finally disagreed as to the amendments to be made in the Bill; or
    c) More than six months elapse from the date of the reception of the Bill by the other House without the Bill being passed by it, the President may, unless the Bill has elapsed by reason of a dissolution of the House of the People, notify to the Houses by message if they are sitting or by public notification, if they are not sitting, his intention to summon them to meet in a joint sitting for the purpose of deliberating and voting on the Bill:

Provided that nothing in this clause shall apply to a Money Bill.

2. In reckoning any such period of six months as is referred to in clause (1), no account shall be taken of any period during which the House referred to in sub-clause (*c*) of that clause is prorogued or adjourned for more than four consecutive days.
3. Where the President has under clause (1) notified his intention of summoning the Houses to meet in a joint sitting, neither House shall proceed further with the Bill, but the President may at any time after the date of his notification summon the Houses to meet in a joint sitting for the purpose specified in the notification and, if he does so, the Houses shall meet accordingly.
4. If at the joint sitting of the two Houses the Bill, with such amendments, if any, as are agreed to in joint sitting, is passed by a majority of the total number of members of both Houses present and voting, it shall be deemed for the purposes of this Constitution to have been passed by both Houses:

Provided that at a joint sitting

a) If the Bill, having been passed by one House, has not been passed by the other House with amendments and returned to the House in which it originated, no amendment shall be proposed to the Bill other than such amendments (if any), as are made necessary by the delay in the passage of the Bill;
b) If the Bill has been so passed and returned, only such amendments as aforesaid shall be proposed to the Bill and such other amendments as are relevant to the matters with respect to which the Houses have not agreed; and the decision of the person presiding as to the amendments which are admissible under this clause shall be final.

5. A joint sitting may be held under this article and a Bill passed thereat, notwithstanding that a dissolution of the House of the People has intervened since the President notified his intention to summon the Houses to meet therein.

Special procedure in respect of Money Bills

1. A Money Bill shall not be introduced in the Council of States.
2. After a Money Bill has been passed by the House of the People, it shall be transmitted to the Council of States for its recommen-

dations and the Council of States shall within a period of fourteen days from the date of its receipt of the Bill return the Bill to the House of the People with its recommendations and the House of the People may thereupon either accept or reject all or any of the recommendations of the Council of States.

3. If the House of the People accepts any of the recommendations of the Council of States, the Money Bill shall be deemed to have been passed by both Houses with the amendments recommended by the Council of States and accepted by the House of the People.

4. If the House of the People does not accept any of the recommendations of the Council of States, the Money Bill shall be deemed to have been passed by both Houses in the form, in which it was passed by the House of the People without any of the amendments recommended by the Council of States.

5. If a Money Bill passed by the House of the People and transmitted to the Council of States for its recommendations is not returned to the House of the People within the said period of fourteen days, it shall be deemed to have been passed by both Houses at the expiration of the said period in the form, in which it was passed by the House of the People.

Definition of "Money Bills"

1 For the purposes of this Chapter, a Bill shall be deemed to be a Money Bill, if it contains only provisions dealing with all or any of the following matters, namely:

a) The imposition, abolition, remission, alteration or regulation of any tax;

b) The regulation of the borrowing of money or the giving of any guarantee by the Government of India, or the amendment of the law with respect to any financial obligations undertaken or to be undertaken by the Government of India;

c) The custody of the Consolidated Fund or the Contingency Fund of India, the payment of moneys into or the withdrawal of moneys from any such Fund;

d) The appropriation of moneys out of the Consolidated Fund of India;

e) The declaring of any expenditure to be expenditure charged on the Consolidated Fund of India or the increasing of the amount of any such expenditure;

f) The receipt of money on account of the Consolidated Fund of India or the public account of India or the custody or issue of such money or the audit of the accounts of the Union or of a State; or

g) Any matter incidental to any of the matters specified in sub-clauses (*a*) to (*f*).

2. A Bill shall not be deemed to be a Money Bill by reason only that it provides for the imposition of fines or other pecuniary penalties, or for the demand or payment of fees for licences or fees for services rendered, or by reason that it provides for the imposition, abolition, remission, alteration or regulation of any tax by any local authority or body for local purposes.

3. If any question arises whether a Bill is a Money Bill or not, the decision of the Speaker of the House of the People thereon shall be final.

4. There shall be endorsed on every Money Bill, when it is transmitted to the Council of States under Article 109, and when it is presented to the President for assent under Article 111, the certificate of the Speaker of the House of the People signed by him that it is a Money Bill.

Assent to Bills—When a Bill has been passed by the Houses of Parliament, it shall be presented to the President, and the President shall declare either that he assents to the Bill, or that he withholds assent therefrom:

Provided that the President may, as soon as possible after the presentation to him of a Bill for assent, return the Bill, if it is not a Money Bill to the Houses with a message requesting that they will reconsider the Bill or any specified provisions thereof and, in particular, will consider the desirability of introducing any such amendments as he may recommend in his message, and when a Bill is so returned, the Houses shall reconsider the Bill accordingly, and if the Bill is passed again by the Houses with or without amendment and presented to the President for assent, the President shall not withhold assent there from.

Procedure in Financial Matters

Annual financial statement

1. The President shall in respect of every financial year cause to be laid before both the Houses of Parliament a statement of the estimated receipts and expenditure of the Government of India for that year, in this Part referred to as the "annual financial statement".

2. The estimates of expenditure embodied in the annual financial statement shall show separately:

   a) The sums required to meet expenditure described by this Constitution as expenditure charged upon the Consolidated Fund of India; and

   b) The sums required to meet other expenditure proposed to be made from the Consolidated Fund of India, and shall distinguish expenditure on revenue account from other expenditure.

3. The following expenditure shall be expenditure charged on the Consolidated Fund of India:

   a) The emoluments and allowances of the President and other expenditure relating to his office;

   b) The salaries and allowances of the Chairman and the Deputy Chairman of the Council of States and the Speaker and the Deputy Speaker of the House of the People;

   c) Debt charges for which the Government of India is liable including interest, sinking fund charges and redemption charges, and other expenditure relating to the raising of loans and the service and redemption of debt;

   d) (*i*) The salaries, allowances and pensions payable to or in respect of Judges of the Supreme Court;

   ii) The pensions payable to or in respect of Judges of the Federal Court;

   iii) The pensions payable to or in respect of Judges of any High Court which exercises jurisdiction in relation to any area included in the territory of India or which at any time before the commencement of this Constitution exercised jurisdiction in relation to any area included in a Governor's Province of the Dominion of India;

e) The salary, allowances and pension payable to or in respect of the Comptroller and Auditor-General of India;

f) Any sums required to satisfy any judgement, decree or award of any court or arbitral tribunal;

g) Any other expenditure declared by this Constitution or by Parliament by law to be so charged.

Procedure in Parliament with respect to estimates

1. So much of the estimates as relates to expenditure charged upon the Consolidated Fund of India shall not be submitted to the vote of Parliament, but nothing in this clause shall be construed as preventing the discussion in either House of Parliament of any of those estimates.
2. So much of the said estimates as relates to other expenditure shall be submitted in the form of demands for grants to the House of the People, and the House of the People shall have power to assent, or to refuse to assent, to any demand, or to assent to any demand subject to a reduction of the amount specified therein.
3. No demand for a grant shall be made except on the recommendation of the President.

Appropriation Bills

1. As soon as may be after the grants under Article 113 have been made by the House of the People, there shall be introduced a Bill to provide for the appropriation out of the Consolidated Fund of India of all moneys required to meet:

    a) The grants so made by the House of the People; and

    b) The expenditure charged on the Consolidated Fund of India but not exceeding in any case the amount shown in the statement previously laid before Parliament.

2. No amendment shall be proposed to any such Bill in either House of Parliament which will have the effect of varying the amount or altering the destination of any grant so made or of varying the amount of any expenditure charged on the Consolidated Fund

of India, and the decision of the person presiding as to whether an amendment is inadmissible under this clause shall be final.

3. Subject to the provisions of Articles 115 and 116, no money shall be withdrawn from the Consolidated Fund of India except under appropriation made by law passed in accordance with the provisions of this Article.

Supplementary, additional or excess grants

1. The President shall:

   a) If the amount authorized by any law made in accordance with the provisions of Article 114 to be expended for a particular service for the current financial year is found to be insufficient for the purposes of that year or when a need has arisen during the current financial year for supplementary or additional expenditure upon some new service not contemplated in the annual financial statement for that year, or

   b) If any money has been spent on any service during a financial year in excess of the amount granted for that service and for that year, cause to be laid before both the Houses of Parliament another statement showing the estimated amount of that expenditure or cause to be presented to the House of the People a demand for such excess, as the case may be.

2. The provisions of articles 112, 113 and 114 shall have effect in relation to any such statement and expenditure or demand and also to any law to be made authorizing the appropriation of moneys out of the Consolidated Fund of India to meet such expenditure or the grant in respect of such demand, as they have effect in relation to the annual financial statement and the expenditure mentioned therein or to a demand for a grant and the law to be made for the authorization of appropriation of moneys out of the Consolidated Fund of India to meet such expenditure or grant.

Votes on account, votes of credit and exceptional grants

1. Notwithstanding anything in the foregoing provisions of this Chapter, the House of the People shall have power:

a) To make any grant in advance in respect of the estimated expenditure for a part of any financial year pending the completion of the procedure prescribed in Article 113 for the voting of such grant and the passing of the law in accordance with the provisions of Article 114 in relation to that expenditure;

b) To make a grant for meeting an unexpected demand upon the resources of India, when on account of the magnitude or the indefinite character of the service the demand cannot be stated with the details ordinarily given in an annual financial statement;

c) To make an exceptional grant which forms no part of the current service of any financial year; and Parliament shall have power to authorize by law the withdrawal of moneys from the Consolidated Fund of India for the purposes for which the said grants are made.

2. The provisions of Articles 113 and 114 shall have effect in relation to the making of any grant under clause (1) and to any law to be made under that clause as they have effect in relation to the making of a grant with regard to any expenditure mentioned in the annual financial statement and the law to be made for the authorization of appropriation of moneys out of the Consolidated Fund of India to meet such expenditure.

Special provisions as to financial Bills

1. A Bill or amendment making provision for any of the matters specified in sub-clauses (*a*) to (*f*) of clause (1) of Article 110 shall not be introduced or moved except on the recommendation of the President and a Bill making such provision shall not be introduced in the Council of States:

Provided that no recommendation shall be required under this clause for the moving of an amendment making provision for the reduction or abolition of any tax.

2. A Bill or amendment shall not be deemed to make provision for any of the matters aforesaid by reason only that it provides for the imposition of fines or other pecuniary penalties, or for the demand or payment of fees for licences or fees for services rendered, or by reason that it provides for the imposition,

abolition, remission, alteration or regulation of any tax by any local authority or body for local purposes.

3. A Bill which, if enacted and brought into operation, would involve expenditure from the Consolidated Fund of India shall not be passed by either House of Parliament unless the President has recommended to that House the consideration of the Bill.

Procedure Generally

Rules of procedure

1. Each House of Parliament may make rules for regulating, subject to the provisions of this Constitution, its procedure and the conduct of its business.
2. Until rules are made under clause (1), the rules of procedure and standing orders in force immediately before the commencement of this Constitution with respect to the Legislature of the Dominion of India shall have effect in relation to Parliament subject to such modifications and adaptations, as may be made therein by the Chairman of the Council of States or the Speaker of the House of the People, as the case may be.
3. The President, after consultation with the Chairman of the Council of States and the Speaker of the House of the People, may make rules as to the procedure with respect to joint sittings of, and communications between, the two Houses.
4. At a joint sitting of the two Houses the Speaker of the House of the People, or in his absence such person as may be determined by rules of procedure made under clause (3), shall preside.

Regulation by law of procedure in Parliament in relation to financial business— Parliament may, for the purpose of the timely completion of financial business, regulate by law the procedure of, and the conduct of business in, each House of Parliament in relation to any financial matter or to any Bill for the appropriation of moneys out of the Consolidated Fund of India, and, if and so far as any provision of any law so made is inconsistent with any rule made by a House of Parliament under clause (1) of Article 118 or with any rule or standing order having effect in relation to Parliament under clause (2) of that Article, such provision shall prevail.

Language to be used in Parliament

1. Notwithstanding anything in Part XVII, but subject to the provisions of article 348, business in Parliament shall be transacted in Hindi or in English:

Provided that the Chairman of the Council of States or Speaker of the House of the People, or person acting as such, as the case may be, may permit any member who cannot adequately express himself in Hindi or in English to address the House in his mother-tongue.

2. Unless Parliament by law otherwise provides, this Article shall, after the expiration of a period of fifteen years from the commencement of this Constitution, have effect as if the words "or in English" were omitted there from.

Restriction on discussion in Parliament.— No discussion shall take place in Parliament with respect to the conduct of any Judge of the Supreme Court or of a High Court in the discharge of his duties except upon a motion for presenting an address to the President praying for the removal of the Judge as hereinafter provided.

Courts not to inquire into proceedings of Parliament

1. The validity of any proceedings in Parliament shall not be called in question on the ground of any alleged irregularity of procedure.
2. No officer or member of Parliament in whom powers are vested by or under this Constitution for regulating procedure or the conduct of business, or for maintaining order, in Parliament shall be subject to the jurisdiction of any court in respect of the exercise by him of those powers.

Chapter III—Legislative Powers of the President

Power of President to promulgate Ordinances during recess of Parliament

1. If at any time, except when both Houses of Parliament are in session, the President is satisfied that circumstances exist which render it necessary for him to take immediate action, he may promulgate such Ordinances, as the circumstances appear to him to require.

2. An Ordinance promulgated under this article shall have the same force and effect as an Act of Parliament, but every such Ordinance:

a) Shall be laid before both Houses of Parliament and shall cease to operate at the expiration of six weeks from the re-assembly of Parliament, or, if before the expiration of that period resolutions disapproving it are passed by both Houses, upon the passing of the second of those resolutions; and

b) May be withdrawn at any time by the President.

Explanation—Where the Houses of Parliament are summoned to re-assemble on different dates, the period of six weeks shall be reckoned from the later of those dates for the purposes of this clause.

3. If and so far as an Ordinance under this article makes any provision which Parliament would not under this Constitution be competent to enact, it shall be void.

Chapter IV—The Union Judiciary

Establishment and constitution of Supreme Court

1. There shall be a Supreme Court of India consisting of a Chief Justice of India and, until Parliament by law prescribes a larger number, of not more than seven[1] other Judges.

2. Every Judge of the Supreme Court shall be appointed by the President by warrant under his hand and seal after consultation with such of the Judges of the Supreme Court and of the High Courts in the States, as the President may deem necessary for the purpose and shall hold office until he attains the age of sixty-five years:

Provided that in the case of appointment of a Judge other than the Chief Justice, the Chief Justice of India shall always be consulted.

Provided further that

a) A Judge may, by writing under his hand addressed to the President, resign his office;

b) A Judge may be removed from his office in the manner provided in clause (4).

2a) The age of a Judge of the Supreme Court shall be determined by such authority and in such manner, as Parliament may by law provide.

3. A person shall not be qualified for appointment as a Judge of the Supreme Court unless he is a citizen of India and:

   a) Has been for at least five years a Judge of a High Court or of two or more such Courts in succession; or

   b) Has been for at least ten years an advocate of a High Court or of two or more such Courts in succession; or

   c) Is, in the opinion of the President, a distinguished jurist.

Explanation I—In this clause "High Court" means a High Court which exercises, or which at any time before the commencement of this Constitution exercised, jurisdiction in any part of the territory of India.

Explanation II—In computing for the purpose of this clause the period during which a person has been an advocate, any period during which a person has held judicial office not inferior to that of a district judge, after he became an advocate shall be included.

4. A Judge of the Supreme Court shall not be removed from his office except by an order of the President passed after an address by each House of Parliament supported by a majority of the total membership of that House and by a majority of not less than two-thirds of the members of that House present and voting has been presented to the President in the same session for such removal on the ground of proved misbehaviour or incapacity.

5. Parliament may by law regulate the procedure for the presentation of an address and for the investigation and proof of the misbehaviour or incapacity of a Judge under clause (4).

6. Every person appointed to be a Judge of the Supreme Court shall, before he enters upon his office, make and subscribe before the President, or some person appointed in that behalf by him, an oath or affirmation according to the form set out for the purpose in the Third Schedule.

7. No person who has held office as a Judge of the Supreme Court shall plead or act in any court or before any authority within the territory of India.

Salaries, etc., of Judges

1. There shall be paid to the Judges of the Supreme Court such salaries, as may be determined by Parliament by law and, until provision in that behalf is so made, such salaries, as are specified in the Second Schedule.
2. Every Judge shall be entitled to such privileges and allowances and to such rights in respect of leave of absence and pension as may from time to time be determined by or under law made by Parliament and, until so determined, to such privileges, allowances and rights, as are specified in the Second Schedule:

Provided that neither the privileges nor the allowances of a Judge nor his rights in respect of leave of absence or pension shall be varied to his disadvantage after his appointment.

Appointment of acting Chief Justice.—When the office of Chief Justice of India is vacant or when the Chief Justice is, by reason of absence or otherwise, unable to perform the duties of his office, the duties of the office shall be performed by such one of the other Judges of the Court, as the President may appoint for the purpose.

Appointment of ad hoc Judges

1. If at any time there should not be a quorum of the Judges of the Supreme Court available to hold or continue any session of the Court, the Chief Justice of India may, with the previous consent of the President and after consultation with the Chief Justice of the High Court concerned, request in writing the attendance at the sittings of the Court, as an *ad hoc* Judge, for such period as may be necessary, of a Judge of a High Court duly qualified for appointment as a Judge of the Supreme Court to be designated by the Chief Justice of India.
2. It shall be the duty of the Judge who has been so designated, in priority to other duties of his office, to attend the sittings of the Supreme Court at the time and for the period for which his attendance is required, and while so attending he shall have all the jurisdiction, powers and privileges, and shall discharge the duties, of a Judge of the Supreme Court.

Attendance of retired Judges at sittings of the Supreme Court.—Notwithstanding anything in this Chapter, the Chief Justice of India may at any time, with the previous consent of the President, request any person who has held the office of a Judge of the Supreme Court or of the Federal Court or who has held the office of a Judge of a High Court and is duly qualified for appointment as a Judge of the Supreme Court to sit and act as a Judge of the Supreme Court, and every such person so requested shall, while so sitting and acting, be entitled to such allowances, as the President may by order determine and have all the jurisdiction, powers and privileges of, but shall not otherwise be deemed to be, a Judge of that Court:

Provided that nothing in this article shall be deemed to require any such person as aforesaid to sit and act as a Judge of that Court unless he consents so to do.

Supreme Court to be a court of record—The Supreme Court shall be a court of record and shall have all the powers of such a court including the power to punish for contempt of itself.

Seat of Supreme Court—The Supreme Court shall sit in Delhi or in such other place or places, as the Chief Justice of India may, with the approval of the President, from time to time, appoint.

Original jurisdiction of the Supreme Court—Subject to the provisions of this Constitution, the Supreme Court shall, to the exclusion of any other court, have original jurisdiction in any dispute:

a) Between the Government of India and one or more States; or

b) Between the Government of India and any State or States on one side and one or more other States on the other; or

c) Between two or more States.

If and in so far as the dispute involves any question (whether of law or fact) on which the existence or extent of a legal right depends:

Provided that the said jurisdiction shall not extend to a dispute arising out of any treaty, agreement, covenant, engagement, *sanad* or other similar instrument which, having been entered into or executed before the commencement of this Constitution, continues in operation after such commencement, or which provides that the said jurisdiction shall not extend to such a dispute.

131A [*Exclusive jurisdiction of the Supreme Court in regard to questions as to constitutional validity of Central laws.*] *Rep. by the Constitution (Forty-third Amendment) Act,* 1977, *s.* 4 (*w.e.f.* 13-4-1978).

Appellate jurisdiction of Supreme Court in appeals from High Courts in certain cases

1. An appeal shall lie to the Supreme Court from any judgment, decree or final order of a High Court in the territory of India, whether in a civil, criminal or other proceeding, if the High Court certifies under Article 134A that the case involves a substantial question of law as to the interpretation of this Constitution.
2. Where such a certificate is given, any party in the case may appeal to the Supreme Court on the ground that any such question as aforesaid has been wrongly decided.

Explanation – For the purposes of this Article, the expression "final order" includes an order deciding an issue which, if decided in favour of the appellant, would be sufficient for the final disposal of the case.

Appellate jurisdiction of Supreme Court in appeals from High Courts in regard to civil matters

1. An appeal shall lie to the Supreme Court from any judgment, decree or final order in a civil proceeding of a High Court in the territory of India if the High Court certifies under Article 134A:
   a) That the case involves a substantial question of law of general importance; and
   b) That in the opinion of the High Court the said question needs to be decided by the Supreme Court.
2. Notwithstanding anything in Article 132, any party appealing to the Supreme Court under clause (1) may urge as one of the grounds in such appeal that a substantial question of law as to the interpretation of this Constitution has been wrongly decided.
3. Notwithstanding anything in this Article, no appeal shall, unless Parliament by law otherwise provides, lie to the Supreme Court from the judgement, decree or final order of one Judge of a High Court.

134. Appellate jurisdiction of Supreme Court in regard to criminal matters

1. An appeal shall lie to the Supreme Court from any judgment, final order or sentence in a criminal proceeding of a High Court in the territory of India, if the High Court:

a) Has on appeal reversed an order of acquittal of an accused person and sentenced him to death; or

b) Has withdrawn for trial before itself any case from any court subordinate to its authority and has in such trial convicted the accused person and sentenced him to death; or

c) Certifies under article 134A that the case is a fit one for appeal to the Supreme Court.

Provided that an appeal under sub-clause (*c*) shall lie subject to such provisions as may be made in that behalf under clause (1) of Article 145 and to such conditions as the High Court may establish or require.

2. Parliament may by law confer on the Supreme Court any further powers to entertain and hear appeals from any judgement, final order or sentence in a criminal proceeding of a High Court in the territory of India subject to such conditions and limitations, as may be specified in such law.

Certificate for appeal to the Supreme Court—Every High Court, passing or making a judgement, decree, final order, or sentence, referred to in clause (1) of Article 132 or clause (1) of Article 133, or clause (1) of Article 134 :

a) May, if it deems fit so to do, on its own motion; and

b) Shall, if an oral application is made, by or on behalf of the party aggrieved, immediately after the passing or making of such judgement, decree, final order or sentence, determine, as soon as may be after such passing or making, the question whether a certificate of the nature referred to in clause (1) of Article 132, or clause (1) of Article 133 or, as the case may be, sub-clause (*c*) of clause (1) of Article 134, may be given in respect of that case.

Jurisdiction and powers of the Federal Court under existing law to be exercisable by the Supreme Court.— Until Parliament by law otherwise provides, the Supreme Court shall also have jurisdiction and powers with respect to any matter to which the provisions of Article 133 or Article 134 do not apply, if jurisdiction and powers in relation to that matter were exercisable by the Federal Court immediately before the commencement of this Constitution under any existing law.

Special leave to appeal by the Supreme Court

1. Notwithstanding anything in this Chapter, the Supreme Court may, in its discretion, grant special leave to appeal from any judgement, decree, determination, sentence or order in any cause or matter passed or made by any court or tribunal in the territory of India.
2. Nothing in clause (1) shall apply to any judgement, determination, sentence or order passed or made by any court or tribunal constituted by or under any law relating to the Armed Forces.

Review of judgements or orders by the Supreme Court.— Subject to the provisions of any law made by Parliament or any rules made under Article 145, the Supreme Court shall have power to review any judgement pronounced or order made by it.

Enlargement of the jurisdiction of the Supreme Court

1. The Supreme Court shall have such further jurisdiction and powers with respect to any of the matters in the Union List as Parliament may by law confer.
2. The Supreme Court shall have such further jurisdiction and powers with respect to any matter as the Government of India and the Government of any State may by special agreement confer, if Parliament by law provides for the exercise of such jurisdiction and powers by the Supreme Court.

Conferment on the Supreme Court of powers to issue certain writs.— Parliament may by law confer on the Supreme Court power to issue directions, orders or writs, including writs in the nature of *habeas corpus, mandamus,* prohibition, *quo warranto* and *certiorari,* or any of them, for any purposes other than those mentioned in clause (2) of Article 32.

Transfer of certain cases

1. Where cases involving the same or substantially the same questions of law are pending before the Supreme Court and one or more High Courts or before two or more High Courts and the Supreme Court is satisfied on its own motion or on an application made by the Attorney-General of India or by a party to any such case that such questions are substantial questions of general importance, the Supreme Court may withdraw the case or cases

pending before the High Court or the High Courts and dispose of all the cases itself:

Provided that the Supreme Court may after determining the said questions of law return any case so withdrawn together with a copy of its judgement on such questions to the High Court from which the case has been withdrawn, and the High Court shall on receipt thereof, proceed to dispose of the case in conformity with such judgement.

2. The Supreme Court may, if it deems it expedient so to do for the ends of justice, transfer any case, appeal or other proceedings pending before any High Court to any other High Court.

Ancillary powers of Supreme Court— Parliament may by law make provision for conferring upon the Supreme Court such supplemental powers not inconsistent with any of the provisions of this Constitution, as may appear to be necessary or desirable for the purpose of enabling the Court more effectively to exercise the jurisdiction conferred upon it by or under this Constitution.

Law declared by Supreme Court to be binding on all courts— The law declared by the Supreme Court shall be binding on all courts within the territory of India.

Enforcement of decrees and orders of Supreme Court and orders as to discovery, etc.

1. The Supreme Court in the exercise of its jurisdiction may pass such decree or make such order as is necessary for doing complete justice in any cause or matter pending before it, and any decree so passed or order so made shall be enforceable throughout the territory of India in such manner, as may be prescribed by or under any law made by Parliament and, until provision in that behalf is so made, in such manner, as the President may by order prescribe.

2. Subject to the provisions of any law made in this behalf by Parliament, the Supreme Court shall, as respects the whole of the territory of India, have all and every power to make any order for the purpose of securing the attendance of any person, the discovery or production of any documents, or the investigation or punishment of any contempt of itself.

Power of President to consult Supreme Court

1. If at any time it appears to the President that a question of law or fact has arisen, or is likely to arise, which is of such a nature and of such public importance that it is expedient to obtain the opinion of the Supreme Court upon it, he may refer the question to that Court for consideration and the Court may, after such hearing as it thinks fit, report to the President its opinion thereon.

2. The President may, notwithstanding anything in the proviso to Article 131, refer a dispute of the kind mentioned in the said proviso to the Supreme Court for opinion and the Supreme Court shall, after such hearing as it thinks fit, report to the President its opinion thereon.

Civil and judicial authorities to act in aid of the Supreme Court.—All authorities, civil and judicial, in the territory of India shall act in aid of the Supreme Court.

144A. *[Special provisions as to disposal of questions relating to constitutional validity of laws.] Rep. by the Constitution (Forty-third Amendment) Act,* 1977, *s.* 5 (*w.e.f.* 13-4-1978).

Rules of Court, etc.

1. Subject to the provisions of any law made by Parliament, the Supreme Court may from time to time, with the approval of the President, make rules for regulating generally the practice and procedure of the Court including:

   a) Rules as to the persons practising before the Court;

   b) Rules as to the procedure for hearing appeals and other matters pertaining to appeals including the time within which appeals to the Court are to be entered;

   c) Rules as to the proceedings in the Court for the enforcement of any of the rights conferred by Part III;

   cc) Rules as to the proceedings in the Court under article 139A;

   d) Rules as to the entertainment of appeals under sub-clause (c) of clause (1) of article 134;

   e) Rules as to the conditions subject to which any judgement pronounced or order made by the Court may be reviewed and the procedure for such review including the time within which applications to the Court for such review are to be entered;

f) Rules as to the costs of and incidental to any proceedings in the Court and as to the fees to be charged in respect of proceedings therein;

g) Rules as to the granting of bail;

h) Rules as to stay of proceedings;

i) Rules providing for the summary determination of any appeal which appears to the Court to be frivolous or vexatious or brought for the purpose of delay;

j) Rules as to the procedure for inquiries referred to in clause (1) of Article 317.

2. Subject to the provisions of clause (3), rules made under this article may fix the minimum number of Judges who are to sit for any purpose, and may provide for the powers of single Judges and Division Courts.

3. The minimum number of Judges who are to sit for the purpose of deciding any case involving a substantial question of law as to the interpretation of this Constitution or for the purpose of hearing any reference under Article 143 shall be five:

Provided that, where the Court hearing an appeal under any of the provisions of this Chapter other than article 132 consists of less than five Judges and in the course of the hearing of the appeal, the Court is satisfied that the appeal involves a substantial question of law as to the interpretation of this Constitution the determination of which is necessary for the disposal of the appeal, such Court shall refer the question for opinion to a Court constituted, as required by this clause for the purpose of deciding any case involving such a question and shall on receipt of the opinion dispose of the appeal in conformity with such opinion.

4. No judgement shall be delivered by the Supreme Court save in open Court, and no report shall be made under Article 143 save in accordance with an opinion also delivered in open Court.

5. No judgement and no such opinion shall be delivered by the Supreme Court save with the concurrence of a majority of the

Judges present at the hearing of the case, but nothing in this clause shall be deemed to prevent a Judge who does not concur from delivering a dissenting judgment or opinion.

Officers and servants and the expenses of the Supreme Court

1. Appointments of officers and servants of the Supreme Court shall be made by the Chief Justice of India or such other Judge or officer of the Court, as he may direct:

Provided that the President may by rule require that in such cases as may be specified in the rule, no person not already attached to the Court shall be appointed to any office connected with the Court, save after consultation with the Union Public Service Commission.

2. Subject to the provisions of any law made by Parliament, the conditions of service of officers and servants of the Supreme Court shall be such as may be prescribed by rules made by the Chief Justice of India or by some other Judge or officer of the Court authorized by the Chief Justice of India to make rules for the purpose:

Provided that the rules made under this clause shall, so far as they relate to salaries, allowances leave or pensions, require the approval of the President.

3. The administrative expenses of the Supreme Court, including all salaries, allowances and pensions payable to or in respect of the officers and servants of the Court, shall be charged upon the Consolidated Fund of India, and any fees or other moneys taken by the Court shall form part of that Fund.

Interpretation—In this Chapter and in Chapter V of Part VI, references to any substantial question of law as to the interpretation of this Constitution shall be construed as including references to any substantial question of law as to the interpretation of the Government of India Act, 1935 (including any enactment amending or supplementing that Act), or of any Order in Council or order made there under, or of the Indian Independence Act, 1947, or of any order made thereunder.

❑❑❑

Chapter 12

Powers and Functions of Parliament and Supreme Court of India

Parliament of India

The **Parliament of India**, also popularly known as **Sansad** (Sanskrit:); is the supreme legislative body in India. The Parliament comprises the President of India and the two Houses-Lok Sabha (House of the People) and Rajya Sabha (Council of States). The President has the power to summon and prorogue either House of Parliament or to dissolve Lok Sabha.

India's Parliament is bicameral; Rajya Sabha is the upper house and Lok Sabha is the lower house. The two Houses meet in separate chambers in the Sansad Bhavan (located on the Sansad Marg or "Parliament Street") in New Delhi. Those elected or nominated (by the President) to either house of Parliament are referred to as Members of Parliament or MPs. The MPs of Lok Sabha are directly elected by the Indian public and the MPs of Rajya Sabha are elected by the members of the State Legislative Assemblies, in accordance with proportional representation. The Parliament is composed of 790 MPs, who serve the largest democratic electorate in the world; 714 million Indians registered to vote in the 2009 general elections.

The Indian Parliament consists of two houses called as Lok Sabha and the Rajya Sabha, and the President of India.

The main Functions and Powers of the Indian Parliament are :

Functions and Powers of the Indian Parliament

The Constitution of India enumerates the powers and functions of the Indian Parliament in Chapter II of Part V of the constitution. Like the British counterpart, the Parliament of India is not a fully sovereign legislature. It does not enjoy unlimited and absolute powers like that of the British Parliament. It is a creation of the Constitution.

It has no natural growth like that of the British Parliament. As it is created by the Constitution, it is bound by the provisions of the Constitution.

The powers and functions of the Indian Parliament may be generalized in the following heads. While discussing these powers, it should be borne in mind that they are enjoyed and exercised by both the Houses of Parliament with a few difference.

a) Law making powers

The Parliament of the Union Government is competent to legislate on all matters that are enumerated in the Union List and the Concurrent List of the Constitution. In the Concurrent List, the Parliament and the State Legislatures have joint jurisdiction. However, in case of conflict over any law made under the Concurrent List, the Union Law will prevail upon the State Law provided the State Law has not received the earlier assent of the President. **The Union Parliament is also competent to make law over the State List under the following circumstances:**

i) When the proclamation of Emergency is in operation, the Parliament can make law in any item included in the State List. In case of the declaration of President's Rule in any State under Article 356 of the Constitution, the Parliament is competent to legislate on any matter included in the State List (Article 250).

ii) In normal times when Rajya Sabha passes a resolution by two-thirds majority of its members present and voting that it is necessary in the national interest that Parliament should make law with regard to any matter enumerated in the State List, then Parliament is competent to make law in that matter for the whole or any part of India (Article 249).

iii) The Parliament is competent to legislate on any matter pertaining to the State List, if such legislation is deemed necessary for the implementation of international treaties or agreements concluded with foreign States (Article 253).

iv) If the legislatures of two or more States pass a resolution to the effect that it is desirable to have a parliamentary law in any matter in the State List, then the Parliament can make law for those States (Article 252).

Except in the above-mentioned occasions, the Parliament of India is not competent to make law in the State List. If at any time, the Parliament encroaches upon the rights of the States, the Supreme Court can prevent such encroachment of the Parliament through its power of Judicial Review. The Parliament must make law in accordance with the provisions of the Constitution.

b) Financial Powers

In the financial domain, the Parliament is the supreme authority. Not a single paisa can be spent by the Executive without parliamentary sanction. The budget is annually prepared by the Cabinet and it is submitted for the approval of the Parliament. The Parliament also approves all proposals of the Union Government to impose taxes.

Money Bills can originate only in the Lok Sabha. After they have been passed by the Lok Sabha, they are sent to the Rajya Sabha for approval. Within 14 days the Rajya Sabha is expected to give its consent. Thus, the power of the Rajya Sabha is limited with regards to money Bills.

Further, to keep a vigil on the way the Executive spends the money granted by the legislature, there are two Standing Committees of the Parliament. They are the Public Accounts Committee and the Estimates Committee. These two Committees exercise legislative control over the Executive on behalf of the Parliament. There are certain items of expenditure included in the Budget which are not votable in the Parliament. These items include salary of the President, the Judges of the Supreme Court, and the members of the Union Public Service Commission, etc. They are charged from the Consolidated Fund of India.

c) Control over the Executive

The Parliament keeps a day-to-day watch over the activities of the Executive. As ours is a parliamentary system of Government, the Executive is responsible to the Parliament for all acts of omissions and commissions.

The Parliament may remove a Cabinet out of power by a vote of no confidence. It may reject a bill or a budget proposal of the Cabinet.

Members of the Parliament have a right to ask questions and supplementary question to the Ministers. Any lapses or mishandling on the part of the Government can be exposed in the Parliament. Adjournment motions may be moved to discuss serious administrative lapses. Through adjournment motions, matters of public importance can be brought to the notice of the Government by the members of the Parliament. There is a Committee on ministerial assurances appointed by the Parliament to see that the promises made to the Parliament by the respective ministers are fulfilled. In this matter, the Lok Sabha is more powerful than the Rajya Sabha.

d) Amending Power

The Parliament is competent to amend the Constitution. Both the Houses have equal powers so far amendment of the Constitution is concerned. A bill to amend the Constitution may originate either in the Rajya Sabha or in the Lok Sabha. Unless it is passed by both the Houses with the required majority, the amendment cannot be effective.

e) Judicial Functions

The Constitution vested in the Parliament the power to impeach the President, the Vice-President, and the other High Federal Officers like the Judges of the Supreme Court and High Courts, Auditor-General, Members of the Public Service Commission, etc. Impeachment is a judicial trial of the Parliament to remove high federal officers. While the resolution for impeachment is moved in one House, the other House sits as a Court of Trial. Approval of both the Houses is necessary for any impeachment.

Further, the Parliament possesses punitive powers to punish its members, and non-members who have broken the privileges of the House. This power is not ordinarily subject to the review of the Court. In a Parliamentary system of Government, legislative privileges are immune from judicial control.

f) Electoral Function

The Parliament participates in the election of the President and the Vice-President. It also elects some of its members to various Committees of the Parliament. The Vice- President is elected by both the Houses of the Parliament. He is removable by a resolution of the Rajya Sabha agreed to by the Lok Sabha.

g) Deliberative Function

The Parliament is a forum for deliberation on questions of public importance. It also serves as a ventilating chamber of public grievances. The Parliament is a mirror of national life. Whatever happens in various parts of the country can be discussed in its forum. It is often described as "a nation in miniature". Of all the functions of the Parliament this is an important function in a democratic country. Resolutions passed by the Parliament after days of deliberation may have the force of law. The Parliament represents the consensus of public opinion in the country, Churchill once described the British Parliament as **"the citadel of liberty".** The Parliament in India also protects the rights and liberties of the people.

Supreme Court of India

The **Supreme Court of India** is the highest judicial forum and final court of appeal as established by Part V, Chapter IV of the Constitution of India. According to the Constitution, the role of the Supreme Court is that of a federal court and the guardian of the Constitution.

Articles 124 to 147 of the Constitution of India lay down the composition and jurisdiction of the Supreme Court of India. The Supreme Court has Original jurisdiction in disputes involving between the Government of India and one or more States or between the Government of India and any State or States on one side and one or more States on the other or between two or more States. The Supreme Court is meant to be the last resort and highest appellate court which takes up appeals against the verdicts of the High Courts and other courts of the states and territories. Also, the Supreme court has the power of Judicial review as per Article 32 of the Constitution. The Supreme Court of India held its inaugural sitting on 28 January, 1950.

The Supreme Court of India came into being on 28 January, 1950. It replaced both the Federal Court of India and the Judicial Committee of the Privy Council which were at the apex of the Indian court system.

Supreme Court Advocates

There are three categories of Advocates. who are entitled to practice law before the Supreme Court of India :

Senior Advocates: These are Advocates who are designated as Senior Advocates by the Supreme Court of India or by any High Court.

Advocate-on-Record: Only these Advocates are entitled to file any matter or document before the Supreme Court.

Other Advocates: These are Advocates whose names are entered on the roll of any State Bar Council maintained under the Advocates Act, 1961 and they can appear and argue any matter on behalf of a party in the Supreme Court but they are not entitled to file any document or matter before the Court.

The Supreme Court Building and its Architecture

The main block of the Supreme Court building was built on a square plot of 22 acres and the building was designed by chief architect Ganesh Bhikaji Deolalikar who was the first Indian to head CPWD and designed the Supreme Court Building in an Indo-British architectural style. He was succeeded by Shridher Krishna Joglekar. The Court moved into the present building in 1958. The building is shaped to project the image of scales of justice with the Central Wing of the building corresponding to the centre beam of the Scales. In 1979, two new wings - the East Wing and the West Wing - were added to the complex. In all, there are 15[3] court rooms in the various wings of the building. The Chief Justice's Court is the largest of the courtrooms located in the centre of the Central Wing.

Composition of Supreme Court of India

Size of the court

As originally enacted, the Constitution of India provided for a Supreme Court with a Chief Justice and seven lower-ranking Judges- leaving it to Indian Parliament to increase this number. In the early years, a full bench of the Supreme Court sat together to hear the cases presented before them. As the work of the Court increased and cases began to accumulate, Parliament increased the number of Judges from the original eight in 1950 to eleven in 1956, fourteen in 1960, eighteen in 1978, twenty-six in 1986 and thirty one in 2008. As the number of the Judges have increased, they have sat in smaller Benches of two or three (referred to as a *Division Bench*) - coming together in larger Benches of five or more (referred to as a *Constitutional Bench*) only when required to settle fundamental questions of law. Any bench may refer the case under consideration upto a larger bench, if the need to do so arises.

Eligibility

- The person must be a citizen of India
- Judge of a High Court or of two or more such Courts in succession for at least five years, or
- An Advocate of a High Court or of two or more such Courts in succession for at least ten years, or
- The person must be, in the opinion of the President, a distinguished jurist.

A Judge of a High Court or retired Judge of the Supreme Court or High Courts may be appointed as an ad-hoc Judge of the Supreme Court.

Appointments and the Collegium

Judges of Supreme Court used to be appointed by the President of India, who acted on the advice of the Union Cabinet. Subsequent to the rulings in the Three Judges Cases (1982, 1993, 1998), the President has to appoint judges who have been chosen by the Supreme Court's collegium-a closed group comprising the Chief Justice of India and the four senior most associate judges of the court.[6] The Union Cabinet and Parliament have almost no role to play in the appointment of judges to the Supreme Court or to any of India's twenty-four High Courts.[7] The position of Chief Justice of India is attained on the basis of seniority amongst the judges serving on the court.

Tenure

Supreme Court judges retire at the age of 65. A judge of Supreme Court can be removed by the procedure prescribed in Article 124(4) of Constitution of India on the ground of proved misconduct or incapacity or judge resigning from his office addressed to the President of India. The procedure prescribed for removal of Supreme Court judge should not be called an impeachment procedure because this procedure is provided only for the removal of the President of India under Article 61 of Constitution of India on ground of violation of the Constitution.

Salary

Article 125 of the Indian Constitution leaves it to the Indian Parliament to determine the salary, other allowances, leave of absence, pension, etc. of the Supreme Court judges. However, the Parliament cannot alter any of these privileges and rights to the judge's disadvantage after his appointment. A judge gets ₹ 90,000 and the Chief Justice gets a sum of ₹ 1,00,000.

Powers and Functions of Supreme Court of India

The constitutional task assigned to the judiciary is in no way less than that of the other two functionaries - legislature and executive.

Indeed, it is the role of the judiciary to carry out the constitutional message, and it is its responsibility to keep a vigilant watch over the functioning of democracy in accordance with the Constitution. **Sir Alladi Krishna swami Ayyar remarked in the Constituent Assembly that, "The Su-preme Court under the Constitution has wide powers, more than the highest court, in any other federation.**

The criticism, if at all, can only be that the powers of the Supreme Court are not wide enough, but that they are too wide" (Constituent Assembly Debates, 1949). The various roles and functions of the Supreme Court are discussed below :

Original Jurisdiction (Article 131)

This refers to the cases that directly originate in the Supreme Court. It has original exclusive jurisdiction in any dispute between (a) the Government of India and one or more States; or (b) the Government of India and any State or States on one side and one or more other States on the other; or (c) two or more States.

Appellate Jurisdiction (Articles 132 to 136)

This refers to the power of reviewing and revising the orders of lower courts and tribunals. This jurisdiction extends to both the civil and the criminal appeals from the High Courts under certification from these courts or, in its absence, permitted by the Supreme Court itself. Normally, these appeals are in cases involving substantial question of law of general importance or interpretation of the Constitution or death penalty awarded by a High Court.

Advisory Jurisdiction

Under Article 143, the Supreme Court has been vested with the power of advisory jurisdiction.

When-ever the President consults the Supreme Court, on any matter of public importance, it gives opinion to the President the Supreme Court may also decline to give its opinion to the President. The advice is not binding on the President.

Supreme Court as a Court of Record

According to Article 129, the Supreme Court shall be a Court of record and shall have all powers of such a Court, including the power to punish for contempt of itself. As a Court of record, it has the power to punish those who are adjudged as guilty of contempt of court.

Appeal by Special Leave

This power has been conferred upon the Supreme Court by Article 136. It may, in its discretion, grant special leave to appeal from any judgments, decree, determination, sentence or order in any cause or matter passed or made by any court or tribunal in the territory of India.

Writ Jurisdiction

The Supreme Court is the guardian of the individual liberties and fundamental rights. It has the power to declare a law passed by any legislature null and void, if it encroaches upon the fundamental rights guaranteed to the people by the Constitution. For the enforcement of fundamental rights, it can issue writs in the nature of Habeas Corpus, Mandamus, Certiorari, Prohibition and Qua-Warrantor.

Besides the above mentioned powers, the Supreme Court has the power of judicial review. It implies the power to review and determine validity of a law or an order. It refers to "the power of a court to inquire whether a law, executive order or other official action conflicts with the written Constitution, and if the court concludes that it does, to declare it unconstitutional and void".

Singh (1994) opines that "judicial review in India is based on the assumption that the Constitution is the supreme law of the land, and all governmental organs, which owe their origin to the Constitution and derive their powers from its provisions, must function within the framework of the Constitution, and must not do anything which is inconsistent with the provisions of the Constitution".

However, the Indian Constitution does not in so many words assign the power of judicial review to the court. There are several specific provisions in the Constitution, which guarantee judicial review of legislation, such as Articles 13, 32, 131-136, 143, 226, 145, 246, 251, 254 and 372. Apart from these Articles, the power of judicial review is derived from the position of Supreme Court as the guardian of the Constitution.

The court can challenge the constitutional validity of a law on the following grounds:

i) The subject matter of the legislation is not within competence of the legislature which has passed it;

ii) It is repugnant to the provisions of the Constitution; or

iii) It infringes one of the fundamental rights.

The power of judicial review, in general, flows from the powers of the courts to interpret the Constitution. As such, it has the final say in the interpretation of the Constitution and by such interpretation; the Supreme Court has extended its power of judicial review to almost all the provisions of the Constitution.

❑❑❑

Chapter 13

State Executive-Governor, Chief Minister, Council of Ministers

(Legislative, Judiciary Powers and Functions)

State Executive - Governor, CM, Council of Ministers

The **governors** and **lieutenant-governors** of the states and territories of India have similar powers and functions at the state level as that of the President of India at Union level. Governors exist in the states while lieutenant-governors exist in union territories and in the National Capital Territory of Delhi. The governor acts as the nominal head, whereas the real power lies in the hand of the chief ministers of the states and the chief minister's Council of Ministers.

In India, a lieutenant governor is in-charge of a Union Territory. However, the rank is present only in the union territories of Andaman and Nicobar Islands, Delhi and Puducherry (the other territories have an administrator appointed, who is an IAS officer). Lieutenant-governors hold the same rank as a governor of a state in the list of precedence.

The governors and lieutenant-governors are appointed by the president for a term of 5 years.

Selection process

Qualifications

Article 157 and Article 158 of the Constitution of India specify eligibility requirements for the post of governor. They are as follows:

A governor must:

1. Be a citizen of India;
2. Be at least thirty-five (35)years old;

3. Not be a member of the either house of the parliament or house of the state legislature.
4. Not hold any other office of profit.

Powers and functions

The governor enjoys many different types of powers:

1. **Executive powers** related to administration, appointments and removals,
2. **Legislative powers** related to law-making and the state legislature, that is Vidhan Sabha or Vidhan Parishad,
3. **Discretionary powers** to be carried out according to the discretion of the governor.

Executive powers

1. The Constitution vests in the governor all the executive powers of the state government. The governor appoints the chief minister, who enjoys the support of the majority in the Vidhan Sabha. The governor also appoints the other members of the Council of Ministers and distributes portfolios to them on the advice of the chief minister.
2. The Council of Ministers remain in power during the 'pleasure' of the governor, but in the real sense it means the pleasure of the Vidhan Sabha. As long as the majority in the Vidhan Sabha supports the government, the Council of Ministers cannot be dismissed.
3. The governor appoints the chief minister of a state. He/she also appoints the Advocate General and the chairman and members of the State Public Service Commission. The president consults the governor in the appointment of judges of the High Courts and the governor appoints the judges of the District Courts.

Legislative powers

1. The governor summons the sessions of both houses of the state legislature and prorogues them. The governor can even dissolve the Vidhan Sabha. These powers are formal and the governor while using these powers must act according to the advice of the Council of Ministers, headed by the chief minister.

2. The governor inaugurates the state legislature by addressing it after the assembly elections and also at the beginning of the first session every year. The governor's address on these occasions generally outlines new policies of the state government. A bill that the state legislature has passed, can become a law only after the governor gives assent. The governor can return a bill to the state legislature, if it is not a money bill, for reconsideration. However, if the state legislature sends it back to the governor for the second time, the governor must assent to it. The governor has the power to reserve certain bills for the president.
3. When the state legislature is not in session and the governor considers it necessary to have a law, then the governor can promulgate ordinances. These ordinances are submitted to the state legislature at its next session. They remain valid for no more than six weeks from the date the state legislature is reconvened unless approved by it earlier.

Financial powers

1. Money bills can be introduced in the State Legislative Assembly only on the prior recommendation of the governor.
2. He also causes to be laid before the State Legislature the annual financial statement which is the State Budget. Further no demand for grant shall be made except on his recommendation.
3. He can also make advances out of the Contingency Fund of the State to meet any unforeseen expenditure. Moreover, he constitutes the State Finance Commission. In Vidhan Sabha, he nominates 1 person.

Discretionary powers

The governor can use these powers:

a) If no party gets an absolute majority, the governor can use his discretion in the selection of the chief minister;

b) During an emergency he can override the advice of the council of ministers. At such times, he acts as an agent of the president and becomes the real ruler of the state;

c) He uses his direction in submitting a report to the president regarding the affairs of the state; and

d) He can with hold his assent to a bill and send it to the president for his approval.

Emoluments

Governor's pay

Date established	Salary (per month)
1 January, 2006	Rs. 1.9 lakh (US$ 2,900)

Various Emoluments, Allowances and Privileges available to a governor are determined by the Governors (Emoluments, Allowances and Privileges) Act, 1982.In addition to the monthly salary, the governor is entitled to rent free official residence, free household facilities and conveyance. The governor and his family are provided with free medical attendance, accommodation and treatment for life.

Removal

The term of governor's office is normally 5 years but it can be terminated earlier by:

1. Dismissal by the president on the advice of the prime minister of the country, at whose pleasure the governor holds office.
2. Resignation by the governor Note: There is no provision of impeachment, as it happens for the president.

Chief Minister

A **Chief Minister** is the elected head of government of a state of India. The chief minister is the head of the state (governor is the nominal head (de jure executive) and does everything under the guidance of the chief minister) Cabinet, and the leader of the state Legislature. By the Constitution of India, the chief minister is appointed by the Governor of the state (Article 164). The parliamentary system in India follows the Westminster system. Hence the chief ministers of the states are elected by the members of the legislature. The people do not elect the head of the government, rather they elect their representatives only. In turn their representatives select the head of the government. But once the head of the government is elected, he or she enjoys almost exclusive executive powers. This is in contrast with the head of the state, the Governor, who is the ceremonial head of state.

Selection process

Eligibility

The Constitution of India sets the principle qualifications, one must meet to be eligible to the office of the Chief Minister. A Chief Minister must be:

1. Should be a citizen of India.
2. Should be a member of the state legislature. If a person is elected chief minister who is not a member of the legislature, then he/she must become a member within six months.
3. Should be of 25 years of age or more

Election

The chief minister is elected through a majority in the state legislative assembly. This is procedurally established by the vote of confidence in the legislative assembly, as suggested by the governor of the state who is the appointing authority.

Oath

Since, according to the constitution, the chief minister is appointed by the governor, the swearing in is done before the governor of the state.

The oath of office

I, <Name of Minister>, do swear in the name of God/solemnly affirm that I will bear true faith and allegiance to the Constitution of India as by law established, that I will uphold the sovereignty and integrity of India, that I will faithfully and conscientiously discharge my duties as a Minister for the State of <Name of the State> and that I will do right to all manner of people in accordance with the Constitution and the law without fear or favour, affection or ill-will.

Constitution of India, Schedule 3, Para 5

The oath of secrecy

I, <Name of Minister>, do swear in the name of God/solemnly affirm that I will not directly or indirectly communicate or reveal to any person or persons any matter which shall be brought under my consideration or shall become known to me as a Minister for the State of <Name of the State> except, as may be required for the due discharge of my duties as such Minister.

Constitution of India, Schedule 3, Para 6

Remuneration

By Article 164 of the constitution of India, remuneration of the chief minister as well as other ministers are to be decided by the respective state legislatures. Hence, this varies from state to state.

Legislative and Judiciary Powers and Functions

The Powers and Functions of Legislative Council (India)

1. Legislative Powers

Non-money bills can be introduced in the Legislative Council. When a non-money bill, passed by the Legislative Assembly, comes to the Legislative Council, the latter can pass it, or can send it back with amendments to the legislative Assembly for its reconsideration. If the bill is passed by the Council, it is sent to Governor for his approval. If the bill is returned by the Legislative Council to the Legislative Assembly for reconsideration, the process of lawmaking is delayed.When, aft reconsideration by the Legislative Assembly, the bill again comes to the Legislative Council the latter may pass it in which case the bill will be sent to the Governor for approval. If, the contrary, the bill is rejected second time by the Legislative Council, the bill is deemed to have been passed by the Legislative Council. Thus the Legislative Council has o delaying power and the Legislative Assembly can override it.

2. Financial Powers

The Legislative Council has only limited powers in financial matters. A Money Bill cannot be introduced in the Legislative Council. It can be introduced only in the Legislative Assembly. When a Money Bill comes from the Legislative Assembly to the Legislative Council, the latter is required to take action on it within 14 days. If the Council passes it, then the bill is sent to the Governor for his assent.If, on the other hand, the Council sends back the Money Bill to the Assembly with some changes and if these changes are not acceptable to the Assembly, then the bill, as originally passed by the Assembly, shall be taken as passed by both the Houses, the Assembly as well as the Council.If the Council does not return the Money Bill to the Assembly within 14 days, then the bill is deemed to have been passed by both the Houses. Money Bills are not sent back to the Legislative Council second time. It is, thus, clear that in the financial field, the Legislative Council has a subordinate status and that the Legislative Assembly has a dominant position.

3. Constituent Power

Some amendments of the constitution need to be ratified by the state legislatures. When such an amendment bill comes to a bicameral state legislature, the bill has to be passed by both Houses of the state legislature. But like ordinary bills, the Legislative Council can delay the passage of the amendment bill, but in case of difference of opinion between the two Houses, the voice of the Legislative Assembly shall prevail.

4. Control over Executive

The Legislative Council does not have much control over the Executive. The Council of Ministers is responsible to the Legislative Assembly. Even if the government is defeated in the Legislative Council, it is not bound to resign. The members of the Legislative Council may elicit information and expose the weakness of the government by asking questions and moving different motions in the Council, but they cannot force the Council of Ministers to resign.

5. Miscellaneous

i) The Legislative Council elects its own Chairman and Deputy Chairman,

ii) The Council discusses technical matters, as there are experts as its members.

Judiciary Powers and Functions

The **judiciary** (also known as the **judicial system**) is the system of courts that interprets and applies the law in the name of the state. The judiciary also provides a mechanism for the resolution of disputes. Under the doctrine of the separation of powers, the judiciary generally does not make law (that is, in a plenary fashion, which is the responsibility of the legislature) or enforce law (which is the responsibility of the executive), but rather interprets law and applies it to the facts of each case. This branch of the state is often tasked with ensuring equal justice under law. It usually consists of a court of final appeal (called the "Supreme court" or "Constitutional court"), together with lower courts. In the 1980s, the Supreme Court of India for almost a decade had been encouraging public interest litigation on behalf of the poor and oppressed by using a very broad interpretation of several articles of the Indian Constitution. The term "judiciary" is also used to refer collectively to the personnel, such as judges, magistrates and other adjudicators, who form the core of a judiciary (sometimes referred to as a "bench"), as well as the staffs who keep the system running smoothly.

Various functions

1. In common law jurisdictions, courts interpret law, including constitutions, statutes, and regulations. They also make law (but in a limited sense, limited to the facts of particular cases) based upon prior case law in areas where the legislature has not made law. For instance, the tort of negligence is not derived from statute law in most common law jurisdictions. The term *common law* refers to this kind of law.
2. In civil law jurisdictions, courts interpret the law, but are prohibited from *creating* law, and thus, do not issue rulings more general than the actual case to be judged. Jurisprudence plays a similar role to case law.
3. In the United States court system, the Supreme Court is the final authority on the interpretation of the federal Constitution and all statutes and regulations created pursuant to it, as well as the constitutionality of the various state laws; in the US federal court system, federal cases are tried in trial courts, known as the US district courts, followed by appellate courts and then the Supreme Court. State courts, which try 98% of litigation, may have different names and organization; trial courts may be called "courts of common plea", appellate courts "superior courts" or "commonwealth courts". The judicial system, whether state or federal, begins with a court of first instance, is appealed to an appellate court, and then ends at the court of last resort.
4. In France, the final authority on the interpretation of the law is the Council of State for administrative cases, and the Court of Cassation for civil and criminal cases.

5. In the People's Republic of China, the final authority on the interpretation of the law is the National People's Congress.

Other countries, such as Argentina have mixed systems that include lower courts, appeals courts, a cassation court (for criminal law) and a Supreme Court. In this system, the Supreme Court is always the final authority, but criminal cases have four stages, one more than civil law does. On the court sits a total of nine justices. This number has been changed several times.

❑❑❑

Chapter 14

Human Rights Commission
(Structure, Power and Functions)

I. Karnataka State Human Rights Commission (KSHRC)

Constitution of KSHRC

Sec. 21 of the Protection of Human Rights Act, 1993, as amended by the Protection of Human Rights (Amendment)Act, 2006 under Chapter V, lays down that the State Government may constitute a Human Rights Commission which shall consist of :

1. A Chairperson who has been a Chief Justice of a High Court;
2. One Member who is, or has been, a Judge of a High Court or District Judge in the State with a minimum of seven years experience as District Judge;
3. One Member to be appointed from amongst persons having knowledge of, or practical experience in, matters relating to human rights;

The Commission has a Secretary, who is the Chief Executive Officer of the State Commission.

Functions of KSHRC

The Commission performs all or any of the following functions:

1. Inquire suo-motu or on a petition presented to it by a victim or any person on his behalf, into complaint of :
   - Violation of human rights or abetment thereof, or
   - Negligence in the prevention of such violation, by a public servant.
2. Intervene in any proceeding involving any allegation of violation of human rights pending before the court, with the approval of such court;

3. Visit, under intimation to the State Government, any jail or any other institution under the control of the State Government, where persons are detained or lodged for purposes of treatment, reformation or protection, to study the living conditions of the inmates and make recommendations thereon;
4. Review the safeguard provided by or under the Constitution or any law for the time-being in force for the protection of human rights & recommend measures for their effective implementation;
5. Review the factors including the act of terrorism that inhibit the enjoyment of human rights and recommend appropriate remedial measures
6. Undertake and promote research in the field of human rights;
7. Spread human rights literacy among various sections of the society and promote awareness of safeguards available for the protection, media, seminar and other available means;
8. Encourage the efforts of non-governmental organizations and institutions working in the field of human rights; and
9. Such other functions, as it may consider necessary for the promotion of human rights.

Powers Relating To Inquires

1. The State Commission shall, while inquiring into complaints under this Act, have all the powers of a Civil Court trying a suit under the Code of Civil Procedure, 1908 and in particular, in respect of the following matters, namely:
   - Summoning and enforcing the attendance of witnesses and
   - Examining them on oath
   - Discovery and production of any document
   - Receiving evidence on affidavits
   - Requisitioning any public record or copy thereof from any Court or office
   - Issuing commissions for the examination of witnesses or documents
   - Any other matter, which may be prescribed

2. The State Commission shall have the power to require any person subject to any privilege which may be claimed under any law for the time being in force, to furnish information on points or matters useful for, or relevant to the subject matter of inquiry.
3. The State Commission also has certain other powers to facilitate the process of inquiry undertaken by it.
4. The State Commission shall be deemed to be a Civil Court and every proceeding before it shall be deemed to be a judicial proceeding within the meaning of Sec. 193 and Sec 228 and for the purpose of Sec. 196 of the Indian Penal Code.

II. National Human Rights Commission of India

The **National Human Rights Commission** (NHRC) of India is an autonomous public body constituted on 12 October, 1993 under the Protection of Human Rights Ordinance of 28 September, 1993. It was given a statutory basis by the **Protection of Human Rights Act, 1993** (TPHRA). The NHRC is the national human rights institution, responsible for the protection and promotion of human rights, defined by the Act as "rights relating to life, liberty, equality and dignity of the individual guaranteed by the Constitution or embodied in the International Covenants".

Since late 2011, the organization has been embroiled in a controversy where leading jurists have sought the resignation of its Chairman, ex-Chief Justice K.G.Balakrishnan, pending investigation into charges of assets disproportionate to his income. In response, NHRC has uploaded details of Justice Balakrishnan's assets.

Functions

TPHRA mandates the NHRC to perform the following functions :

1. Proactively or reactively inquire into violations of human rights or negligence in the prevention of such violation by a public servant
2. By leave of the court, to intervene in court proceeding relating to human rights
3. Visit any jail or other institution under the control of the State Government, where persons are detained or lodged for purposes of treatment, reformation or protection, for the study of the living conditions of the inmates and make recommendations

4. Review the safeguards provided by or under the Constitution or any law for the time being in force for the protection of human rights & recommend measures for their effective implementation
5. Review the factors, including acts of terrorism that inhibit the enjoyment of human rights and recommend appropriate remedial measures
6. Study treaties and other international instruments on human rights and make recommendations for their effective implementation
7. Undertake and promote research in the field of human rights
8. Engage in human rights education among various sections of society and promote awareness of the safeguards available for the protection of these rights through publications, the media, seminars and other available means
9. Encourage the efforts of NGOs and institutions working in the field of human rights
10. Such other function, as it may consider it necessary for the protection of human rights.

Composition

The NHRC consists of :

- A Chairperson who has been a Chief Justice of the Supreme Court of India
- One Member who is, or has been, a Judge of the Supreme Court of India
- One Member who is, or has been, the Chief Justice of a High Court
- Two Members to be appointed from among persons having knowledge of, or practical experience in, matters relating to human rights
- In addition, the Chairpersons of four National Commissions serve as ex-officio members.

Current members

The current chairperson of the NHRC is **K.G Balakrishnan**, and the other members are:

- Babulal Chandulal (B.C.) Patel
- Satyabrata Pal

Ex-officio members

- Wajahat Habibullah, Chairperson, National Commission for Minorities
- Panna Lal (P.L.) Punia, Chairperson, National Commission for Scheduled Castes
- Dr. Rameshwar Oraon, Chairperson, National Commission for Scheduled Tribes
- Mamta Sharma, Acting Chairperson, National Commission for Women.

Appointment

Sections 3 and 4 of TPHRA lay down the rules for appointment to the NHRC. The Chairperson and members of the NHRC are appointed by the President of India, on the recommendation of a committee consisting of:

- The Prime Minister (chairperson)
- The Home Minister
- The Leader of the Opposition in the Lok Sabha (House of the People)
- The Leader of the Opposition in the Rajya Sabha (Council of States)
- The Speaker of the Lok Sabha (House of the People)
- The Deputy Chairman of the Rajya Sabha (Council of States)

Former chairpersons

S.No.	Name	Tenure
1.	Justice Ranganath Misra	12 October 1993 - 24 November, 1996
2.	Justice M N Venkatachaliah	26 November 1996 - 24 October, 1999
3.	Justice J S Verma	4 November 1999 - 17 January, 2003
4.	Dr. Justice A S Anand	17 February 2003 - 31 October, 2006
5.	Justice Dr. Shivaraj Patil*	1 November 2006 - 1 April, 2007
6.	Justice S. Rajendra Babu	2 February 2007 - 31 May, 2009
7.	Justice Govind Prasad Mathur*	1 June 2009 - 6 June, 2010
8.	Justice K G Balakrishnan	7 June 2010 - 11 May, 2015

*Acting Chairperson

International status

The NHRC has been accredited with "A status" by the International Coordinating Committee of National Human Rights Institutions (the ICC), indicating that it is in conformity with the Paris Principles – a broad set of principles agreed upon by a conference of experts on the promotion and protection of human rights, in Paris in October 1991, and subsequently endorsed by the UN General Assembly. The Commission is, thus, entitled to participate in the ICC and in its regional sub-group, the Asia Pacific Forum, and may take part in certain sessions of the UN human rights committees.

References

Administration Report for the Year 1976-77 (Madras, 1983), pp. 14-15.

Administration Report of the Forest Department of the Madras State for the Year Ending 31 March, 1967 (Madras, 1968), p.5.

Administration Report of the Forest Department of the Madras State for the Year Ending 31 March, 1952 (Madras, 1954), p.5.

Administration Report of the Forest Department of the Madras State for the Year Ending 31 March, 1962 (Madras, 1963), pp.24-25.

Brandis, Suggestions Regarding Forest Administration, pp.4-264.

Chhatrapati Singh, Common Property and Common Poverty : India's Forests, Forest Dweller and the Law (Delhi, 1986), pp. 60-71.

Circular, Government of India to Local Governments, No.4-F-70-1, 27 Feb., 1915.

D.K.Pandey, "Forest Policy and Land Management in India", Kurukshetra, Vol. XIV, Nos. 4 and 5 (Jan.-Feb. 1997), pp.60-62.

Dutta, R. and Yadav, B., 2012, Supreme Court on Forest Conservation. Universal Law Publishing Co., New Delhi (India).

Fort St. George Gazette, 6 and 11 July, 1882; 19 Aug., 1882 and 12 Sept., 1882; Brandis, Suggestions Regarding Forest Administration, p.2.

Government of India, The National Forest Policy of India, 1988 (Delhi, 1988), para 1.1.

Government of India, The Old Forest Policy, Circular No.22F, 19 Oct., 1894, para 3.

Government of India, The Wildlife (Protection) Act, 1972 (53 of 1972) (Delhi, 1974).

Government of Madras, The Madras Preservation of Private Forest Act, 1949 (As Modified upto the 15 December, 1966) (Madras, 1967), pp. 1-10.

Government of Tamil Nadu, Policy Note on Forest Department, 1979-80 (Madras, 1979), p.2.

Government of Tamil Nadu, Policy Note on Forest Department, 1980-81 (Madras, 1980), p.5; G.O.No.728, Forests and Fisheries, 17 Aug., 1978.

Government of Tamil Nadu, The Tamil Nadu Hill Areas (Preservation of Trees) Act, 1955 (Madras, 1984). For Rules, G.O.No.2795, Food and Agriculture, 16 Sept., 1957.

Joy, P.P., 2012, Set up your criminal practice. Swamy Law House, Ernakulam (India).

National Forest Policy, 1988, para 4.5; Administration Report of Tamil Nadu Forest Department 1994–95 (Chennai, 1996), p.3.

National Forest Policy, 1988, para 4.9 and 12; Administration Report of Tamil Nadu Forest Department, 1989-90 (Madras, 1991), p.4.

Principal Chief Conservator of Forests, Policy and Implementation, p.8; The Gazette of India, 17 Dec., 1988.

R.C. Agarwal, Constitutional Development and National Movement of India, part III (New Delhi, 2002), pp.96-97 and 103; Main Stream, 25 Feb., 1995.

Ramalinga Reddy, Guide on Forest Law, p. 135.

Resolution, Ministry of Food and Agriculture, Government of India, No. 7-110/51-F, 4 Apr., 1952.

Shetty, B.J. 1985, A Manual of Law for Forest Officers, Sharda Press, Mangalore (India).

Stebbing, The Forests of India, Vol. 1, p.206.

Takwani, C.K.T. and Thakker, M.C., 2012, Takwani Criminal Procedure. Lexis Nexis Butterwarths Wadhwa, Nagpur (India).

Tamil Nadu Forest Department, Sixth Five Year Plan on Forestry (1978-1983) (Madras, 1978), pp. 50, 53-54; State Planning Commission, Toward An Industry Oriented Forestry Policy: Report on Forestry, 1972-1984 (Madras, 1972), pp. 1-2.

Tamil Nadu Forest Department; Sixth Fiver Year Plan on Forestry, pp. 13-14; D. Ramalinga Reddy, Guide on Forest Law (Madras, 1982), p. 87.

Tamil Nadu Government Gazette, 13 Mar., 1974; G.O.No.75, Forests and Fisheries, 15 Feb., 1974.

The committee consisted of the District Collector, the District Forest Officer, the Tehsildar, the Executive Engineer of the Agriculture Department and the Personal Assistant to the Collector of the District who should be secretary of the committee.

The Madras Preservation of Private Forests Act, 1949 (As Modified upto the 15 December, 1966), section 3(2), sections 4,9 and 14.

The Old Forest Policy, 1894, para 4 and 5.

The Old Forest Policy, 1894, para 9.

The population of India had increased by forty per cent between 1894 and 1952.

The Tamil Nadu Hill Areas (Preservation of Trees) Act, section 3 and 4, pp. 4-5.

The Wildlife (Protection) Act, 1972, section 18 and 37.

Troup, The Work of the Forest Department, pp.7-8.

Varghese, M.I., 2012, Treatise on Forest Laws of Kerala. Swamy Law House, Ernakulam (India).

□□□

Chapter 15

Model Questions Bank

Q I. Choose the Correct Answer for the Following

1. As per the forest policy of 1988, the forest area under hilly region should be:

   a) 33% b) 20%

   c) 66% d) 60%

2. First National Forest Policy of independent India promulgated in:

   a) 1988 b) 1894

   c) 1982 d) 1952

3. National Forest Policy 1988 was issued on:

   a) 7th Dec 1988 b) 12th Dec 1952

   c) 15h Dec 1947 d) 14th Dec 1988

4. Improvement on Indian Agriculture was submitted in 1893 by:

   a) Dr. Brandi's b) Mr. Watson

   c) Dr. Voelcker d) None

5. _____ means in simple term "certain guidelines" for the achievement of certain objective:

   a) Law b) Policy

   c) Legislative d) None

6. Preservation of forests, which are essential for the climatic and physical ground, is called:

   a) Protective forest b) Productive forest

   c) a and b d) None

7. In 1988, NFP the national goal should be to have how much land area under forest:

   a) One third b) Two third

   c) Half the area d) None

8. The principles of enumeration and organization of working plan was introduced by:

   a) Dr. Brandi's b) Mr. Watson

   c) Dr. Voelcker d) Dr. Mc. Clelland

9. The Chandra Gupta Maurya came in to power during:

   a) 200 BC b) 300 BC

   c) 400 BC d) 500 BC

10. In India, the highest administrative authority to look after forest department is:

    a) DIG b) IGF

    c) PCCF d) CCF

11. Legal measures will have to be available for protection against this form of abuse:

    a) Over grazing b) Illicit felling

    c) Encroachment d) All

12. Following is not a common form of right and concessions in forest area:

    a) Right of grass cutting b) Right to collect NTFPs

    c) Right to grazing d) Right to poaching

13. Captain Watson of the Police was appointed as India's first:

    a) IGF b) Conservator

    c) DCF d) PCCF

14. First Forest Act was enunciated in the year:

    a) 1865 b) 1947

    c) 1894 d) 1988

15. First Forest Policy was formed in the year:
    a) 1988 b) 1994
    c) 1894 d) 1952
16. Forest (Conservation) Act was enacted in the year:
    a) 1988 b) 1972
    c) 1980 d) 1942
17. Chandragupta Maurya afforded considerable degree of protection to the following animal:
    a) Tiger b) Bird
    c) Elephants d) All
18. Forest laws are:
    a) General law b) Special law
    c) Both a & b d) None
19. Which is controlling ministry for forest and environment at the central Govt. level:
    a) MHA b) MEA
    c) MoEF d) HRD
20. Forest Settlement officer was appointed under:
    a) IFA 1927 b) IFA 1878
    c) FCA 1980 d) None
21. "Chapter of Indian Forestry" was submitted in the year:
    a) 1955 b) 1972
    c) 1855 d) 1952
22. JFM was introduced in the National Forest Policy of :
    a) 1988 b) 1952
    c) 1980 d) 1927
23. Indian Forest Act consists of:
    a) 86 chapter b) 50 chapter
    c) 13 chapter d) 28 chapter

24. The grazing right should always remain related to the land in terms of:

a) Fertility b) Density

c) Carrying capacity d) Flora

25. IPC is a comprehensive criminal law effective since:

a) 1862 b) 1987

c) 1952 d) 1980

26. The maximum number of Anglo Indians who can be nominated to the Lok Sabha are:

a) 3 b) 2

c) 5 d) 4

27. The quorum required to hold meetings of the legislative chambers is what fraction of the total membership of the House?

a) 1/3 b) ¼

c) 1/6 d) 1/10

28. How Many members of the Rajya Sabha are nominated by the President of India?

a) 0 b) 11

c) 12 d) 13

29. Parliament of India is composed of:

a) Lok Sabha only

b) Rajya Sabha only

c) Lok. Sabha and Rajya Sabha

d) Lok Sabha, Rajya Sabha and President

30. What is the minimum age for being the member of the Parliament?

a) 40 years b) 45 years

c) 35 years d) None of these

31. When was the Constitution of India adopted by the Constituent Assembly?

a) 25th Nov., 1949 b) 29th Nov., 1949

c) 26th Nov., 1949 d) 27th Nov., 1949

32. In the Parliament, Lower House is called as:
    a) Legislative Assembly b) Legislative Council
    c) Rajya Sabha d) Lok Sabha

33. In the Constituent Assembly, who was the Head of the Union Constitution Committee?
    a) Jawaharlal Nehru b) Sardar Patel
    c) Subhash Chandra Bose d) None of the above

34. In the Constituent Assembly, which committee recommended that Indian Constitution adopt Parliamentary Form of Executive:
    a) Drafting Committee
    b) Constitutional Committee
    c) Union Constitution Committee
    d) All the above

35. When was the Constitution of India put into effect:
    a) 25th Nov, 1950 b) 26th Jan, 1950
    c) 26th Nov, 1952 d) 26th Nov, 1949

36. The First Forest Policy in India is formulated in the year:
    a) 1988 b) 1952
    c) 1894 d) 1927

37. First Inspector General of Forests in India was:
    a) Mr. Brandis b) Dr. Voelcker
    c) Mr. Watson d) Mr. Connoly

38. The law which pertains to the enforcement of rights of citizen in a country is:
    a) Civil law b) Criminal law
    c) Forest law d) None of these

39. National Forest Policy 1988 was issued on:
    a) 7th Dec, 1988 b) 12th Dec, 1988
    c) 15^{h} Dec, 1988 d) 14th Dec, 1988

40. "Improvement on Indian Agriculture" was submitted in 1893 by:

a) Dr. Brandi's b) Mr. Watson

c) Dr. Voelcker d) None

41. In India, the highest administrative authority to look after Forest Department is:

a) DIG b) IGF

c) PCCF d) CCF

42. Captain Watson of the Police was appointed as India's first:

a) IGF b) Conservator

c) DCF d) PCCF

43. Forest (Conservation) Act was enacted in the year:

a) 1988 b) 1972

c) 1980 d) 1942

44. "Charter of Indian Forestry" was submitted in the year:

a) 1955 b) 1972

c) 1855 d) 1952

45. JFM was introduced in the National Forest Policy of:

a) 1988 b) 1952

c) 1980 d) 1927

46. The First Forest Policy in India is formulated in the year:

a) 1988 b) 1952

c) 1894 d) 1927

47. Indian Forest Act has ________ chapters:

a) 13 b) 14

c) 16 d) 12

48. First Inspector General of Forests in India was:

a) Mr. Brandis b) Dr. Voelcker

c) Mr. Watson d) Mr. Connoly

49. Karnataka Forest Act was enunciated in the year:
    a) 1965 b) 1963
    c) 1964 d) 1966
50. In Karnataka JFPM scheme was started in the year:
    a) 1993 b) 1990
    c) 1992 d) 1991
51. Functional classification of Forests was given in:
    a) First Forest Policy b) Second Forest Policy
    c) Third Forest Policy d) None of these
52. According to Karnataka Forest Rules, 1969, which of the following species does not require transit pass?
    a) Teak b) Rosewood
    c) Honne d) Rubber
53. The law which pertains to the enforcement of rights of citizen in a country is:
    a) Civil law b) Criminal law
    c) Forest law d) None of these
54. Forest Department in India was established in the year:
    a) 1927 b) 1894
    c) 1864 d) 1875
55. VFC stands for:
    a) Village Forest Council
    b) Village Forest Committee
    c) Village Forest Community
    d) Village Forest Corporation
56. The First Forest Policy was formulated based on the recommendations of:
    a) Dr. Voelcker b) Mr. Brandis
    c) Mr. Osmoston d) Mr. Connoly
57. Forest and Wildlife is in which of the list:
    a) State b) Concurrent
    c) Both d) None

58. JFPM scheme was passed in ________ National Forest Policy:

a) First b) Second

c) Third d) Both a & b

59. In India, First Forest Act was enunciated in the year:

a) 1947 b) 1988

c) 1865 d) 1948

60. First Inspector General of Forests in India was:

a) Mr. Brandis b) Dr. Voelcker

c) Mr. Watson d) Mr. Connoly

61. Forest Department in India was established in the year:

a) 1927 b) 1894

c) 1864 d) 1875

62. India has:

a) One Forest Policy b) Two Forest Policies

c) Three Forest Policies d) Four Forest Policies

63. Head of the State Forest Department is:

a) PCCF (HOFF) b) PCCF (Wildlife)

c) APCCF d) Forest Minister

64. JFPM stands for:

a) Joint Forest Management

b) Joint Forest Protection and Management

c) Joint Forest Planning and Management

d) None of these

65. First Inspector General of Forests of Karnataka (Mysore):

a) Mr. Muthanna b) Mr. L. Rickets

c) Mr. Ramarao d) Miller

Q II. Match The Following

Set I

S.No	Part A		Part B
1.	I.P.C.C.	a)	Climate change
2.	Charter of Indian Forestry	b)	1855
3.	First I.G.F.	c)	Dr. Brandie's
4.	Article 48. A	d)	Forests and Wildlife
5.	Productive forest	e)	Commercial forest
6.	Indian Evidence Act	f)	1872
7.	I.P.C.	g)	Mr. Macaulay
8.	Joint Forest Management	h)	Village Forest Committee
9.	Revised National Forest Policy	i)	1988
10.	International year of Forest	j)	2011

Set II

S.No	Part A		Part B
1.	NCA	a)	1976
2.	The wildlife protection act	b)	1972
3.	Captive management	c)	Zoo Authority of Karnataka
4.	Biological Diversity Act	d)	2002
5.	Tribal Act	e)	2006
6.	Tree lands	f)	1952 policy
7.	Forest law	g)	Special law
8.	Joint Forest Management	h)	1988 policy
9.	Forest policy and law	i)	S. S. Negi
10.	Public law	j)	Criminal law

Set III

S.No.	Part A		Part B
1.	Article 48 (A)	a)	Ranchi
2.	Tree Protection Act	b)	Dehradun
3.	Forest Survey of India	c)	1972
4.	Institute of Forest Productivity	d)	1973

5.	The Wildlife Protection Act	e)	2006
6.	Biological Diversity Act	f)	1971
7.	Tribal Act	g)	2009
8.	Project Snow Leopard	h)	Forests and Wildlife
9.	Ramsar Convention on Wetlands	i)	2002
10.	Project Tiger	j)	1976

Set IV

S.No.	Part A		Part B
1.	Article 48 (A)	a)	Ranchi
2.	Tree Protection Act	b)	Dehradun
3.	Forest Survey of India	c)	1972
4.	Institute of Forest Productivity	d)	1973
5.	The Wildlife Protection Act	e)	2006
6.	Biological Diversity Act	f)	1971
7.	Tribal Act	g)	2009
8.	Project Snow Leopard	h)	Forests and Wildlife
9.	Ramsar Convention on Wetlands	i)	2002
10.	Project Tiger	j)	1976

Set V

S.No.	Part A		Part B
1.	Wildlife Protection Act	a)	2002
2.	Indian Evidence Act	b)	Restriction on Trade & Transport of Beete trees or Black wood
3.	Ramsar Convention on Wetlands	c)	Non Bailable Offence came in to force
4.	Montreal Protocal	d)	Bailable Offence
5.	Project Tiger	e)	1987
6.	Biological Diversity Act	f)	1973
7.	Murder	g)	Eviction of Encroachment
8.	Bribery	h)	1972
9.	Section 104-A of KFA	i)	1975
10.	Section 64-A of KFA	j)	1872

Set VI

S.No.	Part A		Part B
1.	Karnataka Tree Preservation Act	a)	2005
2.	Karnataka Forest Act	b)	Restriction on Trade & Transport of Beete trees or Black wood
3.	Indian Forest Act	c)	Non Bailable Offence
4.	Indian Penal Code	d)	Bailable Offence
5.	Criminal Procedure Code	e)	1860
6.	Right to Information Act	f)	1973
7.	Murder	g)	Eviction of Encroachment
8.	Bribery	h)	1976
9.	Section 104-A of KFA	i)	1927
10.	Section 64-A of KFA	j)	1963

Q III. Say the Following Statements True or False

1. NFP, 1988 was formulated to satisfy the needs of British Government.
2. As per the NFP, 1952, the forest area under plain land should be 20 per cent.
3. Tree lands to provide fire wood to released cow dung for green manure.
4. The FBT's are advised to meet their raw materials requirements from the forest.
5. According to NFP, 1988, there is a wide scope for development of urban forestry.
6. The proportion of forest land would naturally same in different region.
7. Forest was considered as "Foster Mother" of Agriculture.
8. Forest policies are differing from country to country.
9. To realizing importance of forests, a separate ministry was created (MOEF) in 1980's.
10. Productive forests must be preserved or created for physical and climatic consideration.
11. Forest laws are defines the limit of forestry.
12. Forest, wildlife and environment are under the concurrent list.

13. The criminal laws are pertaining to the punishment for wrong offences.
14. Biological Diversity Act was signed by India in 2002.
15. Private rights are belonging to a particular person or individual.

Q IV. Fill in the Blanks With Suitable Words

1. The Captain Watson was appointed as first conservator in the year ______________.
2. ____________________ is the controlling ministry for Forests at Central Govt. level.
3. ____________ is the forests which have to be maintained and managed to meet the needs of defence, communications, industry and other general purposes.
4. Functional classification of forest is given in the NFP of ________.
5. India's new forest policy was enunciated in the year ________.
6. Law is a command which obliges a person to a course of conduct is given by _____________.
7. The liberty of doing something with law is called as ____________.
8. The ___________ law is pertains to the enforcement of rights of citizen in a country.
9. Expand CrPC _________________________________.
10. The NFP, 1952 advocated a Functional Classification of Indian Forests to focus attention on the specific object into :

    a) __________________ b) __________________

    c) __________________ d) __________________
11. ________________ is the controlling ministry for Forests at Central Government level.
12. The government owned forests of 1894 policy have been classified into :

    a) __________________ b) __________________

    c) __________________ d) __________________

13. The NFP, 1952 suggested to keep a minimum of 1/3rd of country's total land area under forests with ________% in Himalayas and other hilly tracts and ________% in plain lands.

Q V. Expand the abbreviations & mention their head quarters

IIFM: ____________________

TFRI: ____________________

ICFRE: ____________________

IFGTB : ____________________

IWST: ____________________

MOEF: ____________________

NAEB: ____________________

FRI: ____________________

AFRI: ____________________

FSI: ____________________

IGNFA: ____________________

KSHRC:____________________

NHRC:____________________

Q VI. Define/Answer in One Sentence

1. Forest law
2. Forest policy
3. Legal rights
4. General law
5. National forest
6. Rights
7. Crime
8. Legal rights
9. Tree land
10. Shifting cultivation
11. National Park

12. Biodiversity
13. Criminal law
14. Private right
15. IPC
16. Commercial forest
17. Protective forest
18. Village forest
19. Policy
20. Law
21. Special Law
22. Policy
23. Timber
24. Biological Diversity
25. Arrest
26. CrPC
27. Collusion
28. Confession
29. Confession
30. Summons
31. Special Law
32. Accident

Q VII Answer the Following

1. Write the salient features of National Forest Policy, 1894.
2. Write the characteristics of law.
3. Write the basic needs of NFP, 1988.
4. What is the strategy of 1988 forest policy for area under forests?
5. What is the scope for increasing tree lands in India?
6. Write the difference between rights and privilege.
7. Mention the powers of forest settlement officer.
8. Objectives of forest legislation
9. Qualification of a President
10. What are the Provisions for minorities in the Constitution?
11. Write the Special provisions for SC and ST in the Constitution?

12. What are the factors affecting Forest Policies?
13. Why Forest Law is needed?
14. Charter of Indian Forestry, 1855
15. Wright against exploitation.
16. Forest Policy of 1952.
17. Write the main objectives of National Forest Policy 1988.
18. Explain the application of the Indian Penal Code in forestry.
19. Differentiate between Wrongful gain and Wrongful loss.
20. Essentials of forest management.
21. Applicability of IPC in forest laws/offence.
22. Objectives of First National Forest Policy, 1894.
23. Functions and powers of National Biodiversity Authority.
24. Write the salient features of National Forest Policy, 1894.
25. What is the necessity of Forest Laws? List out.
26. Write the basic needs of NFP 1988?
27. Write the applicability of the Indian Penal Code (IPC) in forest laws / offence.
28. Write the salient features of Forest Conservation Act, 1980.
29. List out the Chapter-wise definition of Wildlife Protection Act, 1972.
30. What is the management strategy of Forest Policy, 1988 for area under forests?
31. Define Law. Write the characteristic features of law.
32. Write the different types of legal rights.
33. List out the types / classes of Criminal Courts.
34. Differentiate between Wildlife Sanctuary and National Park.

Q VIII. Answer the Following

1. What are the objectives of 1988 policy?
2. What is the necessity of forest legislation in India?
3. Write a short note on scope of forest policy.
4. What are the objectives of 1952 policy?

5. Write the functional classification of forest given in the 1952 NFP.
6. Briefly discuss the 1988 NFP strategy towards the tribal people and forest.
7. Biological Diversity Act, 2002.
8. What are the limitations of 1894 policy?
9. Essentials of forest management.
10. Applicability of IPC in forest laws/offence.
11. Objectives of First National Forest Policy, 1894.
12. Functions and powers of National Biodiversity Authority.
13. Forest produce according to KFA
14. Duties of Tree Authority
15. Which are the defects in National Forest Policy of 1894 and 1952?
16. Vital needs given in NFP, 1952
17. Drawbacks of First National Forest Policy, 1894.
18. Applicability of IPC in forest laws/offence

Q IX. Answer the Following

1. Write an essay on National Forest Policy, 1988.
2. Write an essay on National Forest Policy, 1952.
3. What are the basic needs and objectives of NFP, 1988?
4. Write an essay on 1894 Policy.
5. Mention the recommendations of NCA, 1976 on revision of 1952 policy.
6. Write the different types of legal rights.
7. Explain briefly about salient features of National Forest Policy, 1952.
8. Explain the Fundamental Rights guaranteed by the Constitution.
9. What are the Fundamental duties? Explain.
10. Explain the broad comparison between NFP, 1894, NFP, 1952 and NFP, 1988.

❑❑❑

Appendices

Appendix-I

Ban on Green Felling

In 1995, the Government of Sikkim banned the Green felling in forests & no clear felling, only dead, dying and diseased trees were allowed to be removed for the bonafide use. The total ban on green felling for commercial purposes and the defense of this philosophy for over a decade has made our forests in terms of character and composition, an envy of our neighbors. Needless therefore, to mention that planners, scientists and advisors are increasingly of the view that Sikkim is eligible to claim carbon sequestration cost for amelioration of regional climatic conditions by retaining and regenerating forest cover.

Forest protection, wildlife conservation and maintenance of environmental fabric in the hills of Sikkim have attracted the prime focus of the Government over the last several years. Legislations, rules and guidelines have either been put in place or revised and amended to make them more stringent.

The following rules /notifications deserve special mention :

Amendment of Sikkim Forests, Water Courses and Road Reserves (Preservation and Protection) Act, 1988:

The State Government has brought about vital amendments in the present Sikkim Forest Water Courses and Road Reserve (Preservation and Protection) Act, 1988 (Amendment, 2000) to make the specified clause more stringent and harsh in enforcement. Offences such as illegal felling of trees, encroachment and grazing in the Reserve Forest have been made non-bailable. Other important initiatives, measures and actions taken are Intensification of Management & Protection. The overall management of forest land and forestry resources have been intensified by better patrolling, effective forest check posts, check on illegal extraction and transit of forest produce, reporting and recording of all forests offences and other information in Headquarter control room and Division control rooms, registration of forest cases, check on leakage of forest revenue and better communication system.

The Sikkim Forests (Compounding of Offences) Rules, 1998. This rule notified by the government is to make strict rules for offender who commits any forest offence. Thereby keep a check on the offenders for violating the rules.

- The Sikkim Transit of Timber and other Forest Produce Rules, 1999.
- The Sikkim Forest (Detection, Enquiry and Disposal of Forest Offences) Rules, 2002
- The Sikkim Forest Department Reward Rules, 1998
- The Sikkim Forests Cattle Tress Pass Rules, 2000
- The Sikkim Private and Other Non-Forest Lands Tree Felling Rules, 2006
- The Sikkim Forest (Allotment of Areas for Quarrying of Sand and Stone) Rules, 2006.

Appendix-II

List of Agricultural Universities in India

State Agricultural Universities / Central University

1. Acharya NG Ranga Agricultural Univ., Rajendranagar, Hyderabad-500030, A.P
2. Anand Agricultural University, Anand-388110, Gujarat
3. Assam Agricultural University, Jorhat-785013, Assam
4. Bidhan Chandra Krishi Viswavidyalaya, P.O Krishi Viswavidyalaya, Mohanpur, Nadia-741252, West Bengal
5. Birsa Agricultural University, Kanke, Ranchi- 834006, Jharkhand
6. Central Agricultural University, Imphal -795004, Manipur
7. Chandrashekar Azad Univ. of Agriculture & Technology, Kanpur- 208002, U.P
8. Chaudhary Charan Singh Haryana Agricultural University, Hissar-125004,Haryana
9. Chaudhary Sarwan Kumar Himachal Pradesh Krishi Vishvavidhalaya, Palampur, Kangra- 176062, Himachal Pradesh
10. Dr Balasaheb Sawant Konkan Krishi Vidyapeeth, Dapoli, Ratnagiri-415712, Maharashtra
11. Dr Panjabrao Deshmukh Krishi Vidyapeeth, Krishi Nagar, Akola-444104, Maharashtra
12. Dr Yashwant Singh Parmar Univ. of Horticulture & Forestry, Solan, Nauni – 173230, Himachal Pradesh
13. Govind Ballabh Pant University of Agriculture & Technology, Pantnagar, Udhamsingh Nagar-263145, Uttarakhand
14. Guru Angad Dev University of Veterinary and Animal Sciences, Ludhiana-141004, Punjab
15. Indira Gandhi Krishi Vishwavidyalaya, Krishak Nagar, Raipur-492006, Chhattisgarh
16. Jawaharlal Nehru Krishi Vishwavidyalaya, Krishi Nagar, Jabalpur- 482004, M.P.
17. Junagadh Agriculture University, Moti Bagh, Agril. Campus, Junagadh-362001, Gujarat

18. Karnataka Veterinary Animal and Fisheries Science University, P.B. No. 6, Nandinagar, Bidar-585401, Karnataka
19. Kerala Agricultural University, P.O Vellanikkara, Thrissur-680656, Kerala
20. Maharana Pratap Univ. of Agriculture & Technology, Udaipur-313001, Rajasthan
21. Maharashtra Animal Science & Fishery University, Nagpur, Maharashtra
22. Mahatma Phule Krishi Vidyapeeth, Rahuri-413722, Maharashtra
23. Marathwada Agricultural University, Parbhani -431402, Maharashtra
24. Narendra Deva University of Agriculture & Technology, Kumarganj, Faizabad- 224229, Uttar Pradesh
25. Navsari Agricultural University, Vijalpore, Navsari-396450, Gujarat
26. Orissa Univ. of Agriculture & Technology, Siripur, Bhubaneswar-751003, Odisha
27. Punjab Agricultural University, Ludhiana -141004, Punjab
28. Rajasthan Agricultural University, Bikaner -334006, Rajasthan
29. Rajendra Agricultural University, Pusa, Samastipur-848125, Bihar
30. Sardar Vallabh Bhai Patel Univ of Agriculture & Technology, Modipuram, Meerut-250110, Uttar Pradesh
31. Sardarkrushinagar-Dantiwada Agricultural University, Sardarkrushinagar, Dantiwada, Banaskantha-385506, Gujarat
32. Sher-E-Kashmir Univ. of Agricultural Sciences & Technology, Railway Road, Jammu- 180012 (J&K)
33. Sher-E-Kashmir Univ. of Agricultural Sciences & Technology, Shalimar, Srinagar- 191121, (J&K)
34. Sri Venkateswara Veterinary University, Tirupati, Chittoor-517502, A.P.
35. Tamil Nadu Agricultural University, Coimbatore-641003, Tamil Nadu
36. Tamil Nadu Veterinary and Animal Sciences University, Madhavaram Milk Colony, Chennai- 600051, Tamil Nadu

37. University of Agricultural Sciences, Dharwad, Karnataka
38. University of Agricultural Sciences, Banglore- 560065, Karnataka
39. UP Pandit Deen Dayal Upadhaya Pashu Chikitsa Vigyan Vishwa Vidhyalaya Evam Go Anusandhan Sansthan, Mathura- 281001, Uttar Pradesh
40. Uttar Banga Krishi Vishwavidyalaya, P.O. Pundibari, Distt. Cooch Behar-736165, West Bengal
41. West Bengal University of Animal & Fishery Sciences, 68 KB Sarani, Kolkata-700037, West Bengal
42. University of Horticultural Sciences, Venkataramnagudem, West Godavari, A.P.
43. Rajmata VRS Agricultural University, Gwalior-474002, Madhya Pradesh
44. University of Horticultural Sciences, Navanagar, Bagalkot-587101, Karnataka
45. University of Agricultural Sciences, Raichur-584102, Karnataka

Deemed-to-be Universities

1. Indian Agricultural Research Institute, Pusa-110012, New Delhi
2. Indian Veterinary Research Institute, Izatnagar, Bareilly-243122, Uttar Pradesh
3. National Dairy Research Institute, Karnal-132001, Haryana
4. Central Institute of Fisheries Education, Mumbai-400061, Maharashtra
5. Allahabad Agricultural Institute, Allahabad-211007, Uttar Pradesh.

Central Universities with Agriculture Faculty

1. Banaras Hindu University, Varanasi, U.P.
2. Aligarh Muslim University, Aligarh, U.P.
3. Vishwa Bharti, Shantiniketan, West Bengal
4. Nagaland University, Medizipherma, Nagaland

□□□